Worldwide Destinations Casebook

Worldwide Destinations Casebook

The geography of travel and tourism

Brian Boniface and Chris Cooper

ELSEVIER
BUTTERWORTH
HEINEMANN

AMSTERDAM   BOSTON   HEIDELBERG   LONDON   NEW YORK   OXFORD
PARIS   SAN DIEGO   SAN FRANCISCO   SINGAPORE   SYDNEY   TOKYO

Elsevier Butterworth-Heinemann
Linacre House, Jordan Hill, Oxford OX2 8DP
30 Corporate Drive, Burlington, MA 01803

First published 2005
Reprinted 2005, 2006

British Library Cataloguing in Publication Data
A catalogue record for this book is available from the British Library

Library of Congress Cataloguing in Publication Data
A catalogue record for this book is available from the Library of Congress

ISBN 0 7506 6440 1

For information on all Elsevier Butterworth-Heinemann
publications visit our website at www.books.elsevier.com

Working together to grow
libraries in developing countries

www.elsevier.com | www.bookaid.org | www.sabre.org

ELSEVIER · BOOK AID International · Sabre Foundation

Typeset by Newgen Imaging Systems (P) Ltd, Chennai, India
Printed and bound in Italy

Contents

List of figures

List of tables

Part 1
Introduction

1.1

How to use this book

Introduction

This book provides you with a variety of case studies based on the geography of travel and tourism. The book is designed to be used as a companion volume with the core text – *Worldwide Destinations: The Geography of Travel and Tourism* (4th edition, 2005). However, as the case studies cover destinations, key issues in the geography of travel and tourism and contemporary points of debate, you can also use this book on its own. In this section we outline the benefits and uses of case studies, and provide some hints and tips on how you can get the most out of the case study approach.

The case study approach

Case studies are an important element in the teaching and learning of the geography of travel and tourism. In particular they enhance and enliven the subject area by examining stimulating issues in real-life situations, illustrating the key elements of tourism destinations and effectively bringing the real world into the classroom, without the need for extensive international travel (Swarbrooke and Horner, 2004).

Case studies also play a key role in teaching learning strategies for the geography of travel and tourism for three important reasons:

1 One of the problems of teaching the geography of travel and tourism is that in lesson or lecture presentation, the various elements of the body of knowledge have to be separated out; the

economic, social and environmental impacts of tourism, for example, are treated individually, yet in real life they are all linked. Case studies allow us to demonstrate these important linkages and relationships and to see 'the big picture'. Case studies work especially well for destinations at the local scale by drawing together the many different elements of tourism as they focus on one particular place.

2 As well as encouraging integration of tourism material, case studies also allow that material to be linked to other subject areas – for example, finance or human resources. Effectively cases can act as a 'capstone' to teaching and learning programmes by drawing all the elements of a programme together for either teaching and learning, or for the purpose of assessment, where they are ideally suited to creative forms of assessment on tourism programmes.

3 Using case studies as a form of assessment gets around the more arid and theoretical ways of assessing students' understanding of the geography of travel and tourism – for example, cases lend themselves to 'open book' tests. Their role in assessment schemes needs careful thought however. It is important that cases fit into the progression of assessment for a programme and that care is given to the nature of assessment (Cooper *et al.*, 1996). There are two key uses for cases in assessment. The first is where they are used to *deepen understanding* of a particular issue; these are sometimes known as 'intrinsic cases'. On the other hand they can be used to *integrate material* across a range of subjects, such as the major elements of the body of knowledge of tourism at a particular destination.

However they are approached, cases bring a range of benefits to the classroom and by encouraging active learning they allow students to gain valuable experience in:

- problem solving and decision making
- focusing on key issues within a clearly defined situation
- teamwork
- roles and role play
- working to deadlines for, say, reports or presentations
- the development of critical thinking skills
- presentation skills
- recognizing that there is no one 'correct' answer to a problem
- judging the relevance of different types of evidence and techniques.

Whilst case studies do much to bring the real world into the classroom, they do differ from reality in a number of ways. For example, the student is provided with the facts and the background to the problem and then asked to come up with a solution. In real life the problem often emerges first, and the facts and relevant background information then have to be sought out in an attempt to address the issue. Similarly, in many cases the student is provided with more information than would be available in reality. One way around this is to design a case where students have to purchase extra information to a budget. Finally, from a teaching and learning point of view the success of the case is very dependent on the communications skills of the teacher, the dynamics of the student group, and the interaction between the two.

Hints and tips on how to get the most out of case studies

Case studies are complex and cannot be solved quickly or simply; so do not rush into a solution. When working on the cases in this book try to use the following guidelines (Seperich *et al.*, 1996; Swarbrooke and Horner, 2004):

- **Read the case carefully**, making brief notes as you do so. You may need to read the case more than once to ensure that you fully understand the issues. To help you, we have identified as many as five key issues in some of the case studies.
- **Be prepared for the first session** – case studies are often made available to you or your group before the session when the case will be introduced and discussed. Make good use of the extra time to arrive prepared for the session. In this first session the teacher will brief you on the task that you are expected to complete. It is important that this is clearly stated and that you understand exactly what you are being asked to do. Make sure that you fully know the assessment guidelines – for, say, a report or presentation.
- **Discuss the case with your group**, and if possible arrange a meeting before class to 'warm up' on the issues. Identify any barriers and problems that may prevent you recommending particular solutions. In many of the cases in this book political realities act in this way. This also means avoiding the 'easy option' solutions, such as 'fire the president', 'demolish the hotel' or 'do more research'.
- **Think about all the relevant – and realistic – alternatives**. For example, at a congested natural attraction or 'beauty spot' is it best to *either* 'spread the load' of tourists away from the attraction *or* make the site more robust, and manage it in such a way to increase its *capacity* to take more visitors?
- **Select the best alternative** by evaluating each option against the situation outlined in the case.
- **Develop and implement a planned solution**. Often when students present a solution to a problem they miss the all-important element of how to implement it. For example, you may recommend that a town council designs a community tourism plan, but unless it can be put into practice within reasonable financial or other constraints the plan will simply be shelved and be a waste of effort.
- **Be prepared to present your ideas either in a report or as a presentation**. No matter how good your understanding of the case and your ideas, if they are poorly communicated you will fail to convince other people. You may also have to defend your ideas to the rest of the class, as their solutions may well be different from yours. Often, students will be assessed on the case as if they were a consultant or senior manager in an organization or at a destination. This is good discipline as it forces you not simply to repeat the case in a presentation or report, but to show that you can think creatively and 'add value' – after all that is why consultants are paid a fee. Think about the following checklist when you are finalizing your presentation or report:
  1 Do you fully understand the facts and the issues of the case?
  2 Is your presentation or report correctly structured with a logical flow?
  3 Is your solution consistent with the situation of the case?

    4 Is your analysis of the situation comprehensive, taking into account all possible circumstances?

    5 Have you been able to use material, ideas and concepts from other parts of your course to assist you with this case?

    6 Have you made the most of the information provided to you in the case?

- **Closure**. In the final session, the teacher will bring the case to a close, summarizing the main points and the groups' responses.

The structure of the book

The cases

This book presents a range of case studies covering a wide variety of destinations, key issues in the geography of travel and tourism and contemporary points of debate, each designed to support courses in the geography of travel and tourism. We have chosen cases that are based on real life situations and

- have been carefully planned and designed
- incorporate two or more elements of the body of knowledge of the geography of travel and tourism
- illustrate the general principles which emerge from the case study
- have clear learning outcomes.

In order to assist you in getting the most out of the book, each case study has been structured to include:

- key learning outcomes
- key issues of the case
- the main body of the case
- reflections to draw the case to a close
- case discussion points/assignments
- key sources to support your work on the case.

Structure of the book

The book has been organized to reflect the structure of the core text – *Worldwide Destinations: The Geography of Travel and Tourism* – and we hope that this also reflects the way that the subject is taught.

    Part 2 presents cases that illustrate the basic elements of the geography of travel and tourism. This section has three components – tourism demand and definitions, tourism destinations and tourism destination futures.

    Part 3 presents case studies drawn from Europe, the Americas and other world regions. Some of these focus on particular issues while others give an in-depth view of a particular destination.

    In Part 4 we have provided a compendium of resources that can be used to obtain further support material for all of the cases in the book. This is not meant to be comprehensive; as you proceed with your research you will become aware of many other sources of information that may not appear – at first sight – to be directly related to tourism. To get 'the big picture' our subject matter has to be very wide in scope, to include for example transport developments and demographic changes, as well as environmental and cultural issues. Our focus will also shift from the local to the global in terms of scale. In addition to newspaper travel supplements, leisure interest magazines, which cover a vast range of sports and outdoor activities from angling to windsurfing, usually feature particular destinations. Specific information of this type may prove more useful than travelogue videos, guidebooks and the superficial or generalized descriptions given in travel magazines. Radio and television documentaries that deal with business and environmental issues often have a tourism component, providing fresh insights on a particular destination. These documentaries invariably provide more material for discussion than most travel or holiday programmes on TV, which are often presented by 'celebrities' rather than professionals from the tourism industry. Finally, as geographers we should not overlook the valuable information provided by maps and a good atlas!

References

Cooper, C., Shepherd, R. and Westlake, J. (1996) *Educating the Educators in Tourism: A Manual of Tourism and Hospitality Education*. World Tourism Organization, Madrid.

Seperich, G. M., Woolverton, M. J., Beierlein, J. G. and Hahn, D. E. (eds) (1996) *Cases in Agribusiness Management*. Gorsuch Scarisbrick Publishers, Scottsdale, AZ.

Swarbrooke, J. and Horner, S. (2004) *International Cases in Tourism Management*. Elsevier Butterworth-Heinemann, Oxford.

Part 2
Cases Illustrating the Elements of the Geography of Travel and Tourism

2.1

Tourism demand and definitions

Case 1

Mobilities: concepts of travel, tourism and migration

Introduction

This case introduces the complex task of defining tourism, both in terms of who a tourist is, and also how we can define the tourism sector. Whilst these tasks may seem straightforward, in fact they have proved difficult and only in recent years have definitions been agreed at an international level. On completion of this case you will:

1 Be able to distinguish between the terms leisure, recreation and tourism and relate them to a recreation activity continuum.
2 Have a clear understanding of the various technical terms involved in defining and measuring tourism.
3 Be aware of the issues involved in defining a tourist.
4 Be aware of the fact that there are different types of travellers as well as tourists.
5 Understand the approaches to defining the tourism sector.

Key issues

The five key issues in this case study are:

1 Tourism is complex and can be thought of as a leisure activity on one hand, but on the other it is also a business activity.
2 Tourism, travel and recreation are all related in our lives and it is the distance travelled that helps to explain their differences.
3 Because of the many different technical terms – such as tourist, traveller, excursionist – we must be very clear in our understanding of these terms.

4 Defining both the tourist and the tourism sector is a complex task as so many different variables (such as length of stay, for example) are involved.

5 Only in recent years have definitions of tourism and the tourism sector been agreed at an international level. Until then, definitions varied internationally, making standardization of statistics difficult.

Leisure, recreation and tourism

What exactly is meant by the terms leisure, recreation and tourism and how are they related? **Leisure** is often seen as a measure of time and usually means the time left over after work, sleep and personal and household chores have been completed (Figure 1.1). In other words, leisure time is free time for individuals to spend as they please. This does, however, introduce the problem of whether all free time is leisure. A good example of this dilemma is whether the unemployed feel that their free time is in fact 'enforced' leisure, or whether volunteers at a sporting event see their activity as 'serious leisure'. This has led to the view that leisure is as much an attitude of mind as a measure of time, and that an element of 'choice' has to be involved. Of course, these relationships have changed over time – the Industrial Revolution, for example, brought about a sharp contrast between the workplace and the leisure environment, whereas in pre-industrial societies the pace of life is attuned less to 'clock time' and more to the rhythm of the seasons.

Recreation is normally taken to mean the variety of activities undertaken during leisure time (Figure 1.1). Recreation refreshes a person's strength and spirit and can include activities as diverse as watching television to holidaying abroad. We can make a useful distinction between physical recreation including sport, and activities that involve the arts, culture and entertainment. We can be active participants, or passive spectators and recipients.

If we accept that leisure is a measure of time and that recreation embraces the activities undertaken during that time, then **tourism** is simply one type of recreation activity. It is, however, more difficult to disentangle the meanings of the terms recreation and tourism in practice. Perhaps the most helpful way to think about the difference is to envisage a spectrum with, at one end, recreation based either at home or close to home, and at the opposite end recreational travel where some distance is involved and overnight accommodation may be needed. This is based on the time required for the activity and the distance travelled, and it places tourism firmly at one extreme of the *recreational activity continuum* (Figure 1.1). The idea of a spectrum is helpful as, for example, it allows us to consider the role of same-day visitors or excursionists. These travellers are increasingly a consideration in the geography of tourism – they visit for less than 24 hours and do not stay overnight. In other words, they utilize all tourism facilities except accommodation, and put pressure on the host community and the environment.

Clearly, tourism is a distinctive form of recreation and demands separate consideration. In particular, from the geographical point of view, tourism is just one form of 'temporary or leisure mobility', and in defining tourism it is therefore important

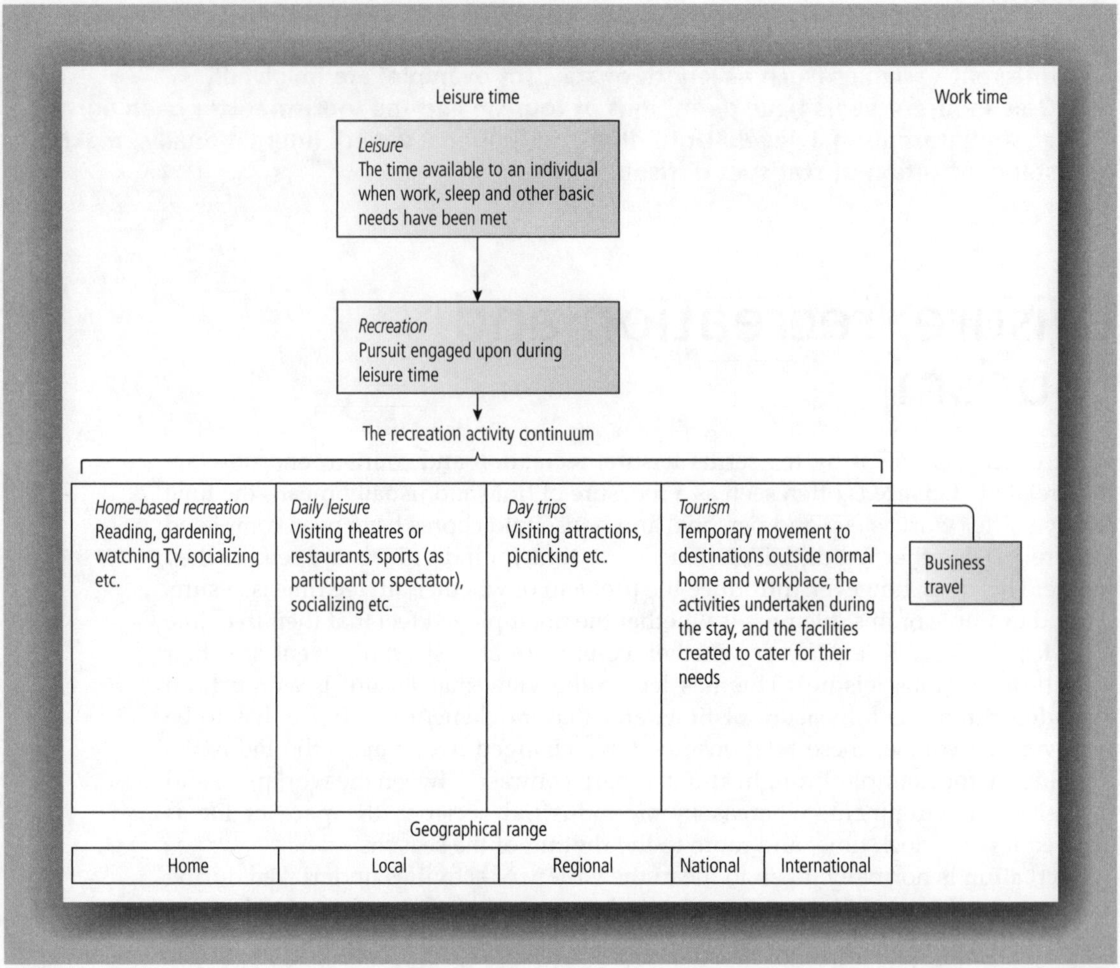

Figure 1.1 Leisure, recreation and tourism

to distinguish it from other types of travel. While the dramatic increase in mobility has facilitated modern tourism, it has also blurred the distinction between home, work and tourist destinations; and between differing types of traveller – whether they are commuters, shoppers or migrants.

This makes the drawing up of definitions of tourism problematic, simply because certain mobile groups have to be excluded from tourism statistics. Figure 1.2 shows the various classifications of travellers who are both included and excluded in official tourism statistics, but we need to look more closely at the following categories:

- **Travellers** The term 'traveller' has a very wide definition here and includes 'nomads' – people constantly on the move – who as hunters and herders have origins pre-dating civilization itself. In all periods of history some travellers have been motivated by *wanderlust* or curiosity, in contrast to the great majority whose journeys were regarded as essential – merchants, missionaries, diplomats, soldiers and sailors. Visitors to remote parts of the world often see themselves as 'travellers' or even 'explorers', rather than as tourists, and their journeys as 'expeditions' rather than

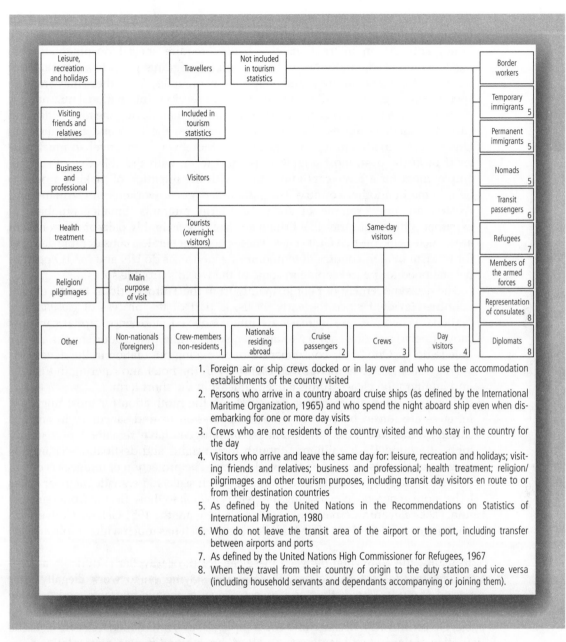

Figure 1.2 Classification of travellers
Source: World Tourism Organization

tours. They would argue that tourism nowadays has become altogether too commercialized, comfortable and predictable, and that real travel should involve an element of hardship and improvisation, as in the past. The fact remains that from an official viewpoint these self-styled travellers still count as tourists.

• **Migrants** Migration is clearly different from tourism in terms of purpose and length of stay and migrants are excluded from tourist statistics. Migration can be defined as travel with a commitment to live and work in another country, or another region (internal migration). People leaving their home country or region are emigrants, whereas on arrival in their place of adoption they become immigrants. At an international level, they require special documentation to legally enter, reside and work in that country. Emigrants provide a great deal of business for some airlines and shipping companies, and they may require specialized freight forwarding and resettlement services. International migration is subject to more restrictions in the new millennium than during the nineteenth and early twentieth centuries – for example, Australia, the USA and the European Union place strict controls on immigration. Moreover, with travel so much easier than in the past, most migration is short term, with the objective of seeking employment for a few years rather than with the intention of making a permanent home in another country. The *gastarbeiter* (guest workers) of Germany and Austria are one example of such short-term migrants. Smaller numbers of expatriates from countries like Britain are working as highly paid professionals in areas such as the oil-rich Gulf states. These people generate a considerable demand for tourism in their country of temporary residence, as do UN and NATO personnel stationed for peacekeeping in some of the world's 'trouble spots'.

The mass movement of people, mainly from the Third World to the developed countries, evident since the early 1990s, is part of the process of *globalization*. National economies are increasingly interconnected, and since capital can now move freely from one country to another, some argue that labour should also be able to do so. One of the consequences of an ageing population in the developed world is a shortage of manpower, especially in the hotel and catering industries, and immigration clearly fulfils a need, at least in the short term.

- **Refugees** Although economic pressures are the motivation for most migrants, refugees are forced by war or political oppression to find sanctuary in another country. Since the 1950s the numbers of refugees have remained persistently high, at around 15–20 million, although their origins and destinations change as new 'trouble spots' appear on the world scene. The protection of refugees is one of the responsibilities of the United Nations, which seeks to persuade member states to be more generous in extending the *right of asylum* to those fleeing from persecution. (The relevant international agreements here are the 1951 Geneva Convention on Refugees and the 1976 New York Protocol, which has much wider implications.)

In reality, the distinction between these categories of traveller is difficult, as visitors often evade visa restrictions, for example staying on to work illegally after a period of study. The distinction between illegal economic migrants, and genuine refugees – whose circumstances prevent them from obtaining documentation – is also subject to controversy. Because of these complex issues, international debate as to the definition of tourism still continues, and there are many different interpretations.

Defining tourists and the tourism sector

Why should we be so concerned with definitions? There are a number of reasons:

- Until we can define tourism or the tourism sector, we cannot measure it. This means that other, more straightforward economic sectors, for example the oil industry, will be able to claim how important they are to the government, while tourism fails to make its case.

- Until we can define tourism and the tourism sector, we will not be able to pass legislation that applies to either the individual traveller or the businesses in the sector.
- Until we are able to solve the conundrum of 'what is tourism' we can never have a true sense of professionalism.

There are two key approaches to definitions. First, we can define tourism from the **demand side**, i.e. the person who is the tourist. This approach is well developed and the United Nations Statistical Commission now accepts the following definition of tourism:

> *The activities of persons travelling to and staying in places outside their usual environment for not more than one consecutive year for leisure, business and other purposes.*

This definition raises a number of issues:

- What is a person's *usual environment*?
- The inclusion of 'business' and 'other' *purposes of visit* demands that we conceive of tourism more widely than simply as a recreation pursuit.
- Certain types of traveller are excluded from the definition. Tourism itself is only one part of the spectrum of travel, which ranges from daily travel to work or for shopping to migration, where the traveller intends to take up permanent or long-term residence in another area.

Secondly, we can define the tourism sector from a **supply side** point of view. Here the difficulty lies in disentangling tourism businesses and jobs from the rest of the economy. After 20 years of debate, the accepted approach is the Tourism Satellite Account (TSA), adopted by the United Nations in 2000. The TSA measures the demand for goods and services generated by visitors to a destination. It allows tourism to be compared with other economic sectors by calculating its contribution to investment, consumption, employment, the gross domestic product (GDP) and taxation.

Reflections on the case

Whilst definitions and terms may seem very 'dry', they are essential for the measurement and clear understanding of tourism. This case has shown how leisure recreation and tourism are linked in a continuum of activity and we can also think of different types of mobility or travel that do not count as tourism but which are important in our lives. Fortunately international agreement has now been reached on definitions of both the tourist and the tourism sector and this will go a long way to recognize tourism as an important economic contributor to economies in the world.

Discussion points/assignments

1 Make a list of all your trips away from home in the last month and classify them on the recreation activity continuum. Thinking about the last month, estimate roughly how much of your time was truly spent 'at leisure'. Compare notes with your classmates and explain the differences.

2 The people running a tourist attraction in your local area have asked you to design a visitor survey for them. What questions would you ask to be able to classify the visitors into local residents, day excursionists and tourists?

3 Thinking about your own town, or a town nearby, make a list of all the elements of the tourism sector – not forgetting to include catering and local government services. Against each category estimate the percentage of activity that derives from tourism and the percentage of activity that relates to other sources.

4 Using the WTO website, draft a briefing note for your local tourist board on the use and benefits of tourism satellite accounts.

5 Draft a checklist of the characteristics of the following types of mobility – migration, commuting, shopping, day excursion, leisure tourism, business tourism.

Key sources

Gilbert, D. (1990) 'Conceptual Issues in the Meaning of Tourism', in C. Cooper (ed.), *Progress in Tourism, Recreation and Hospitality Management*. Belhaven, London, ch. 1, pp. 4–27.

Hall, C. M. and Page, S. (2002) *The Geography of Tourism and Recreation*. Routledge, London.

Rojek, C. and Urry, J. (1997) *Touring Cultures – Transformations of Travel Theory*. Routledge, London.

Urry, J. (2000) *Sociology Beyond Societies. Mobilities for the Twenty First Century*. Routledge, London.

Williams, S. (1998) *Tourism Geography*. Routledge, London.

World Tourism Organization (1995) *Concepts, Definitions and Classifications for Tourism Statistics*. WTO, Madrid.

World Tourism Organization (2001) *Basic Concepts of the Tourism Satellite Account (TSA)*. WTO, Madrid.

World Tourism Organization and UNSTAT (1994) *Recommendations on Tourism Statistics*. WTO, Madrid and United Nations, New York.

Case 2

Understanding the 'new tourist'

Introduction

This case study analyses the driving factors behind the 'new tourist' phenomenon, dissects their characteristics and looks at the implications of this change in consumer behaviour. On completion of this case you will:

1 Recognize the significance of the changing consumer behaviour of tourists.
2 Understand the underlying causes of the changed consumer behaviour.
3 Be able to explain the key features of the new tourist.
4 Be aware of the implications of the new tourist for destinations.
5 Be aware of the implications of the new tourist for tourism marketing.

Key issues

With a maturing tourism market, consumer behaviour has changed. With increased travel experience consumers have learnt how to get the best from technology and the travel sectors; they are discerning in their choice of destination and increasingly they are demanding that the environment and communities in the destinations are given due concern.

1 There are a number of driving factors influencing the new tourist; these are inter-linked and have resulted in the changed consumer behaviour outlined in the case study.
2 The new tourists have a variety of key characteristics that set them apart from the tourists of earlier decades. In particular they are flexible and they demonstrate different values, emphasizing sustainability.

3 The new tourist has implications for how destinations and products are developed, in particular in terms of a greater emphasis on activity and sustainable tourism and away from passive, mass tourism.

4 The new tourist has to be approached differently by tourism marketing organizations and enterprises. They are familiar with information technology and understand the workings of the travel sector.

The drivers of consumer change

The tourism market has matured in the past 25 years and one of the key features of this maturity has been the changing consumer behaviour of the tourist. In recent years, a large number of tourists have become frequent travellers, both internationally and domestically. Increased travel has made them experienced, discerning and increasingly caring of the destinations that they visit. Poon (1993), for example, argues that the standardized mass tourism of the 1960s and 1970s is being superseded by a new tourism revolution. This represents a sea change in the nature of tourism demand that has implications not only for the planning and management of tourism destinations, but also for the way that the tourism sector operates. A range of key influences can be identified which have encouraged the growth of this *new tourist*.

- Trip frequency (both leisure and business), and therefore travel experience, has increased.
- New destinations, particularly long haul, are within reach of the mass market.
- The selling of travel has become technologically-driven, allowing individual access to computer reservation systems and the Internet.
- The media and pressure groups (such as Tourism Concern) have taken a real interest in the responsible consumption and development of tourism, raising the profile of sustainability and placing issues such as the environment and concern for host populations centre-stage. The WTO's Global Code of Ethics for Tourism has set a new standard here and a number of tourism companies now have their own codes of practice for responsible travel.
- Deregulation in the tourism sector has allowed the individual consumer access to efficient direct reservation systems and Internet booking sites – particularly those offering, for example, 'last minute' air fares and hotel room availability.
- Concentration in the industry has meant that one group of companies can offer a complete range of travel options.
- Emergence of the knowledge-based society creates a demand for authentic and well-interpreted experiences, as the passive beach holiday becomes less popular in certain market segments.
- Changing demographics in many key tourist-generating regions with ageing populations, smaller household sizes and higher discretionary incomes all combine to change lifestyles and the nature of tourism needs.

Characteristics and behaviour of the new tourist

These drivers of change have created a new breed of tourist who:

- Are critical and discerning – they have travelled frequently and know what they want. They seek quality, good service and value for money as they are *empowered* by their experiences elsewhere. They also know their rights and will complain if the experience is not as expected or advertised. In this respect, their experience allows them to make comparisons with other destinations and products. They therefore often adopt a *high-satisfaction/low-loyalty* travel pattern of purchasing behaviour.
- Have considerable consumer and technology skills, for example in manipulating their trip to take advantage of last minute bargains. They are prepared to be flexible in travel arrangements – for example, they will travel at short notice or even spontaneously.
- Are motivated by *wanderlust* – they travel out of curiosity and cultural reasons rather than for *sunlust*. This means that tourism destinations and products must build in an element of interpretation, education and seeing the 'real' place. They will seek out activity and adventure vacations and involvement in the destination – they no longer wish just to relax on a beach for 14 days. They are also motivated to search for the authentic and the natural experience at the destination.
- Have values which encourage the *ethical consumption* of tourism, and they will choose destinations and companies on this basis. Their values are oriented to the environment and reflect a changing lifestyle.

The implications of the new tourist

Poon sees the new tourist as the driving force of change behind the new tourism revolution as the sector metamorphoses from the rigid, packaged tourism of the 1960s and 1970s to a new flexible form of tourism. This revolution in tourism demand has implications for both destinations and the tourism sector itself.

- **Destinations** will need to recognize that these *critical consumers* seek quality, sound environmental and sustainable practices, ease of access to reservation systems, good websites and authentic, well-managed experiences. As Poon (1994) states 'travellers are increasingly prepared to shun over-commercialized and polluted resorts' (p. 91).
- **The tourism sector** will need to rethink its marketing strategies and provide tailor-made, customized vacations which demonstrate an understanding of the motivations and needs of the new tourist – in other words, the way that the new tourist thinks, feels and behaves. This will involve sophisticated approaches to the *segmentation* of the tourism market as well as development of customer databases and relationship marketing where customer loyalty is encouraged. In addition, the

new tourist renders traditional market research techniques of classifying individuals obsolete, for example by age or occupation, or by categories such as leisure, business and visiting friends and relatives. Instead, more sophisticated (and expensive) techniques are needed to expose underlying values and motivations.

Reflections on the case

This case has shown how much consumer behaviour in tourism has changed over recent decades. With more frequent travel, consumers are now experienced and know what they want. Their preferences for travel are changing to more active, experience-oriented products. The real lesson here is the need for both the tourism sector and tourism destinations to understand this sea change in the market place and develop appropriate destinations and products.

Discussion points/assignments

1 The Brown family are the classic breed of new tourist – draft an itinerary for them to tour Spain. Show how this itinerary might differ from one made for a typical family in the 1960s.
2 Using the Internet, identify up to three companies that you feel are providing products for the new tourist. Establish the key elements of the product – features, price, distribution channels and target markets. Summarize your findings in a product/market fit table with one column listing the characteristics of the new tourist (the market) and the other the features of the products which meet these characteristics.
3 Select a tourism destination that you know well. Draft a report to the destination manager suggesting how it might be repositioned to appeal to the new tourist.
4 Using travel brochures or the Internet, find four examples of codes of conduct set out by tourism companies for the 'consumption of tourism' or 'responsible tourism/travel codes of behaviour'. Compare these with the WTO's Global Code of Ethics for Tourism (available on the WTO website). How does the private sector approach differ from the WTO?
5 Think of tourism 20 years from now. How might tourism consumer behaviour be different to that of today?

Key sources

Poon, A. (1993) *Tourism, Technology and Competitive Strategies*. CAB, Wallingford.

Poon, A. (1994) The New Tourism Revolution. *Tourism Management*, 15 (2), 91–92.

Swarbrooke, J. and Horner, S. (1999) *Consumer Behaviour in Tourism*. Butterworth-Heinemann, Oxford.

World Tourism Organization (2001) *Tourism 2020 Vision – Global Forecast and Profiles of Market Segments*. WTO, Madrid.

Case 3

Analysing the world pattern of international tourism flows

Introduction

This case study is designed to illustrate and explain the patterns of international tourism demand in both time and space. On completion of the case you will:

1 Be aware of the historical growth of international tourism demand.
2 Be able to reflect on the role of crises and terrorism in affecting tourism demand.
3 Understand how tourism demand varies across world regions.
4 Explain why some countries are major generators of international tourism and some are leading destinations.
5 Be able to explain the underlying causes of these patterns.

Key issues

The five key issues in this case study are:

1 Compared to domestic tourism, international tourism trends are relatively well documented because measurement is standardized across the world and more straightforward than domestic tourism measurement.
2 The growth of international tourism since 1950 has been phenomenal, driven by social, technological and economic factors.
3 In recent years, 'shocks' to the tourism system such as '9/11' have set back these rates of growth.
4 The determinants of demand, allied to the characteristics of the mosaic of tourism destinations around the world, combine to produce global rhythms and patterns of tourism.
5 Understanding these global patterns of international tourism demand is essential for the successful marketing and development of tourism destinations.

Why international flows?

This case is confined to *international* tourism flows and receipts, as the collection and estimation of statistics of international tourism is more accurate than that for *domestic* tourism. The collection and aggregation of statistics into six world regions by the World Tourism Organization necessarily means that their regions, whilst failing to conform to geographical logic, are used throughout this case study.

The historical trend at the world scale

The end of the Second World War represented the beginning of a remarkable period of growth for international tourism, with an annual average growth rate approaching 7 per cent for the second half of the twentieth century (Table 3.1). Until the early years of the twenty-first century international tourism was remarkably resilient to factors that might have been expected to depress growth – recession, oil crises, wars and terrorism. However, in 2001 9/11 represented the first shock to the tourism system and demand fell as a result.

- **The 1950s** In 1950, international tourist arrivals stood at 25.3 million. Growth of international tourism was sluggish as the world recovered from the Second World War. However, the adoption of the jet engine for civil aviation in the closing years of the decade provided an important technological enabling factor for international travel.
- **The 1960s** By 1960, arrivals had reached 69.3 million. The decade of the sixties saw demand for international tourism realized by:
  - *demand-side factors* – large numbers of those living in the developed world had the desire, time and income to travel

Table 3.1 International tourism arrivals: the historical trend

Year	International tourism arrivals (millions)	International tourism receipts (US$ millions)
1950	25.3	2100
1960	69.3	6867
1970	159.7	17 900
1980	284.8	102 372
1985	321.2	116 158
1990	454.8	255 000
1995	567.0	372 000
2000	696.8	477 000
2001	692.6	463 000
Forecast for 2020	1560.0	N/A

o *supply-side factors* – the response by the tourism industry to develop the 'standardized' approach of inclusive tours offered at a competitive price.

Business travel also emerged as an important sector of the market.

- **The 1970s** In 1970, international arrivals had risen to 159.7 million. Growth slowed due to the oil crisis in 1974 and economic recession at the end of the decade. However, recession demonstrates the 'ratchet' effect of tourism demand with an increasing rate of growth in times of prosperity, and at times of recession, demand remains fairly constant, as consumers are reluctant to forego travel.
- **The 1980s** By 1980, international arrivals had reached 284.8 million and growth rates began to slow as the market moved towards maturity. The mid-1980s were a period of substantial travel with European destinations experiencing record years. However, in 1986 the Chernobyl incident, the Libyan bombing and the fall in the US dollar saw a shift in demand away from Europe and North Africa. The late 1980s saw a return to the normal pattern of tourism flows, and accelerating growth, only to be disrupted by the Gulf War.
- **The 1990s** In 1990 international arrivals stood at 454.8 million. The decade opened with the Gulf War that severely depressed international travel and had a long-term impact upon tourism enterprises such as airlines. Over the decade, growth of arrivals was strong and a shift in patterns of demand was evident with the opening up of the former Eastern bloc, and the expansion of tourism in the Pacific Rim countries. In the closing years of the decade, the Asian currency crisis depressed intra-regional travel in Asia, though inbound travel was boosted as prices fell.
- **The New Millennium** Tourism grew substantially in 2000 to reach almost 700 million international arrivals. This growth continued in 2001 until the shock of 9/11, which depressed travel significantly in the final quarter of the year and resulted in the first recorded annual decrease in international arrivals since 1982. Further shocks to the tourism system then ensued with the war in Afghanistan, bombings in Bali in 2002 and in 2003, the outbreak of Severe Acute Respiratory Syndrome (SARS) and the Iraq War. It is the climate of uncertainty created by these events that has had the greatest impact on international travel.

It is difficult to generalize about the pattern of international tourism flows as individual countries display marked differences and contrasts. Similarly, each destination receives a distinctive mix of tourist origins and modes of transport. On a world basis it is estimated that:

- 80 per cent of international arrivals are by surface transport
- 20 per cent are by air
- 30 per cent of international arrivals are for business purposes
- 70 per cent are for pleasure.

However, it is also true that the impact of 9/11 completely changed the international tourism market as symbols of tourism – aircraft – were used as weapons. The impact was such that major international airlines were bankrupted, many destinations and companies saw their markets devastated and consumer confidence in travel was severely tested. The effects of 9/11 can be summarized as:

- A worldwide decrease in international arrivals of 0.6 per cent in 2001 – somewhat less than initially feared.
- Regionally, the Americas were the hardest hit (a decrease of 6 per cent of international arrivals), followed by South Asia (−4.5 per cent) and the Middle East (−2.5 per cent).
- Some destinations with Muslim populations suffered, whilst others, such as Australia, were perceived as safe havens.
- Destinations that were hit the hardest were those dependent on the North American market and those dependent upon the long-haul market. Also preferences changed and consumers sought out 'greener' destinations.
- In many countries, demand switched from international travel to domestic, partly as a result of the reduced availability of airline seats, but also because domestic travel, often by surface transport, was perceived as safer.
- Governments and international agencies put into place 'crisis recovery strategies', including support for the tourism sector, subsidies for airlines and marketing campaigns.

The changing regional picture

Determinants of tourism demand include both lifestyle factors such as income and mobility as well as life cycle factors such as a person's age or family circumstances. These determinants, when allied to the characteristics of the mosaic of tourism destinations around the world, combine to produce global rhythms and patterns of tourism. International tourism arrivals and departures are concentrated into relatively few countries, mainly in Europe and North America. This produces an unbalanced picture that favours developed Western economies and disadvantages the developing world, which is left to compete for the long-haul market – and this accounts for a minor share of the total market. For both generators and destinations of international tourism, as more countries have entered the market, so the dominance of the leading players has been gradually reduced.

Generators

The major tourism-generating countries are those in the *high mass consumption stage* of economic development, although as countries reach the *drive to maturity stage* they become significant generating markets. For any particular destination country, a typical list of the top generating markets would contain neighbouring states together with at least one from a list containing Germany, the UK, Japan and the USA. However, it is clear that in the next 20 years, China will become a major generating country. In part, the pattern of generating countries is explained by two conflicting trends:

- The importance, though declining, of short-haul travel to neighbouring countries, which represents up to 40 per cent of total international trips.
- A substantial growth in long-haul travel. This is due to both consumer demand for new, more exotic destinations and the response from the travel industry to

package long-haul destinations. Aircraft technology and management can now deliver these at a price and length of journey acceptable to the consumer.

Destinations

The post-war period has been marked by the rapid emergence of the East Asia and the Pacific region (EAP) as an international tourism destination, largely at the expense of the Americas and Europe (Table 3.2).

East Asia and the Pacific

In 1950 the EAP region had a share of less than 1 per cent of international tourism; yet, despite SARS, which has had a short-lived impact, by the year 2010 this share is forecast to exceed 20 per cent. The key factors in the region's success are:

- a number of rapidly developing countries with large populations
- well-managed airlines based in the region
- an exotic culture (at least as perceived by the West)
- world-class natural attractions
- good quality tourism infrastructure such as airports
- dynamic societies with positive, welcoming attitudes to tourism, including newly emergent destinations such as China and Vietnam
- favourable exchange rates
- competitively priced inclusive tours
- high-quality accommodation products and cuisine.

Europe's traditional pre-eminence in international tourism has been eroded since the 1960s. While Europe still has the largest volume of international arrivals, growth has been at a slower rate than regions such as the EAP. The trend of new destination regions taking market share from Europe is clear and will

Table 3.2 International tourism arrivals – the changing regional picture: percentage share of international arrivals by WTO region

Region	1950 (%)	1960 (%)	1970 (%)	1980 (%)	1990 (%)	2000 (%)	Forecast for 2010 (%)
Europe	66.5	72.5	70.5	68.4	63.5	57.8	50.2
Americas	29.6	24.1	23.0	18.9	18.8	18.4	18.6
East Asia & Pacific (EAP)	0.8	1.0	3.0	7.0	11.4	15.7	22.1
Africa	2.1	1.1	1.5	2.5	3.4	3.9	4.4
Middle East	0.9	1.0	1.4	2.4	2.1	3.3	3.5
South Asia	0.2	0.3	0.6	0.8	0.7	0.9	1.0

continue. None the less, Europe still dominates world tourism flows simply because it contains:

- many of the world's leading generating countries
- a number of relatively small but adjacent countries generating considerable volumes of cross-border travel
- a mature travel and transport industry
- natural and cultural attractions of world calibre
- many themed attractions, such as Disneyland Paris
- attractive capital cities
- emerging destinations, such as the former Eastern bloc countries
- a variety of tourism products from beach to winter sports holidays
- a mature tourism infrastructure, including the Channel Tunnel and other transport developments
- highly trained personnel
- a developing pan-European currency in the form of the euro
- an integrated industrial base which is important for business tourism.

Elsewhere in the world, the **Americas** account for a significant share of international tourism activity, with an increasing volume of inbound travel to supplement the huge domestic market, but this masks major differences between the USA and Canada on the one hand and the economically much less prosperous Latin American countries. The North American domestic market has benefited from the fall in outbound travel resulting from the fear of terrorism. In **Africa**, due to the prevailing political instability and poor infrastructure, tourism growth is relatively stagnant. The majority of arrivals are in North Africa, but the newly emergent and 'politically acceptable' South Africa is shifting the emphasis of tourism. In the **Middle East**, the stop–go nature of the peace process inevitably has an impact on tourism demand and supply, while in **South Asia** – a region with poor infrastructure and political instability – most activity focuses on India.

Reflections on the case

This case shows that world patterns of international tourism demand are not random. They follow predictable patterns that are related to the different pattern of tourism destinations around the world and to the social and economic characteristics of generating countries. However, the various 'shocks' to the tourism system are rewriting these rules and patterns of demand are changing. It is important to understand the global picture of international tourism demand because they determine tourism flows and the fortunes of all tourism destinations.

Discussion points/assignments

1 This case is dependent upon accurate statistics of international tourism demand. Make a checklist of ways to measure international tourism demand – which is the most accurate? How is international tourism demand measured in your country?

2 Plot the growth of international tourism demand since 1950 on a graph, supplementing the data in this case with that from the WTO website. Explain why the growth rate was more rapid in the first 25 years and slower in later years.

3 On the graph pinpoint dates when growth was checked – identify the events that caused these checks. Choose one event and explain its effect on tourism in your own country.

4 Identify the 'top ten' tourist generators and the ten leading tourism destinations in the world. This is available from the WTO website or their publications. Explain why the leading generators tend to be from developed Western economies. How is the pattern of destinations changing and why?

5 Taking your own country as the example, compile a statistical report on tourism demand (including domestic tourism if the information is available). Write a brief report explaining the patterns you have found and comparing them to the world pattern of demand.

Key sources

Books and reports

Frechtling, D. (2001) *Forecasting Tourism Demand*. Elsevier Butterworth-Heinemann, Oxford.

Lennon, J. J. (2003) *Tourism Statistics*. Allen and Unwin, St Leonards.

Page, S. (2003) *Tourism Management: Managing for Change*. Elsevier Butterworth-Heinemann, Oxford.

Page, S., Brunt, P., Busby, G. and Connell, J. (2001) *Tourism. A Modern Synthesis*. Thomson Learning, London.

Witt, S. and Witt, C. (1991) *Modelling and Forecasting Demand in Tourism*. Academic Press, New York.

World Tourism Organization (1999) *Changes in Leisure Time*. WTO, Madrid.

Statistics of international tourism demand

Organization for Economic Cooperation and Development (annual) *Tourism Policy and International Tourism in OECD Member Countries*. OECD, Geneva.

Pacific Asia Travel Association (annual) *Annual Statistical Report*. PATA, Bangkok.

World Tourism Organization (annual) *Compendium of Tourism Statistics*. WTO, Madrid.

World Tourism Organization (annual) *Tourism Highlights*. WTO, Madrid.

World Tourism Organization (annual) *Yearbook of Tourism Statistics*. WTO, Madrid.

World Tourism Organization (monthly) *World Tourism Barometer*. WTO, Madrid.

World Tourism Organization (1994) *Recommendations on Tourism Statistics*. WTO, Madrid.

World Tourism Organization (1999) *Tourism Market Trends*, 6 vols. WTO, Madrid.

World Tourism Organization (2000) *Data Collection and Analysis for Tourism Management, Marketing and Planning*. WTO, Madrid.

World Tourism Organization (2001) *Tourism 2020 Vision – Global Forecast and Profiles of Market Segments*. WTO, Madrid.

World Tourism Organization (2001) *Tourism Forecasts*, 6 vols. WTO, Madrid.

Website

http://www.world-tourism.org

2.2
Tourism destinations

Case 4

The Galapagos Islands: balancing resource conservation and tourism development

Introduction

This case is focused upon the unique wildlife of the Galapagos Islands as a tourism resource. The case raises important issues about how unique natural resources should be conserved and managed for tourism, with the associated conflicts over management priorities. On completion of this case you should:

1 Understand the significance of the Galapagos Islands as a natural tourism resource.
2 Be aware of the impact of visitors upon wildlife.
3 Recognize the variety of approaches to conserving wildlife resources.
4 Understand the fact that unique tourism resources are the focus of a wide range of interest groups.
5 Recognize that political and economic realities intervene in the management of tourism resources.

Key issues

The five key issues in this case are:

1 The fact that the tourism attraction of the Galapagos Islands is focused upon its unique wildlife resources, which are vulnerable to increasing numbers of visitors.
2 Visitor impacts on both the wildlife and the community have been significant.

3 The management of the islands' wildlife resources has been implemented through the designation of national park status as well as international recognition as a World Heritage Site and Biosphere Reserve.
4 Visitor management is achieved through the use of qualified guides, strict regulations on visitor activity, and the zoning of the national park, as well as using price and permits as a means of restricting the numbers of visitors.
5 There are a range of stakeholders involved in the management of the Galapagos Islands as a tourism resource, but there is considerable disagreement between them over priorities for the islands.

The Galapagos Islands

The Galapagos Islands lie in the Pacific Ocean about 1000 kilometres west of Guayaquil on the South American mainland (see Figure 4.1). The unique wildlife of the Galapagos is a world-class attraction and a non-reproducible resource, which has been given international recognition as a World Heritage Site and Biosphere Reserve. Most of the animals have no fear of man, as there are no natural predators. Although the islands are situated on the Equator, penguins and sea lions flourish alongside species more closely associated with the tropics, due to the cold ocean currents offshore. The best-known animals are the marine iguanas and giant

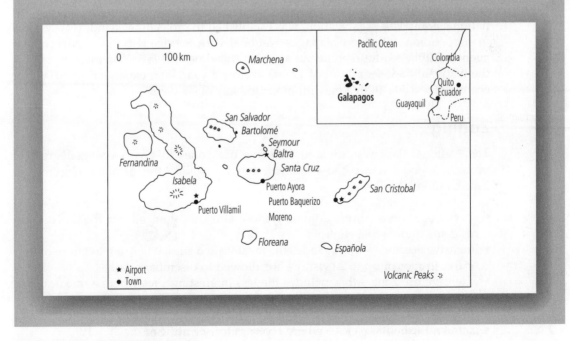

Figure 4.1 The Galapagos Islands

tortoises, of which there are fourteen distinct species on the different islands. This provided the inspiration for Darwin's theory of evolution by natural selection, and the islands' scientific value has long been recognized. Until recently the Galapagos were protected by their remoteness and the human impact was relatively slight. Since the 1970s the growing popularity of ecotourism has focused public interest on the islands, providing support for conservation but posing a greater threat to the fragile ecosystems than the occasional havoc wreaked by pirates and whalers in the past. The widespread perception that the islands are a 'tropical Eden' is far from the reality. The climate is dry, and since the islands are volcanic, the scenery is for the most part barren and rugged. The plants and animals are well adapted to the conditions, including the regular heavy rains and warmer temperatures resulting from the periodic weather event known as El Niño, but their survival is affected by a number of serious problems due to human interference with the environment. Introduced plant and animal species may soon outnumber those native to the islands.

Managing the resource

National park designation

In Europe and North America conservationists and even representatives of the travel industry are seriously considering the introduction of 'no-go areas' for tourists as a solution to the damage caused by tourism to fragile physical and cultural resources. In the Galapagos this has been the policy for many years. As early as 1959, when the number of visitors was less than 1000 a year, the Ecuadorian government designated 97 per cent of the archipelago, excluding only those areas already settled, as a National Park. In 1968 the Charles Darwin Foundation, an international non-profit organization, was established to protect the islands' ecosystems in cooperation with the Galapagos National Park Service (GNPS), a government agency. Organized tourism began at about this time and in 1974 a master plan for the National Park set a limit of 12 000 visitors a year, later expanded to 40 000 for economic reasons, with a maximum visitor stay of six days.

Zoning

The National Park was divided into five use zones to give varying degrees of protection and balance the needs of tourists against the primary objective of conservation, as follows:

- special use zones – areas adjoining those already colonized, for the use of local residents under strict controls
- intensive use zone – this includes the most visited sites, where a maximum of four or five groups of up to 20 visitors are allowed to disembark daily
- extensive use zone – this includes the less interesting sites where a maximum of twelve visitors are allowed to disembark daily
- primitive use zones – where access is prohibited without special permit
- primitive scientific zones – where access is for scientific research only.

Visitor management

Tourism is controlled in the interest of conservation, through:

- the National Park guide programme
- strict regulations to prevent any contamination and disturbance to the wildlife (see Figure 4.2)
- the paperwork necessary for tour vessels to leave port.

Access is also controlled by price; it costs almost as much for foreign tourists to reach the Galapagos by air or cruise ship from the mainland of Ecuador as it does to fly from Europe to Quito or Guayaquil. Foreign visitors to the National Park have to pay a substantial entrance fee (currently US$100). The majority of tourists find accommodation on the cruise ships and yachts that tour the islands. Tourists are restricted to some 54 visitor sites designated by the GNPS; these are reached from the ship by *pangas* (motorized dinghies) – and usually involve a 'wet landing'

The Galapagos Islands are one of the few places in the world that remain relatively untouched by human exploitation. Leave nothing behind but your footprints and take nothing from the islands but photographs. Everyone can help to maintain the islands' fragile ecosystem by following some simple rules. Their future depends on you.

1. Be careful not to transport any live material to the islands, or from island to island (insects, seeds). If you have a pet, do not bring it to the islands. It will not be allowed.
2. No plants, rocks, animals or their remains, such as bones, pieces of wood, corals, shell, or other natural objects, should be removed or disturbed. You may damage the islands' ecological conditions.
3. Animals should not be touched or handled. A sea lion pup will be abandoned by its mother, for example, if she smells the scent of man on her young. The same applies to chicks of birds.
4. Animals may not be fed. It may alter their life cycle, their social structure and affect their reproduction.
5. Do not disturb or chase any animal from its resting or nesting spot. This is especially true for birds such as boobies, cormorants, gulls and frigates. The nests should be approached carefully, keeping a distance of 1 to 2 metres. If disturbed, the bird will flee and abandon its egg or chick, which could die under the hot sun within 30 minutes.
6. A qualified guide approved by the National Park must accompany all groups that visit the National Park. The visitor should follow the trail, marked with small black and white posts, never leave it. If you do so, you may destroy nests without being conscious of it (e.g. marine iguanas nest in the sand).
7. Follow the guide; stay with him for information and advice. He is responsible for you, if he does not follow the rules himself, report him to the National Park.
8. Litter of all types must be kept off the islands. Disposal at sea must be limited to certain types of garbage, only to be thrown overboard in selected areas. Keep all rubbish (film wrappers, cigarette butts, chewing gum, tin cans, bottles, etc.) in a bag or pocket, to be disposed of in your boat. Do not throw anything on the islands or overboard. It could end up at the coast or the beach, or eaten by sea turtles or sea lions. A sea lion may play with a tin can found at the bottom and cut its sensitive muzzle. Sea turtles may die from swallowing a plastic bag.
9. Do not paint names or graffiti on rocks. It is against the law, and you will be fined for it.
10. Do not buy souvenirs or objects made from plants or animals of the islands (with the exception of articles made from wood). Among such articles are turtle shells, sea lion teeth and black coral. This is the best way to discourage such trade.
11. To camp, you need a permit from the National Park Service (for sites on Santa Cruz, San Cristobal and Isabela). Do not make fires, but use a gas stove instead.
12. Do not hesitate to show your conservationist attitude. Explain these rules to others, and help to enforce them.

The Galapagos National Park thanks you for respecting these rules. Think about others who come after you; they'll be grateful to you for your conservationist attitude.

Figure 4.2 Rules for visitors to the Galapagos National Park
Source: Adapted by courtesy of Tourism Concern, 1999

through the surf rather than a 'dry' landing at a jetty. At each visitor site a rough waymarked trail provides the sole access to the wildlife, unusual plants and volcanic landforms of the Galapagos. Tourists are always accompanied by a naturalist-guide licensed by the GNPS with a maximum of 20 visitors per guide. Itineraries for tourists on cruise ships visiting a large number of sites, or on day excursions based at island hotels, are arranged well in advance by the tour operator. Those arriving in chartered yachts and other small vessels are allowed some flexibility in organizing their own itineraries subject to a maximum number of sites per boat.

Visitor impacts

Ecotourism in the Galapagos was worth an estimated $105 million to Ecuador in 1995. In fact tourism is one of the few commercial uses of the islands' limited resource base – various attempts at agricultural development in the past have met with failure. Most foreign visitors are high-income, middle-aged Europeans and North Americans. The value to the national economy is even greater if we consider that most of these tourists spend three days in mainland Ecuador, principally in the cities of Quito and Guayaquil, as part of their holiday. Conservationists are concerned that this controlled 'educational tourism' could grow to become conventional tourism. At present visitors to the pristine beach at Gardner Bay on Española Island – one of the most popular sites – are outnumbered by sea lions. There are no clearly defined limits on the annual number of visitors, and the planned limit of 40 000 has long been exceeded (see Figure 4.3). The number of tour vessels has not increased since the mid-1990s, but tour companies are now tending to use larger, more luxurious ships than before. There is some evidence that the environmental capacity has already been reached in the most visited areas, with disturbance to nesting birds and path erosion.

From the viewpoint of the islanders there is little to attract conventional tourists, and passengers from cruise ships stay only a few hours ashore in Puerto Ayora, the largest community, and Puerto Baquerizo Moreno, the administrative capital. Only a small proportion of the visitor spend actually benefits the local economy, as most tourist requirements have to be imported from the mainland and ecotourism creates relatively few jobs. Recreational activities are limited to scuba diving, snorkelling and sport fishing. Further growth in these and land-based activities such as horse riding will generate a demand for more facilities. At present the three port communities offer little more than basic amenities and small hotels of varying standard. Puerto Ayora, with 10 000 inhabitants – over half the population of the islands – has the most potential for development as a resort, with a recreational business district (RBD) in the making near the harbour, between the road to Baltra Airport and the Charles Darwin Research Station. Facilities here include *cybercafes* that are part of the worldwide support network for backpackers. So far proposals for intensive development here and elsewhere have been resisted, and the only resort hotel offering luxury accommodation is located in the interior of Santa Cruz Island.

Ecuadorians and foreign visitors evaluate the islands' resources in different ways. Domestic tourists, for example, are much more likely to buy black coral souvenirs from local traders, which is illegal. Tourism has resulted in an influx of workers from the mainland, helped by subsidized domestic air fares. They are attracted by the prospect

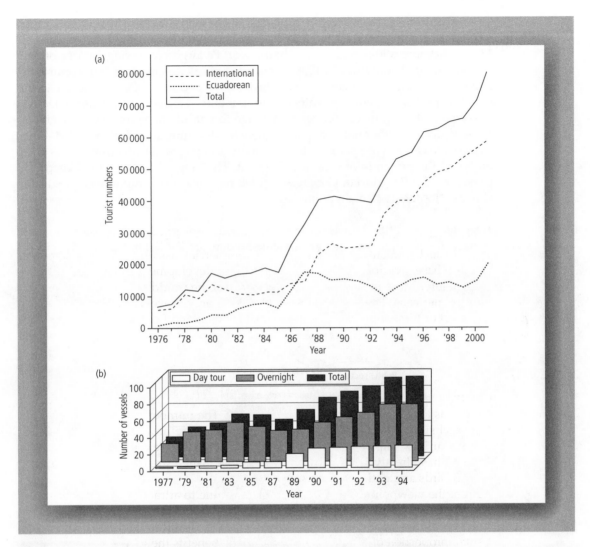

Figure 4.3 The growth of tourism to the Galapagos: (a) total tourist numbers;
(b) number of vessels calling at the islands
Source: (a) 1976–1995 statistics from Jackson, 1997: 251; 1996–2001 statistics from CETUR (Ecuadorian tourist organization); (b) MacFarland and Cifuentes, 1995

of short-term financial gain and a climate that is free of tropical diseases. The population is growing at the rate of 8 per cent a year. This puts pressure on scarce resources such as water, foodstuffs and building materials, and increases the risk of oil spillage from the supply ships (as indeed occurred in January 2001 off San Cristobal Island). All of which further tips the balance against the survival of the islands' wildlife.

The stakeholders

Conservation is also vital for the surrounding seas, and tourism has to share use of this resource with the important fishing industry; this includes both small-scale local operators and large, well-equipped ships based on the mainland and supplying international markets. In 1986 the government established the Galapagos Marine Resources Reserve, reputedly the world's largest, covering an area of over 130 000 square kilometres. In 1995 a concerted effort was made to ban commercial fishing, especially of sea cucumbers which are valued in the Far East as an aphrodisiac. In protest, islanders threatened the staff of the GNPS and the Charles Darwin Research Station, causing deliberate damage to wildlife habitats. Similar incidents have occurred in other national parks where local communities feel excluded – such as the Coto Doñana in Spain. In the case of the Galapagos the government has taken on board the principle of local involvement. The 'Special Law for the Galapagos' passed by the Ecuadorian Congress in 1998 recognizes the importance of sustainable development. Its main points are:

- greater cooperation between the organizations concerned with conservation and tourism development (the various stakeholders are shown in Figure 4.4)

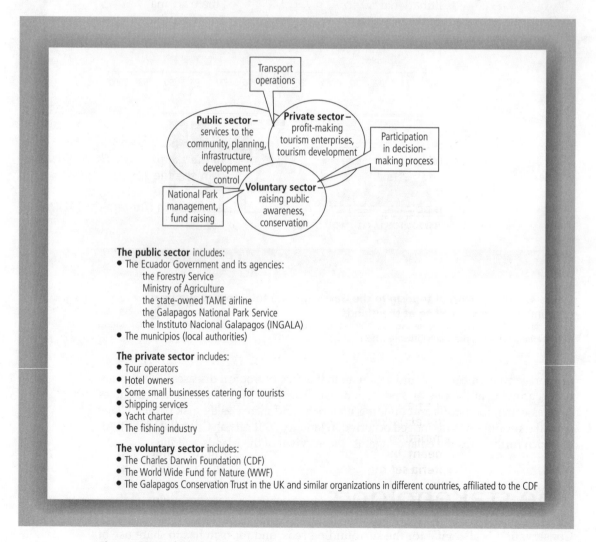

The public sector includes:
- The Ecuador Government and its agencies:
    the Forestry Service
    Ministry of Agriculture
    the state-owned TAME airline
    the Galapagos National Park Service
    the Instituto Nacional Galapagos (INGALA)
- The municipios (local authorities)

The private sector includes:
- Tour operators
- Hotel owners
- Some small businesses catering for tourists
- Shipping services
- Yacht charter
- The fishing industry

The voluntary sector includes:
- The Charles Darwin Foundation (CDF)
- The World Wide Fund for Nature (WWF)
- The Galapagos Conservation Trust in the UK and similar organizations in different countries, affiliated to the CDF

Figure 4.4 Stakeholders in Galapagos tourism

- promotion of locally based nature tourism
- greater control over tourism development by INGALA, the regional planning agency, which will require environmental impact statements from developers
- stabilization of population growth by making it more difficult to obtain rights of residence in the islands
- allocation of 40 per cent of the visitor entrance fee to the GNPS for conservation
- protection of native island species to be achieved through prevention by stricter quarantine regulations against plant and animal imports, and damage limitation by eradication of introduced species.

It remains to be seen how effective the Special Law will be in practice. Like other developing countries, Ecuador takes pride in its heritage, but has limited financial resources to set aside for conservation when there are more pressing economic and social problems. It may also be difficult to find experienced professional workers to enforce the regulations in the face of opposition from local politicians, an inefficient bureaucracy and the multinational corporations. It is clear that there are many interests in the conservation of the islands, of which tourism is an important, but not the only, stakeholder.

Reflections on the case

The Galapagos Islands are a unique tourism resource, but this case highlights the difficulties of conserving and managing such a resource in the face of multiple priorities from a range of different stakeholders. In particular we can see the different effectiveness of the various measures used to limit visitor impacts. The Galapagos are an excellent example of political and economic realities intervening in attempts to sustain the islands' wildlife resources.

Discussion points/assignments

1 Using the Internet and travel brochures, put together a full tour itinerary for a visit to the Galapagos for a tourist based in New York. Include all stop-overs and transfers and a detailed itinerary for the visit to the islands themselves.
2 Discuss whether the regulations for visitor management in the Galapagos (see Figure 4.2) are specific enough and can be effectively enforced. How applicable are they to other national parks, and would you suggest additional rules and guidelines to prevent contamination and disturbance to wildlife?
3 Define what is meant by 'national park' and investigate whether the Galapagos satisfies all the criteria set out by the IUCN compared to, say, national parks in Europe or North America.
4 Draw up a list of the positive and negative effects of tourism upon wildlife generally – how many of these effects would you expect to find on the islands?

5 The Galapagos are home to a community of islanders – in class have a debate about the pros and cons of tourism and assign key roles to members of the class. These roles might include the local mayor, business people, fishermen, farmers, other members of the local community, and GNPS staff.

Acknowledgement

We appreciate the help given by the Galapagos Conservation Trust in researching this case study.

Key sources

Chapman, M. (2003) Islands of the fittest, *National Geographic Traveler*, April, 46–57.

Crowley, P. (1999) *The Galapagos: Tourism at the Crossroads*. Tourism Concern, London.

Hall, C. M. and McArthur, S. (1998) *Integrated Heritage Management*. The Stationery Office, London.

Jackson, M. (1997) *Galapagos: A Natural History*. University of Calgary Press, Calgary.

MacFarland, C. and Cifuentes, M. (1995) Case study: Ecuador, in V. Dempka (ed.), *Human Population, Biodiversity and Protected Areas: Science and Policy Issues*. American Association for the Advancement of Science, Washington, pp. 135–188.

Website

www.galapagosonline.com

Case 5

The impact of climate change on tourism

Introduction

Climate change is one of the most significant events facing mankind. This case introduces the causes of climate change and looks at its effects upon tourism and tourists. On completion of this case you will:

1 Recognize the significance of climate change for tourism.
2 Understand the key elements of climate change and their causes.
3 Be aware of the consequences of global warming for tourism.
4 Be aware of the consequences of the thinning of the ozone layer for tourism.
5 Recognize the response required by destinations and the tourism sector to climate change.

Key issues

The five key issues in this case are:

1 Climate change is already a significant factor in human life and is set to become more important. Climate change effects are generally taken to involve a combination of global warming and the thinning of the ozone layer.
2 Global warming is thought to be caused by the burning of fossil fuels creating a greenhouse effect which prevents heat escaping from the earth. Its impact on tourism includes the flooding of low-lying resorts as the sea level rises and the decline of ski resorts as the snowline recedes.
3 The thinning of the ozone layer is caused by the emission of gases into the atmosphere by such devices as aerosols and refrigerators. Its effects on tourism include

increased exposure to ultraviolet radiation at resorts and severe damage to resources such as the bleaching of coral reefs.

4 Climate change is prompting a change in tourism behaviour, with sunbathing becoming less popular.

5 There is a need for some destinations to change their products away from the beach.

Climate change

The various elements of the climate, such as air and sea temperatures, sunshine, wind speed and direction, humidity (the amount of moisture in the air) and precipitation in the form of rain and snow, all play an important role in determining the best conditions for different types of outdoor recreation. Although artificial snow can be manufactured for indoor ski centres, this is expensive and an imperfect substitute for the real thing – a mountain landscape such as the Alps in winter. We could make similar observations, for example, about artificial surf in leisure centres and artificial reefs for scuba diving. In Mediterranean countries and tropical islands the climate at the present time is one of their main assets, a *pull factor* attracting tourists, whereas the cold winters and cloudy skies characteristic of northern countries like Britain act as a powerful incentive or *push factor* for outbound tourism. Although average temperatures etc. are usually considered when we describe the climate of a destination, climate change means that extreme weather events such as heatwaves will become much more frequent in the future.

The impact of climate change upon tourism is potentially very significant and is already being felt in some parts of the world. Whereas in the past, climate changes took place over long periods of time, there is now considerable evidence that the rate of change is accelerating, due to man's interference with the natural environment. The two key dimensions of climate change can be thought of as:

- global warming, and
- thinning of the ozone layer.

Global warming: the causes

Since the beginning of the twentieth century, average temperatures worldwide have increased by about 0.5 °C and may rise by another 2.0 °C in the twenty-first century. The causes and effects of this *global warming* are as yet not fully understood. Some scientists link the rise in temperature directly to major increases in emissions of carbon dioxide, methane and nitrous oxide into the atmosphere. These in turn have resulted from the burning of fossil fuels such as oil and coal by transport, industry and domestic consumers, or from the widespread forest clearance that is taking place throughout the tropics. It is known that carbon dioxide is largely responsible for the *greenhouse effect* of the atmosphere, which prevents excessive radiation of heat from the earth's surface back into space.

The evidence for climatic change is not one-way and is capable of several interpretations. Some scientists believe that the recent changes are well within the limits of fluctuations that have occurred over the last millennium, as evidenced by the advance and retreat of glaciers in the Alps. Even if global warming is now taking place, the release of methane from the thawing permafrost beneath the tundra and greatly increased snowfall resulting from higher temperatures in the Arctic might lead to another Ice Age. According to this scenario the flow of the iceberg-laden Labrador Current would strengthen, deflecting the warm Gulf Stream well to the south of its present path across the North Atlantic. It is not difficult to predict areas in northern latitudes experiencing a general deterioration of the climate.

Global warming: the impact on tourism

Ski resorts

The effects of global warming appear to be most obvious in mountain regions, where glaciers have retreated, the permafrost at high altitudes has thawed, and the risk of avalanches has increased. Many ski resorts, especially those situated at low altitudes, and in marginal areas such as Scotland and the Australian Alps, are becoming unprofitable as the snow cover becomes less reliable.

Rising sea level

The Antarctic Peninsula is a good example of the situation in high latitudes; here the ice cap is melting back rapidly and possibly becoming unstable. Full-scale melting of the polar ice would result in a rise in sea levels worldwide, spelling disaster for many low-lying island destinations, such as the Maldives and Micronesia. The Mediterranean zone would become hotter and drier, aggravating already serious water shortages in some resort areas. These would be less popular with visitors from northern Europe, who conceivably could bask in subtropical warmth in their own seaside resorts, benefiting from an extended summer season. The relationship between tourism and climate change is summarized in Figure 5.1.

Undesirable side-effects include:

- invasions of insects, and pathogens spreading disease (such as the West Nile virus that afflicted much of North America following a prolonged drought in 2002)
- possible ecological disaster for native plants and animals
- prolonged heat waves, especially in cities, with episodes of poor air quality
- increased storm activity and consequent coastal erosion
- increased algal growth at the coast depleting water quality.

Air travel is also likely to become more expensive, due to the penalties imposed on the use of environmentally damaging aircraft fuel.

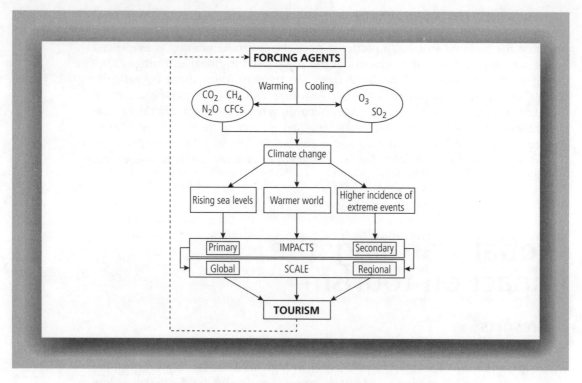

Figure 5.1 The relationship between climate change and tourism
Source: Giles and Perry, 1998: 76

El Niño

A graphic reminder of the power of ocean currents and minor shifts in the atmospheric circulation to influence the weather is shown by the El Niño phenomenon in the eastern Pacific. Named after the Christ Child – because it occurs around Christmas, at intervals of three to seven years – El Niño is characterized by a weakening of the trade winds, a reversal of the surface ocean currents, and a surge of abnormally warm water toward the west coast of South America. El Niño displaces the cold Peruvian Current, bringing heavy rain to the arid coastal belt and destruction of marine life. This spells economic disaster for the beach resorts and the vital fishing industry of Ecuador and Peru. The effects of El Niño are not confined to the Pacific coast of South America, as the weather system characterized by the trade winds is generally stable and spans the entire tropical zone and beyond. The collapse of this system has almost a global impact, affecting areas as far apart as California, southern Africa, Indonesia, Australia and Polynesia with unseasonal floods, droughts and hurricane-force winds. The El Niño of 1997/98 was blamed for the intensity of the forest fires and smog conditions that afflicted South-East Asia. Elsewhere, heavy rains combined with warmer temperatures are putting greater numbers of people at risk from diseases such as dengue fever. In the Pacific Ocean, corals, which can only tolerate a small range of temperature, have been devastated. An El Niño event is usually followed by La Niña, a period of exceptionally cool sea surface temperatures off South America, which causes a reversal of the previous situation.

The severity of El Niño episodes in the 1990s increases the probability that the world can expect more extreme fluctuations in weather conditions and this poses serious problems for resort planners, developers and the tourism industry generally.

Thinning of the ozone layer

The causes

The thinning of the ozone layer in the stratosphere was first discovered over Antarctica in winter but is now noticeable year-round, and to a lesser extent over the Arctic. The causes of the thinning are thought to be the emission of chlorofluoro-carbons (CFCs) from devices such as air conditioners, refrigerators, freezers and aerosols. Of course, tourism must be a contributory factor here. In the meantime action is being taken by governments, industry and consumers, mainly in the developed countries, to curb the use of CFCs, but it remains to be seen whether a world-wide ban on CFCs can be made effective. A start was made in this respect with the adoption of the First International Protocol for Control of Greenhouse Gases at Kyoto, Japan, in 1996.

The impact on tourism

The ozone layer filters out the lethal UVC rays and reduces the impact of the harmful UVB rays of the sun. As so-called *ozone holes* have been identified certain destinations already pose a health hazard to visitors – for example, parts of the Southern Hemisphere such as Australia, New Zealand, South America and even the cool and cloudy Falkland Islands. (You should note that the thinning of the ozone layer has no effect on air and sea surface temperatures and is unrelated to global warming.) There is little doubt that increased ultraviolet radiation is causing a higher incidence of skin cancer and eye cataracts worldwide. Fair-skinned people risk sunburn within 15 minutes of initial exposure, while the use of oils and creams with a high sun-protection factor (SPF) will not prevent long-term damage to the skin. Media interest in the problem may eventually affect attitudes to sunbathing, and to beach tourism in the following ways:

- excessive exposure of the skin may become unfashionable as holidaymakers see the advantages of wearing clothing with a high SPF
- destinations that have traditionally relied on beach tourism will need to diversify by offering *beach plus* products and tours.

Reflections on the case

This case has demonstrated the significance of climate change for tourism, and the fact that weather events will be increasingly erratic and more severe in the future. Effectively, tourism is affected by climate change through changes to its resource base – such as the receding snowline, and also the increased strength of the sun as the ozone layer thins. Tourism is beginning to respond to these challenges in a number of ways, including diversifying activities at beach resorts. None the less, as this case fore-shadows, future climate change will require a shift in thinking on the part of both the tourism sector and the tourist.

Discussion points/assignments

1 Draft a memo to the manager of a beach resort in southern Europe outlining the potential impacts of climate change for the market and the response that should be taken by the resort.

2 A significant amount of tourism investment is at the coast. Using an atlas, locate the destinations that might be at risk from a rise in sea level.

3 You are the manager of a ski resort in the Australian Alps. What measures would you take to counteract the threat posed by global warming and ensure a profitable tourist season?

4 (i) Assess the suitability of the present climate for tourist activities in the following destinations:
   (a) East Africa as a destination for safari tourism (note that the year is divided into rainy and dry seasons).
   (b) The Gambia as a 'winter sun' holiday destination for Europeans, compared to either the Caribbean or Queensland (note the reversal of the seasons in the Southern Hemisphere).
   (c) The Red Sea for scuba diving compared to Queensland.
   (d) Cornwall for surfing compared to northern California.
   (e) Lapland (northern Scandinavia) as a skiing destination compared to either the Austrian Alps or the Australian Alps.
   (f) Ibiza as a destination for 'summer sun' package holidays compared to Brittany as a destination for independent summer holidays.
   You will need to obtain information on average temperatures, relative humidity, sunshine and precipitation for these destinations, which can then be plotted in graph form to make comparisons easier.
   (ii) Investigate the possible impact of global warming on these destinations and tourist activities.

5 Research the phenomenon of 'coral bleaching' and write a briefing note to the Australian Minister for the Environment on the impact of coral bleaching on tourism to the Great Barrier Reef.

Key sources

Bunyard, P. (2001) The truth about climate change. *The Ecologist*, November, pp. 4–11.

Giles, A. and Perry, A. (1998) The use of a temporal analogue to investigate the possible impact of projected global warming on the UK tourist industry. *Tourism Management*, 19 (1), 75–80.

Henson, R. (2002) *The Rough Guide to Weather*. Rough Guides, London.

Lynas, M. (2003) Winter tourism feels the heat. *Geographical*, 75 (10), 97–105.

Pearce, E. A. and Smith, C. G. (1990) *The World Weather Guide*. Hutchinson, London.

Rogers, D. (2004). Going to extremes. *Condé Nast Traveler*, May, 93–105.

The Royal Meteorological Office (1970–) *Tables of Temperature, Relative Humidity and Precipitation for the World*. HMSO, London.

Soplee, C. (1999) El Ninõ/La Niña: nature's vicious cycle. *National Geographic*, 195 (3), 73–95.

Viner, D. and Agnew, M. (2000) *The Implications of Climate Change on Tourism Markets and Demand*. Climate Research Unit, University of East Anglia, Norwich.

World Tourism Organization (2003) *Climate Change and Tourism*. WTO, Madrid.

Case 6

Managing transport at the tourism destination

Introduction

With the high profile given to air travel, it is easy to forget that most international tourist journeys as well as domestic trips are undertaken by surface modes of transport. This case study examines the issues relating to motor vehicles at the destination and the various approaches to transport management. On completion of this case study you will:

1 Understand the benefits of motorized travel for the tourist.
2 Be aware of the problems that motorized transport poses at the destination.
3 Recognize the benefits of managing transport at the destination by creating new facilities and separating tourist traffic from local traffic.
4 Recognize the benefits of park and ride schemes where motor vehicles are separated from the attraction.
5 Understand the success criteria for the various approaches to traffic management.

Key issues

The five key issues in this case are:

1 Motorized transport is the dominant mode of travel to both domestic and international destinations, as most tourist trips are over short distances.
2 This form of transport causes a range of problems at tourism destinations, including safety, intrusion and congestion.

3 By separating out tourist traffic through such management solutions as scenic drives and tourist routes, the trip becomes a valued travel experience in its own right and the transport problems are reduced.

4 By persuading tourists to separate from their vehicles and visit the destination using another form of transport (such as park and ride schemes), the impact on environmentally sensitive areas is reduced.

5 Each of these management approaches is appropriate in particular circumstances and each is associated with a variety of issues and success criteria.

Motorized transport at the destination

The vast majority of travel at the destination takes place by surface transport, predominantly by car but with coaches/buses playing a significant role. This immediately creates a number of issues and problems for tourism destinations:

- **Safety** The car is more dangerous than other modes of transport, causing an average of a quarter of a million deaths and seven million serious injuries worldwide every year, with young children featuring prominently among the victims. Clearly, unrestricted use of the car is not conducive to safe and secure holiday destinations or attractions.
- **Speed** Holiday driving is on average 10 per cent slower than normal driving and visitors are often uncertain of their route.
- **Facilities** Cars need facilities such as car parks that are often visually intrusive. In coastal resorts, a busy highway along the seafront acts as a barrier separating the tourist accommodation, retailing and other activities from the beach.
- **Visual intrusion** Cars parked en masse are brightly coloured and reflect light, often creating an eyesore adjacent to a natural or historic attraction, or within a resort or historic town.
- **Congestion** Cars cause traffic congestion on the approach routes and at the destination itself.
- **Environmental impact** Cars are a source of pollution in destination areas, with their noise and exhaust fumes.

Yet the reasons that cars are used at the destination are compelling:

- They allow door-to-door flexibility, providing much more privacy than any form of public transport and the freedom to travel at will.
- They are perceived as an inexpensive form of travel, especially for family groups, because running costs and vehicle depreciation are not seen as part of the cost of individual trips.
- They allow unparalleled viewing.
- They can comfortably contain luggage, pets, and recreational equipment as well as people (including the elderly or the handicapped who otherwise may not have access to tourism destinations).

- They can be used to tow caravans, trailer tents or boats.
- They act as a secure base for the tour – whilst picnicking, or enjoying an attraction.

Management solutions at the destination

Nonetheless, the impact of the car has become severe at many tourism destinations. As a result, transport management measures are now being adopted to solve these problems and balance the needs of local community traffic with those of visitors. Implementation of these measures can be difficult, as motorists are often resistant to restrictions. We seem able to accept restrictions on motoring for business or every-day domestic travel, but are rather less willing to comply when we are 'at leisure'. Even so, our increasing desire for a quality experience at destinations will inevitably lead to the demand that leisure traffic is also 'managed'.

There are two key management approaches.

1 Separate visitors from their cars
Park and ride schemes
These involve the provision of an alternative form of transport for the visitor. Normally, the visitors are invited to park their car and to travel to the attraction by bus, or some other form of transport. Park and ride schemes need a number of conditions to be successful:

- A road configuration that prevents 'short circuiting the system'.
- Local resident and business community support – often such schemes are seen as an infringement of residents' freedom and businesses worry that trade will be lost.
- Effective and visible marketing, publicity, signposting and information.
- Visitors who are prepared to sacrifice their own freedom to travel at will for an enhanced experience at the destination.
- A landscaped yet secure parking area, adjoining weatherproof waiting areas/bus stops.
- A regular shuttle service to the attraction – a key benefit of park and ride schemes is that the numbers of visitors arriving at the attraction can be monitored and controlled.

Park and ride schemes are well suited to destinations such as historic towns and villages where the streets are narrow and access is difficult; natural attractions where the presence of traffic is intrusive; and family-based attractions or des-tinations where children's safety needs to be given special consideration. Park and ride is a flexible management option, as it can be used only at peak times if necessary – weekends and busy holiday periods, for example.

Provision of alternative forms of transport

The imaginative provision of alternative forms of transport also acts as an effective management tool at the destination to separate visitors from their cars, for example:

- Circular sight-seeing city bus and boat tours with regular 'hop-on-hop-off' stops at key tourist 'sights' as in London and New York, many historic cities and also rural areas such as the UK's Peak District National Park.
- Public transport that meets the needs of the user, as, for example, at Hadrian's Wall, a heritage attraction of Roman origin in the north of England. Here a bus service calls at key points along the Wall to save visitors from having to make repeat journeys back to their cars.
- Journey planner computer discs to make the public transport system 'legible' at tourist destinations.
- Novelty forms of transport such as cable cars, horse-drawn trams, recreational road trains or steamboats. Monorails are used in some theme parks and exhibition sites but tend to be too intrusive and costly for most attractions.

2 Separate visitor traffic from local traffic

Scenic drives

The creation and development of scenic drives allows the separation of touring traffic from local traffic. Given that tourism traffic drives more slowly and is seeking to enjoy the drive, rather than simply to get from A to B as quickly as possible, it is logical to create special linear attractions for the holidaymaker touring by car. These are known as scenic drives and are designed primarily to provide a distinctive driving experience for pleasure travel. They allow the destination manager to control the numbers of vehicles entering the drive and environmental impact can be reduced, as visitors tend to stay within their vehicles.

Scenic drives are often provided with a range of facilities and features:

- interpretation and information for the visitor
- frequent stopping places for views, picnics and barbecues
- landscaped and purpose-designed driving experiences to maximize the impact of the scenery
- motels, shops and cafes.

Scenic drives are found mainly in North America – the Blue Ridge Parkway is a good example; snaking through Virginia and North Carolina, it is often used in car advertisements. They are much less common in Europe and other parts of the world.

Reflections on the case

There is no doubt that motorized transport is the preferred mode of transport to destinations by tourists, simply because of the benefits that it delivers. However, as this case shows, motor vehicles pose a range of management issues for destinations, not least those of safety, intrusion and congestion. This means that if the quality of the experience at the destination is to be maintained, then tourists will have to accept management restrictions on their driving freedom. With imagination, this can be turned into an opportunity to create attractive scenic drives and linear attractions, as well as great travel experiences when the car is left behind.

Discussion points/assignments

1 From your own experience make a checklist of the advantages and disadvantages of the car as a form of tourist transport.
2 Devise a class debate on the trade-off *between* (i) the freedom to drive anywhere and thus perhaps spoil some tourism experiences *versus* (ii) the need for individual freedom to be curtailed in order to create better experiences at the destination, and perhaps also improve the quality of life for the residents of the places we visit.
3 In your local area select a transport scheme that has been implemented at a tourism destination or attraction. Assess the benefits and costs of the scheme from a tourism point of view.
4 A number of park and ride schemes have failed due to objections from local residents. Argue the case for either the advantages or the disadvantages of park and ride schemes for local residents at a destination.
5 Take a popular destination or attraction in your region. Analyse the traffic issues at that destination and draft a report recommending the most appropriate solutions.

Key source

Tolley, R. (ed.) (1990) *The Greening of Urban Transport*. Belhaven, London.

European policy and tourism

Introduction

The European Union is one of the few regions in the world to have attempted to devise a policy for tourism which is truly international in its scope. This case study traces the history of the policy and examines the issues surrounding tourism in Europe. On completion of the case you will:

1 Be aware of the role and importance of tourism in the European Union (EU).
2 Understand the background to the formation of the European Community.
3 Understand the role of various European institutions managing tourism in the EU.
4 Be aware of the tourism policy initiatives in the EU.
5 Recognize the influence of other areas of EU policy in tourism matters.

Key issues

There are five key issues in this case:

1 Europe remains the world's most significant tourism region.
2 The European Union is a union of sovereign states and is unusual in having a tourism policy that covers all states.
3 Tourism has few statutory rights under the EU constitution.
4 Most issues that affect tourism are dealt with by other areas of policy such as transport or regional development.
5 Tourism has a chequered history regarding policies in the EU.

Tourism in Europe

Europe is a region of immense economic, social and cultural diversity. In part this diversity explains why Europe continues to be a crucible of conflict, with two world wars during the twentieth century, which ended with a civil war in the Balkan region. Europe is also under economic pressures from both North America and the newly industrializing countries of South-East Asia. Here, Europe's failure to perform as a region is brought into clear focus when shares of international tourism are examined:

- In 1960 Europe accounted for 72 per cent of international tourism arrivals.
- By 2000 this share had fallen to 58 per cent.

None the less, Europe continues to dominate world tourism. This is despite the fact that Europe accounts for less than 10 per cent of the world's population and an even smaller share of its total land area. In 2000 it received over 400 million of the world's 697 million international tourist arrivals, and accounted for almost 50 per cent of the world's receipts from international tourism. The strong economies in the region account for most of the world's top tourist generating countries, dominating the outbound flow of international travel, and are also estimated to generate massive demand for domestic trips.

Europe is pre-eminent in the world's tourism system for the following reasons:

- Most of the region's economies are in the high mass consumption stage, or in the drive to maturity. The population, though ageing, is in general affluent, mobile and has a high propensity to travel.
- Europe consists of a rich mosaic of languages, cultural resources and tourist attractions of world calibre.
- The adoption of the single European currency, the euro, in many European countries in 2002 has facilitated tourism.
- Europe comprises many relatively small countries in close proximity, encouraging a high volume of short international trips.
- The region's climatic differences are significant, leading since the 1950s to a considerable flow of sun-seeking tourists from northern Europe to the south.
- Europe's tourism infrastructure is mature and of a high standard.
- The tourism sector throughout most of the region is highly developed, and standards of service – though not the best in the world – are good.
- Most European governments have well-funded, competent tourist authorities with marketing and development powers.

Background to the policy

The impetus for a united Europe emerged from the devastation of the Second World War. The idea of a customs union for coal and steel dates back to 1951 and led to the European Coal and Steel Community (ECSC). The ECSC was successful and as more countries joined it broadened to other sectors of the economy. This led to the signing of the Treaty of Rome in 1957 as the basis of all European legislation;

however, tourism was not included as a policy area in the original Treaty. The Treaty of Rome founded the European Economic Community which became the present European Union (EU) and in the ensuing decades the number of members grew from the original six signatories to 15 in 1994. By the mid-1980s impetus for a Single European Market led to the Single European Act that aimed to abolish the following barriers to movement in Europe by the end of 1992:

1 physical barriers
2 technical barriers
3 fiscal barriers.

The Single European Market operates within a framework of European organizations and decision-taking bodies, each of which has a role in tourism:

- **The European Commission** Based in Brussels, the Commission was created to implement the Treaty of Rome and is effectively the 'civil service' of Europe. Its remit is to provide the *European* dimension by initiating, implementing and policing EU legislation. It is made up of a series of departments – or Directorates. Tourism is in Directorate General XXIII.
- **The European Parliament** The Parliament is based in Brussels and Strasbourg. It is an elected body and debates and amends European legislation. The Parliament has traditionally been supportive of tourism initiatives at Community level.
- **The Council of Ministers** The Council makes decisions about European legislation, once it has been initiated by the Commission and debated by Parliament. The Council acts as a counterbalance to the unifying role of the Commission by representing the *national* interest of member countries. Statements by the Council relating to tourism have triggered significant policy initiatives.
- **The European Court of Justice** The European Court is based in The Hague with the remit to interpret the Treaty of Rome and make judgments. The Court would make judgments over any dispute concerning tourism policy or related policy as it impacts upon tourism.
- **European Investment Bank (EIB)** The EIB provides long-term loans and supports regional development in the EU. Tourism projects benefit from regional development schemes.
- **Committee of the Regions** The Committee comprises representatives of regions and cities across the EU, and is an increasingly important forum for tourism initiatives.
- **The Economic and Social Committee** This advisory committee is focused on social and employment issues – both critical areas for tourism.

In the early years of the twenty-first century the impetus for a united Europe has spread to countries of the former Eastern bloc and those on the fringes of Europe such as Malta and Cyprus. The entry of these countries may re-focus the distribution of regional funds away from the original members of the EU. The following countries, some of which are significant tourism destinations, became part of an enlarged European Union in 2004:

- Cyprus
- Czech Republic
- Estonia

- Hungary
- Latvia
- Lithuania
- Malta
- Poland
- Slovakia
- Slovenia

The implications of European policies for tourism

The legislation and initiatives that have created the Single European Market have had a number of implications for tourism. These can be considered in terms of:

1 Tourism policy – which is a minor element of the Community's business and budget.
2 Other policy areas – such as transport and regional development – which have considerable influence and budgets.

Tourism policy in the European Union

The fact that Europe has a supra-national tourism policy that relates to all member states is unusual if we compare it to other geographical regions of the world. It reflects the importance of tourism in the EU, estimated to directly generate over 8 million jobs and account for at least 5 per cent of gross domestic product. However, the tourism policy for Europe is relatively recent and has undergone a number of changes over time; indeed it has been criticized as being piecemeal and ad hoc. Equally, the policy has had much less impact upon the tourism sector than some of the other policies we later outline in Part 2. This is partly because, at European level, there is no legal authority to act in the tourism field, and the view has been that the 'subsidiarity' principle operates – i.e. that tourism is a matter for member states and not for Europe as a whole.

Significant events in the development of a tourism policy for Europe include:

- **1980** Establishment of a Tourism Commissioner.
- **1982** *Initial Guidelines on a Community Policy for Tourism*, stressing: the need for freedom of movement; the importance of social tourism; improving working conditions in the tourism sector; the problem of seasonality; regional development; and the importance of cultural tourism.
- **1984** European Court judgment that the EU could intervene in tourism matters under the principle of free movement of persons, services and capital. The Council of Ministers emphasized the need for tourism to be given greater consideration in the Community.
- **1986** *Community Action in the Field of Tourism* was published, setting out the Commission's objectives in tourism as: freedom of movement; addressing temporal and spatial imbalances; providing information and protection for tourists; improving working conditions; and improving tourism statistics. This document

firmly established tourism as an element of Community policy and saw an increase in the tourism budget.

- 1988 – Proposal for the European Year of Tourism to be held in order to stress preparations for the 1992 initiative; this would promote tourism generally, but with an emphasis on different cultures and lifestyles, and a more even distribution of tourism, both seasonally and by region.
- **1989** Directorate General XXIII (DG XXIII) of the Commission was established to implement the European Year of Tourism. Also the Council of Ministers made a statement on the direction that tourism should take in the Community, emphasizing the following:
  - ○ the subsidiarity rule for tourism
  - ○ cooperation between member states on tourism strategy
  - ○ a Community tourism policy benefiting the individual traveller and tourism enterprises
  - ○ the need for a better distribution of tourism
  - ○ the need to invest in human resources in tourism
  - ○ the setting up of a statistical action plan for tourism
  - ○ the need to coordinate Community policies in terms of infrastructure for tourism.
- **1990** European Year of Tourism – not an unqualified success.
- **1991** *The Community Action Plan to Assist Tourism* was published based on the Council of Ministers' statement in 1989. The plan ran from 1993 to 1995 aiming to: improve tourism statistics; stagger holidays; encourage cooperation between members; offer consumer protection; raise awareness of tourism and the environment; encourage cultural tourism, rural tourism, social tourism, youth training and promotion of Europe as a destination.
- **1995** A Green Paper was published on *The Role of the Union in the Field of Tourism*. This advisory document laid out four options for future EC involvement in tourism ranging from effectively doing nothing and leaving tourism to member states (option 1), to a full treatment of tourism at Community level (option 4).
- 1996 – *The First Multiannual Programme to Assist European Tourism – Philoxenia* (literally from the Greek 'hospitality towards visitors') was proposed by the Commission as a new programme to ensure continuity of action in tourism. This also addressed issues such as the impact of tourism, competitiveness and quality.
- **1997** The European Parliament voted for option 4 in the 1995 Green Paper, effectively creating a new tourism role for the European Commission working together with member states. This implies that the Treaty of Rome would need to be revised to include a 'tourism competence'. This year also saw the publication of the first in a series of European Commission reports on employment in tourism – *Employment in Tourism – Guidelines for Action*.
- **1999** A significant year for tourism in the EU. First, it saw the introduction of the 'euro' as the European Union's currency with major implications for tourism. Secondly, for the first time the Council of Ministers failed to support tourism and rejected Philoxenia – the European programme to assist tourism. As a result, the policy focus shifted towards tourism as an employment generator with the publication of the European Commission's document *Enhancing Tourism's Potential for Employment*.
- **2001** Establishment of DG XXIII working groups to examine the future of tourism in Europe. These informed the Commission's policy paper on *Working Together for the Future of European Tourism*. This document stressed the need for

partnerships and cooperation in the tourism sector and for the sustainability and competitiveness of European tourism.

- **2002**   Adoption of Council of Ministers' decision to support *Working Together for the Future of European Tourism*, the closer monitoring of the impact of EU policy on tourism, and examination of the promotion of Europe as a destination.

Related policy issues that affect tourism

Removal of physical barriers

- **Legislation**   Legislation to remove barriers to travel and the free movement of goods and services allows for the free movement of travellers between member states and implies the abolition of border controls and customs within the EU.
- **Transport policy**   Transport policy has had a major effect upon tourism in two ways:
  - First, through the creation of free movement by enhancing surface travel 'through routes' across Europe.
  - Secondly, through the deregulation of transport. The major development here has been the three-stage deregulation of European air transport, with the effect of enhancing the role of regional airports, supporting smaller airlines and changing the patterns of air travel across Europe.

Removal of technical barriers

- **Regional development**   The different types of structural funds are designed to remove regional disparities across Europe. Tourism is a major beneficiary through the encouragement of small enterprises, the regeneration of rural, urban and declining industrial areas, and through job creation.
- **Environmental legislation**   A range of environmental initiatives have influenced tourism, in particular directives on water quality, environmental impact and auditing legislation, and benchmarking exercises such as the 'Blue Flag' beach scheme.
- **Social legislation**   Here tourism is affected through the provisions to enhance the working conditions of part-time and temporary workers and the mutual recognition of qualifications across member states. This will encourage labour mobility in tourism across the EU. However, some argue that restrictions on working hours, in an industry that is characterized by 'anti-social' hours, could make Europe less competitive with North America and the EAP region in maintaining its share of the international tourism market.
- **Consumer protection policy**   This has important implications for tourism. The Package Travel Directive is designed to provide protection for those booking inclusive tours; the Timeshare Directive protects those purchasing timeshare accommodation and there are a range of information initiatives which involve tourism.

Removal of fiscal barriers

- **Economic and Monetary Union**   The introduction of a Single European Currency (the euro) and the creation of a 'euro-zone' has facilitated travel throughout Europe by doing away with currency exchange. It also acts as a basis for fare construction and encourages pan-European travel companies.

- **Harmonization of taxes and duties**   Here there are a range of policies that aim to provide a 'level playing field' for competition across Europe. There are two areas where tourism is directly affected:
  - The removal of duty free allowances for travellers between member states is a contentious issue as transport operators and terminals make a large profit on duty free goods.
  - The harmonization of value-added taxes on the sale of goods and services (VAT) across Europe will impact upon tourism enterprises and the government revenue of member states.

Reflections on the case

There is no doubt that tourism is a very important element of the European Union's economy and society, and this is reflected in the fact that the EU is one of the few regions of the world to attempt a transnational tourism policy. However, the constitution of the EU has meant that tourism has been sidelined from a policy point of view and most significant decisions affecting tourism take place in other legislative areas of the EU such as transport and regional development.

Discussion points/assignments

1 Using WTO sources, draw a map of the key international tourism flows within and into Europe. Identify the major generating countries for Europe and the major destination countries on the map.

2 Choose one of the countries admitted to the EU in 2004 and draft a checklist of the effects EU entry will have on tourism in that country.

3 List the achievements of European tourism policy and rank the list in terms of (i) effective initiatives and (ii) significant initiatives. For example, the European Year of Tourism may or may not have been effective, but was it significant when set against other issues such as seasonality?

4 Draft a table with the most significant European policy initiatives for tourism that have been implemented as the columns, and the policy area (tourism, transport, consumer protection etc.) as the rows. What does this table tell us about the difficulties of devising policy for a fragmented sector such as tourism?

5 What do you understand by the 'subsidiarity principle' and do you believe that it is right to apply it to tourism in the EU?

Key sources

Davidson, R. (1998) *Travel and Tourism in Europe*. Addison Wesley Longman, Harlow.

Horner, S. and Swarbrooke, J. (1996) *Marketing Tourism, Leisure and Hospitality in Europe*. International Thomson Business Press, London.

Montanaria, A. and Williams, A. (1995) *European Tourism: Regions, Spaces and Restructuring*. Wiley, Chichester.

Pompl, W. and Lavery, P. (1993) *Tourism in Europe: Structures and Developments*. CAB, Wallingford.

Williams, A. M. and Shaw, G. J. (1991) *Tourism and Economic Development: Western European Experiences*. Belhaven, London.

World Tourism Organization (2004) *European Integration in the Era of the European Union's Enlargement and the Development of Tourism*. WTO, Madrid.

Website

http://Europa.eu.int

Case 8

Crisis and risk management in tourism

Introduction

Since 2001, the tourism sector has been affected by a series of 'shocks', including '9/11' and the Bali bombings. This case shows how the sector has come to terms with the inevitability of such events and the process of crisis management. On completing the case you will:

1 Recognize that crises can be either man-made, natural, or a combination of both.
2 Understand the severity of the impact of major crises on the tourism sector.
3 Be aware of the process of crisis management and the stages of planning following a crisis.
4 Be familiar with tourism sector's response to 9/11.
5 Evaluate the response to health crises that can disrupt international tourism.

Key issues

There are five key issues in this case:

1 Crises are now seen as an inevitable part of doing business in tourism, but this fact means that the tourism sector must plan to anticipate crises and manage them better when they occur.
2 There have been a series of shocks to the tourism sector since 2000, including 9/11 and the Bali and Madrid bombings. It is these shocks that have prompted the tourism sector to engage in crisis management.

3 The impact of the major crises that have occurred since 2000 has been severe, driving airlines into bankruptcy and affecting tourism flows around the world.
4 Crisis and risk management has been embraced by the tourism sector as it struggles to come to terms with recent events. This planning approach is a disciplined one with a series of stages and guidelines for anticipating and dealing with crises.
5 Not all crises are a result of terrorist acts, but crisis management provides a framework to deal with different types of crisis, such as the SARS epidemic, or natural disasters, such as earthquakes.

Tourism and crisis

Tourism is potentially at risk from natural and man-made disasters, particularly in developing countries that can ill-afford the loss of foreign exchange. The vulnerability of the tourism sector has been highlighted since 2001 through several major events. The first of these was the terrorist attack on the Twin Towers of the World Trade Center in New York and the Pentagon building in Washington on 11 September 2001 followed by the war in Afghanistan, the Bali nightclub bombings in October 2002, the bombing of an Israeli-owned hotel in Mombasa, the SARS epidemic in 2003 and the Iraq War. The Bali atrocity was disastrous for the economy of Indonesia and beach resorts in other parts of Asia; the SARS outbreak severely affected demand throughout Asia, particularly to the destinations most affected – China, Hong Kong and Singapore – and also Toronto in Canada, where cases of the disease were identified. But it was 9/11 that had the most impact, with international tourism demand falling dramatically in the last quarter of 2001. This crisis forced a number of airlines into bankruptcy and reduced the profitability of tourism businesses worldwide. Travellers deferred their trips, initially through fear of further attacks, and later by anxiety that their jobs might be at risk in the subsequent downturn of the global economy.

The incidents had a number of significant effects on tourism:

1 There was an immediate response on behalf of governments and international agencies to put together rescue packages for the tourism industry.
2 There was a call for better market intelligence in all sectors of tourism.
3 The term 'crisis and risk management' entered the vocabulary of tourism.
4 Security measures and immigration procedures were tightened.

You should be aware of the many other crises and natural disasters that have a more localized effect, such as the following:

• Man-made crises, such as fires, riots, prolonged strikes, kidnappings, air crashes and other transport disasters, business failures, oil spillages destroying beaches and ecosystems.
• Natural disasters, such as earthquakes and volcanic eruptions, floods (which devastated Dresden and Prague in the summer of 2002) and hurricanes.
• Crises that are partly man-made and partly due to natural causes, such as widespread power blackouts disrupting transport, and most forest fires.

Crisis and risk management planning

Crisis and risk management recognizes that we must be prepared for crises and lays down a response pattern to such events. A risk management plan allows a destination or organization to prepare for and manage a crisis and so reduce its potential impacts. Such impacts can be severe, not simply in terms of loss of life or damage to property, but also in negative media coverage.

The Pacific Asia Travel Association (PATA) defines a crisis as 'any situation that has the potential to affect long-term confidence in an organisation or a product, or which may interfere with the ability to continue operating normally' (PATA, 2003, p. 2).

Crisis and risk management plans are now in place for many destinations. International agencies such as the WTO, UNCTAD and PATA are publishing guidelines for the sector on the development of such plans. The essence of risk management is to assess what can go wrong at a destination or in an organization, to determine the most significant risks and implement strategies to deal with those risks. However, once a crisis occurs, then a crisis management plan is put into action. This typically demands strong leadership from within the organization and often the formation of a crisis management team. The template for a crisis management plan normally contains the following elements – sometimes known as 'the four Rs of crisis management':

1 **Reduction**   The initial identification of potential crises and risks, and also the strengths and weaknesses of the destination or organization, in order to reduce the impact of a crisis.
2 **Readiness**   The development of a plan and continual assessment of response tactics and strategies.
3 **Response**   If a crisis occurs, this takes effect in the immediate aftermath of the event. It involves an operational response focused on damage limitation, and a communications response focusing on reassurance.
4 **Recovery**   In the event of a crisis, a useful gauge of the effectiveness of the plan is the speed with which the organization re-assumes normal operations and business returns to pre-crisis levels. It is interesting that business in the tourist sector has returned to normality more quickly after each successive crisis following 9/11.

The US security response to 9/11

The events of 9/11 underscored the lack of such crisis management planning for tourism and the need to put into effect elements 3 and 4 (Response and Recovery) of a crisis management plan after the event. This was particularly true of the USA, where 9/11 highlighted the lack of security procedures at airports; it was less evident in the EU where security systems were already in place as a result of the bombing of a Pan-Am airliner in 1988. Although the Federal Aviation Administration (FAA) had for long been the agency responsible for the safety of air travel, it now came under scrutiny, with many alleging that it was too sympathetic to the commercial interests of the airlines and therefore too lax in the enforcement of security measures. In the wake of 9/11 a new federal agency – the Transport Security Administration (TSA) – was set up by Congress to oversee airport security. This included taking over responsibility for baggage checks from private companies and training airport staff in security procedures. In 2002 the TSA came under the direction of the Department of Homeland Security, which has a coordinating role in bringing together the array of agencies concerned with immigration, customs and emergency services, as well as domestic security. The response to 9/11 includes the following:

- Intelligence-led measures, such as the profiling of airline and airport employees as well as passengers to identify those considered a high risk, using ID cards containing biometric data.
- More effective crowd control in terminals, separating passengers from 'meeters and greeters'.
- The installation of automated baggage screening systems at airports.
- Anti-terrorism training for cabin crews, backed up on some flights by armed air marshals or 'skymasters' employed by the federal government. (The use of air marshals has been standard practice for many years on flights by El Al, the Israeli national airline.)
- Restrictions on airspace over metropolitan areas and those installations considered most at risk.

Cost-effective security is problematic, however, in view of the vast scale of air travel in the USA. For example:

- At noon on a typical day over 6000 commercial and general aviation aircraft are flying in US airspace.
- Commercial airlines operate out of 429 airports, but in addition there are some 8000 small airports and airfields that are more difficult to police effectively. These are used by charter airlines catering mainly for business executives, who are trying to avoid the security delays prevalent since 9/11 at the larger airports.

At least in the short term, most Americans are prepared to accept some inconvenience to their travel arrangements as part of the war on terrorism. However, some see the gathering of data on passengers by government agencies as surveillance, inappropriate in a free society, and a threat to civil liberties.

The response to health crises

The connection between foreign travel and the spread of infectious disease has been recognized for centuries with the imposition of quarantine restrictions on travellers arriving at a country's ports. These originated in medieval Venice, where ships had to wait for 40 days (*quaranta giorni* in Italian) before passengers and crew were permitted to land, in order to protect the city from plague. The recent outbreak of SARS (severe acute respiratory syndrome) is a reminder of how rapidly disease can spread in the age of jet travel. The authorities were able to contain the epidemic, helped by the coordinating role of the World Health Organization, while the wearing of surgical masks by people flying to and from Asian countries also proved fairly effective in limiting the spread of infection. In theory bio-terrorists might get hold of the smallpox virus, which is much more readily transmitted through the air than other diseases. Of more everyday concern to customs officers are the illegal imports of plant and animal materials by travellers – such as 'bushmeat' from West Africa – that can contaminate a country's agricultural products.

The security measures now being taken at airports and seaports around the world show how seriously the tourism sector is taking the threat of future crises and the lengths to which it will go to prevent them. The terms 'crisis', 'risk' and 'security' have become much more significant since 2001, and this is likely to continue.

Reflections on the case

Crises are now seen as an inevitable part of the business of tourism. The tourism sector therefore recognizes the need for effective crisis and risk management at both destination and company levels. This is an important step forward, ensuring that the sector is better prepared for future disasters and hopefully more capable of reducing their impact.

Discussion points/assignments

1 Draft a report to the mayor of New York outlining how consumer behaviour has changed in tourism as a result of 9/11 and the impact that this has had on the city since the event.
2 Draw up a classification of the major crises that can affect tourism and against each draft a brief paragraph explaining how crisis management might help to reduce their impact.
3 Take a recent crisis that has affected the tourism industry and, using the Internet and media sources, plot a timeline of how the major events affecting tourism unfolded following the crisis. Compare notes with others in the class – is there a common pattern to the timeline?
4 Take a tourism destination that you know well and draft a report to the manager outlining 'the four Rs' of crisis management and how that resort might use 'the four Rs' to plan for a future crisis.
5 Why do you think it took an event of such magnitude as 9/11 to prompt the tourism sector to take crisis management seriously?

Key sources

Bierman, D. (2002) *Restoring Tourism Destinations in Crisis: A Strategic Marketing Approach*. CABI, Wallingford.

Keller, P. (2003) *Crisis Management in the Tourism Industry*. Elsevier Butterworth-Heinemann, Oxford.

Pacific Asia Travel Association (2003) *Crisis: It Won't Happen to Us!* PATA, Bangkok.

Pizam, A. and Mansfield, Y. (1996) *Tourism, Crime and International Security Issues*. Wiley, Chichester.

Wilks, J. and Page, S. (2003) *Managing Tourist Health and Safety in the New Millennium*. Elsevier Butterworth-Heinemann, Oxford.

Withers, R. (2002) Managing the impact of natural and man-made disasters on tourism. *Tourism-2002*, MICG Publishing and the Tourism Society, pp. 28–30.

World Tourism Organization (1996) *Tourist Safety and Security: Practical Measures for Destinations*. WTO, Madrid.

World Tourism Organization (1998) *Handbook on Natural Disaster Reduction in Tourist Areas*. WTO, Madrid.

2.3
Tourism destination futures

Case 9

Space: the final tourism frontier?

Introduction

This case study analyses the future activity of space tourism by referring to Leiper's (1979) tourism system and the tourist area life cycle. On completion of the case you will:

1 Be aware of the history of space tourism as an idea.
2 Understand the barriers to space tourism.
3 Be aware of the various stages of the life cycle of space tourism.
4 Be able to identify the various components of the space tourism system.
5 Have an awareness of the future of space tourism.

Key issues

There are five key issues in this case:

1 Space tourism has long been the goal of many individuals and corporations, but the practicalities of sending tourists into space are difficult.
2 Space tourism can mean many different things, including Earth-based space tourism attractions as well as actually travelling into space.
3 The barriers to space tourism are significant and include both the cost and the safety aspects of space travel.
4 There is no doubt that space tourism will become a reality in the future when technological and cost barriers have been reduced.
5 The future of space tourism is assured with not only low orbit activity but also visits to the Moon and possibly Mars.

Space tourism

Space tourism has been defined (Collins and Ashford, 1998) as:

The taking of short pleasure trips in low earth orbit by members of the public.

'Space' begins at an altitude of 100 kilometres, where air density ceases to have any effect on the movement of aircraft and the stars are always visible in the black sky. On a sub-orbital flight to just above this altitude in 'near space' you would experience a few minutes of weightlessness before your craft re-entered the atmosphere at 'Mach 5' (five times the speed of sound).

Space travel emerged from the realms of science fiction with the unmanned Russian Sputnik launch in 1957, followed by the first cosmonaut flight in 1961 and the success of NASA's Apollo missions in landing a total of 12 American astronauts on the Moon between 1969 and 1972. However, the 'space race' was inspired by the Cold War rivalry between the two superpowers, and the momentum for further exploration was not maintained. The space race – this time for tourism – has been boosted since 1996 by the 'X prize' – a US$10 million award by an American foundation to the first entrepreneur to build a craft that can carry three passengers into space, return them safely and make another voyage within two weeks. The first space tourist did not appear on the scene until May 2001, paying US$20 million to visit the International Space Station for a week, but there is now the very real possibility of space tourism subsidising the costs of space exploration. According to the Space Tourism Society we are seeing an emerging type of tourism that not only includes sub-orbital and orbital voyages in near space, but also related activities here on Earth, such as simulated space experiences (for example, Disney's new ride SPACE, simulating a mission to Mars), and tours of space research centres. The goal of the Space Tourism Society is:

To conduct the research, build public desire, and acquire the financial and political power to make space tourism available to as many people as possible as soon as possible.

But if space tourism has attracted so much attention – and is technically feasible – why has it taken so long to be realized? We can identify a number of key reasons for this:

- **Cost and investment** Space tourism is prohibitively expensive, because of the high cost of launches and the fact that space vehicles are not yet truly 'reusable'. Powering a spacecraft requires vast amounts of heavy fuel. To date, space programmes have relied on ballistic missile technology to launch or service satellites and space stations. This is both costly and wasteful, as the launch rockets are destroyed each time they are used, while NASA's space shuttles have to jettison their fuel tanks during each launch. The development of rocket-propelled *spaceplane*s as re-usable launch vehicles (RLVs) would greatly reduce costs, with a turnaround of a few days between landing and re-launch. Even so, they would need significant demand to make them profitable. This is where the private sector would provide the marketing expertise, with access to venture capital for investment in spaceplane development. However, entrepreneurs would also need the cooperation of government space agencies, who generally have shown little interest in space tourism.
- **Health and safety issues** Incidents such as the *Columbia* shuttle disaster in 2002 mean that safety will continue to be a real issue for space tourism, in terms of

consumer perceptions, and the willingness of insurance companies to become involved. Spaceplanes would be a much lower risk than the existing shuttles, which have had a fatal accident rate 10 000 times higher than commercial airliners (Ashford, 2003, p. 89). Health issues in space also act as a constraint, as does the noise associated with the launch. Space exploration results in a number of changes to the human body due to zero gravity such as a loss in bone density. Astronauts adapt quickly to weightlessness, but exposure to solar and cosmic radiation is a more insidious problem. None of these would constitute a health risk to tourists, as distinct from crew members, on a sub-orbital flight lasting a few hours, but the situation might well be different for those staying at a 'space hotel' or undertaking longer orbital voyages.

The life cycle of space tourism

We can broadly envisage the life cycle of space tourism as four phases of development:

- **Pioneer phase**   Here the price per trip ranges from $100 000 to $20 million, but even so the market is currently estimated to be 10 000 a year in the USA alone, and many of these prospective travellers have already paid thousands of dollars as a deposit for their first adventure in space. Elaborate facilities will not be required or developed in this phase, and it is likely that wealthy tourists would ride in spare seats on existing space missions, so that accommodation would be spartan rather than 'de luxe'.
- **Exclusive phase**   By now the price has fallen to $10 000–$100 000 per trip, attracting a wider market. The trips will be available on a regular basis, with greater levels of comfort and attention to issues such as the quality of the experience. Facilities will be more extensive and accommodation could be in clusters of pre-fabricated modules.
- **Mature phase**   The price has fallen to $2000–$10 000 with significant growth in the market, fuelled by competition between the various suppliers. Facilities would be available on a large scale with accommodation constructed in orbit for hundreds of guests.
- **Mass market phase**   This phase is reached when sub-orbital space trips become the equivalent of the air inclusive tour of the late twentieth century, with tens of millions of passengers every year. We can then expect segmentation of the market to cater for different interest groups.

The components of a mature space tourism system

Using Leiper's tourism system we can analyse space tourism in terms of the generating region, the destination region and the transit zone.

The generating region for space tourism

The actual volume of demand for space tourism will depend upon price, the length of stay in space and the associated facilities. Also, medical advances, such as drugs to combat motion sickness, would make the flight more appealing. On Earth, demand will be stimulated by the development of spaceports in countries as diverse as Tonga and Kazakhstan, and space-tourism centres – such as Florida's 'Space Coast' – where prospective tourists can experience simulated space flights. We can expect the USA and Japan to be among the leading generators of space tourism, followed by a shortlist that would probably include China, the UK, France, Germany, Russia and Brazil – countries at the forefront in space research.

The destination region for space tourism

Accommodation may be expected to grow from orbiting hotels for a few hundred guests, to orbiting resort-theme parks with accommodation for thousands of guests. On offer is the experience of a lifetime, including:

- viewing 'Spaceship Earth', with a constantly changing panorama
- astronomy
- recreation activities designed to make use of micro-gravity, such as swimming, gymnastics, new forms of dance, unassisted human flight and ball games
- spacewalks 'on the outside' (wearing a pressure suit)
- simulated exotic worlds using hydroponics to grow low-gravity plants, possibly as an experiment in *'terraforming'* – with the eventual aim of making Mars habitable.

The transit zone

By the mature phase of space tourism, transportation will involve *shuttle ferries* to take passengers to their orbiting hotel/resort, as well as cargo vehicles for launching the accommodation modules. By this stage, the ferries will operate like airlines with substantial numbers of craft. The flight experience will be designed to provide moderate acceleration during boost and re-entry, and the ferries would have the capability to operate from conventional airports.

Mars: the next frontier?

According to the WTO, tourism in near space (defined as anywhere closer than the Moon) should be almost commonplace by 2020. Travel in outer space on the other hand will probably not be feasible for at least another generation. A spaceship would take nine months to reach Mars, plus a stay of at least a year on the 'red planet', waiting for orbital alignment with the Earth, before the return voyage could take place. Nevertheless, there will inevitably be a demand for voyages beyond low orbit from the adventurous, 'elite' type of tourist, and this will provide the impetus for a technological breakthrough in space travel. Robot 'landers' will provide a great deal of information about Mars – its immense volcanoes and other landscape features, some Earth-like, others completely alien – but only a human visitor can communicate the *experience* of actually being there.

Reflections on the case

Space tourism has long been the dream of many, but the significant technological, cost and safety barriers have meant that it is yet to be a reality for all but a handful of millionaires. However, as this case shows, by taking a longer look into the future and applying the life cycle concept, space tourism will be a reality at some point in the future once these barriers have been overcome.

Discussion points/assignments

Draft a timeline of the events surrounding the history of space travel using the Internet and other sources. Extrapolate events on the timeline into the future using the life cycle concept.

1 Draw up a brochure for a short, low orbit space tourism product. Focus your product *either* on the whole experience from Earth to space and back; *or* on the space experience element of the product at the destination.
2 Choose an Earth-based tourism attraction and analyse its success in terms of visitor numbers, the experience and its economics. Do you think that these Earth-based attractions are a substitute for space travel?
3 Draw up a market segmentation for space tourists in the mature stage of the space tourism life cycle.
4 Debate in class the WTO's assertion that space tourism will be commonplace by 2020.

Key sources

Ashford, D. (2003) *Spaceflight Revolution*. Imperial College Press, London.

Collins, P. and Ashford, D. (1998) Space tourism. *Ada Astronautica*, 17 (4), 421–431.

Crouch, G. (2001) The market for space tourism: early indications. *Journal of Travel Research*, 40 (2), 213–219.

Leiper, N. (1979) The framework of tourism. *Annals of Tourism Research*, 6 (4), 390–407.

Monbiot, G. (2000) Space tourism: burning up the planet. *Contours*, 10 (3), 17–18.

Newberry, B. (1997) The ultimate room with a view. *Geographical*, 69 (10), 9–14.

Smith, V. L. (2000) Space tourism: the 21st century 'Frontier'. *Tourism Recreation Research*, 25 (3), 5–15.

Websites

http://www.spacetourismsociety.org
http://www.xprize.org
http://www.spaceadventures.com

Case 10

Tourism as agent of poverty alleviation

Introduction

Poverty has become one of the world's major challenges. This case study outlines recent attempts to use tourism as one means of alleviating poverty. On completion of the case you will:

1 Understand the definition of poverty.
2 Recognize the benefits that tourism can bring to alleviating poverty.
3 Understand the various strategies that can be used by tourism to alleviate poverty.
4 Be aware of some of the difficulties in implementing these strategies.
5 Be aware of some of the scepticism surrounding the use of tourism as an agent of poverty alleviation.

Key issues

There are five key issues in this case:

1 Poverty can be defined in a number of different ways, but international agencies recognize that, however defined, it is important to address poverty.
2 The nature of tourism as an activity means that it lends itself well to being used as an agent of poverty alleviation. It is, for example, labour-intensive and requires little in the way of skills.
3 There is a variety of strategies that can be adopted for pro-poor tourism. These include boosting local employment, incomes, lifestyle and involvement.
4 A number of issues affect the success of pro-poor tourism strategies including the distribution of benefits, ownership of the activity and the area's access to tourism resources.
5 There are a number of significant barriers to the successful adoption of pro-poor tourism.

Poverty

Poverty has become one of the world's major challenges. The World Bank's definition of poverty is anyone living on less than one US dollar per day. But poverty is much more than just an economic issue – other ways of thinking about poverty include issues of living conditions and access to resources. One of the conclusions of the World Summit on Sustainable Development held in Johannesburg in 2002 was the recognition that tourism could make a real contribution to poverty reduction. Yet surprisingly, the role of tourism in poverty alleviation is a recent initiative. In the past, economic, regional and environmental issues dominated thinking on tourism development. However, the Johannesburg agenda is emerging as a central issue for tourism in the future – the role of tourism development as a means of reducing world poverty.

Pro-poor tourism

Sometimes called 'pro-poor tourism' (PPT), this new agenda has been enthusiastically embraced by the developing world and international agencies (including the WTO, UNCTAD and the World Bank). The WTO, for example, has developed a programme 'sustainable tourism – eliminating poverty' (ST–EP).

PPT is an approach, not a product or a type of tourism – a good definition is 'tourism that results in increased net benefits for poor people'. The critical issue is 'how can tourism reduce poverty at the local level, and therefore what policies, strategies and plans can be put into place to enhance poverty alleviation?' As yet there is little real experience of operating pro-poor tourism and the answers to these questions represent a steep learning curve for aid agencies and destinations alike.

Tourism has many advantages as a sector for pro-poor development:

- Tourism is produced where it is consumed – the tourist has to visit the destination, allowing opportunities for economic gain.
- Tourism is labour-intensive and employs a high percentage of women.
- Tourism is naturally attracted to remote, peripheral areas where other economic options are limited.
- Tourism is significant and growing in the developing and least-developed countries (LDCs), such as most of the 12 countries that are home to 80 per cent of the world's poorest people (see Table 10.1). These include China, Vietnam, Laos,

Table 10.1 Relative importance of tourism compared to exports of goods in 2000

	OECD countries	European Union	Developing countries	Least Developed Countries (LDCs)
Tourism receipts as percentage of export earnings	8.0	7.5	8.5	11.3

Cambodia, Myanmar and a number of Pacific islands. (On the other hand, many of the LDCs in Africa have failed to develop a significant tourism sector so far.)

Strategies for pro-poor tourism

We can classify pro-poor strategies into three types:

- Delivering economic benefits such as:
  - creating jobs allowing a measure of security in household income
  - providing opportunities for small businesses both directly and indirectly supplying tourists with goods such as handicrafts and food
  - development of local cooperatives
  - increasing the economic benefits for the whole community – by renting communal land for camping, for example.
- Delivering improved living conditions:
  - training and education, reducing environmental impacts of tourism, reducing competition for natural resources, and improved access to services such as schooling, health care, communications and infrastructure improvements.
- Delivering participation and involvement benefits:
  - changing the policy and planning framework to allow participation by local communities, increasing participation in decision making and developing partnerships with the private sector.

Delivery of pro-poor tourism will depend upon the types of strategic objectives taken from the above list:

- Destination-based strategies work well for poverty alleviation in particular groups, encouraging economic linkages between, say, tourism businesses and local farmers to reduce leakage through imports, boosting partnerships, developing local enterprises and increasing community pride.
- National policy-based strategies are preferred for objectives such as changing systems of land tenure, improving planning procedures, training and education, and infrastructure development.

Successful implementation of these strategies will depend upon some key principles, recognizing:

- the imperative of local ownership and control
- that tourism is a system demanding access to transport, accommodation and the wider range of support services and products
- that the principles of pro-poor tourism are the same everywhere, but that their implementation will vary according to the type of tourism product from, say, small-scale ecotourism to mass tourism
- the need to develop partnerships with the private sector on an equitable footing
- not all the poor will benefit equally
- the focus must be on delivering benefits, not just cutting costs.

However, there are barriers to the implementation of pro-poor tourism strategies. These include:

- a perception by aid agencies that tourism is for the wealthy
- significant economic leakages out of the local community, reducing the net benefits of tourism
- lack of education, training and understanding about pro-poor tourism
- lack of investment and low interest loans to allow local tourism enterprises to get under way
- lack of infrastructure and basic services in very poor areas.

But despite these barriers, the idea of pro-poor tourism is gaining momentum and should be central to the agenda of tourism development in the future.

Reflections on the case

There is no doubt that poverty is one of the world's major challenges. Recent international initiatives have shown that tourism can play an important role in alleviating poverty. This is known as pro-poor tourism and well-tried strategies now exist to use tourism in this way. However, despite the optimism surrounding the idea of pro-poor tourism, there are a number of barriers that will have to be overcome, if tourism is to become an effective agent of poverty reduction.

Discussion points/assignments

1 Using the Internet and other media sources, identify a tourism project that is designed to alleviate poverty. Identify the type of pro-poor strategy that is being used and draft a list of possible issues that may affect the success of the project.
2 Design a brochure for a tourism experience that contains a significant pro-poor element. Think carefully about how tourist spend can best benefit the host country. Websites from organizations such as OXFAM may help here.
3 Draft a code of conduct for a tour operator to give to their clients visiting poverty stricken countries. The code should identify appropriate forms of behaviour, and strategies for ensuring that the tourists' expenditure and activity benefits the poorer people in the community.
4 Utilizing United Nations sources, identify the countries with the most severe poverty problems on a world map. From your knowledge of the world's tourist-generating countries and destination countries (the WTO website will help here), how much hope is there that the two maps may one day look similar?
5 Draft a report to the sceptical head of a large charity justifying why you feel tourism could play a role in the charity's key objective of reducing poverty in Africa.

Key sources

Ashley, C., Boyd, C. and Goodwin, H. (2000) Pro-poor tourism: putting poverty at the heart of the tourism agenda. *Natural Resource Perspectives*, 51 (March), 1–12.
World Tourism Organization (2002) *Sustainable Tourism – Eliminating Poverty*. WTO, Madrid.

Websites

http://www.adb.org/Documents/Policies/Poverty_Reducation/default.asp
http://www.propoor tourism.org.uk
http://www.worldbank.org/poverty
http://www.world-tourism.org

Part 3

Cases Illustrating Regional Travel and Tourism Geography

3.1
Europe

Case 11

London Docklands: waterfront regeneration and tourism development

Introduction

This case presents the London Docklands as an excellent example of the way that tourism has contributed to the regeneration of an urban area. On completion of this case you will:

1 Understand how the London Docklands has been regenerated.
2 Recognize the role of tourism in the regeneration of London Docklands.
3 Understand the role of transport in the development of London Docklands.
4 Be aware of the distinctive nature of the tourist attractions in the London Docklands, many of which appeal to the local community.
5 Be aware of some of the constraints upon Docklands from a tourism development point of view.

Key issues

The five key issues in this case are:

1 London Docklands is an example of urban regeneration with a significant tourism component.
2 The transport system of the Docklands has been the subject of considerable development, but the main artery of the area – the River Thames – has been neglected.

3 A range of tourist attractions have been developed in the London Docklands and adjacent areas such as Greenwich, although the most significant – the Millennium Dome – has not been a success.
4 Most of the tourism developments have been designed to attract the local community as well as visitors from outside the area.
5 The London Docklands has a number of problems as a location for tourism development, including geographical location issues and the local authority management of the area.

Background

London Docklands is an example of tourism on a local scale, focusing on a small area. On the other hand this is also one of the world's largest projects for inner city regeneration, involving the redevelopment of almost 90 kilometres of waterfront, mainly for commercial or residential use. Although tourism has been something of an afterthought rather than part of the original scheme, the new developments attract over 1.5 million visitors a year to a neglected part of London.

As officially designated, London Docklands extends along both banks of the River Thames. As well as Wapping, the Isle of Dogs and the Royal Docks – which are generally regarded as part of the East End – it also includes the former Surrey Docks and a substantial area extending south of the river from London Bridge to Deptford (see Figure 11.1). Although physically separate, these areas have a shared history of domination by the shipping industry, social deprivation and marginalization from the rest of London.

The first enclosed docks were built in the early 1800s to alleviate the acute congestion of the shipping in the Pool of London (the section of the Thames between London Bridge and the Tower of London) and prevent theft of valuable cargoes. The last of the Royal Docks – the King George V – was not completed until shortly after the First World War. In the meantime the docks played a major role in Britain's overseas expansion and industry grew up nearby, along with low-grade housing to accommodate a vast pool of unskilled labour. Docklands – and the East End generally – had few amenities other than 'gin palaces'. St Saviour's Dock in Bermondsey was the setting for one of London's most notorious slums – Jacob's Island – described by Charles Dickens in *Oliver Twist*, while Whitechapel was the location for the 'Jack the Ripper' murders in the 1880s.

Docklands suffered severely from bombing during the Second World War, and although a considerable amount of slum clearance took place in the post-war period, the area remained visually unappealing and was shunned by tourists, partly because it was perceived to be crime-ridden. Also, the docks themselves had high fortress-like walls and security arrangements that prevented public access. The same was true of the waterfront of the Thames itself, an almost unbroken barrier of wharves and warehouses. The River Thames was no longer the transport artery for Londoners that it had been in the eighteenth century. Docklands was not easily accessible by public transport, with few Underground and suburban railway services compared to Central London. By the 1960s the enclosed docks had become obsolete due to the introduction of container ships requiring deepwater harbours.

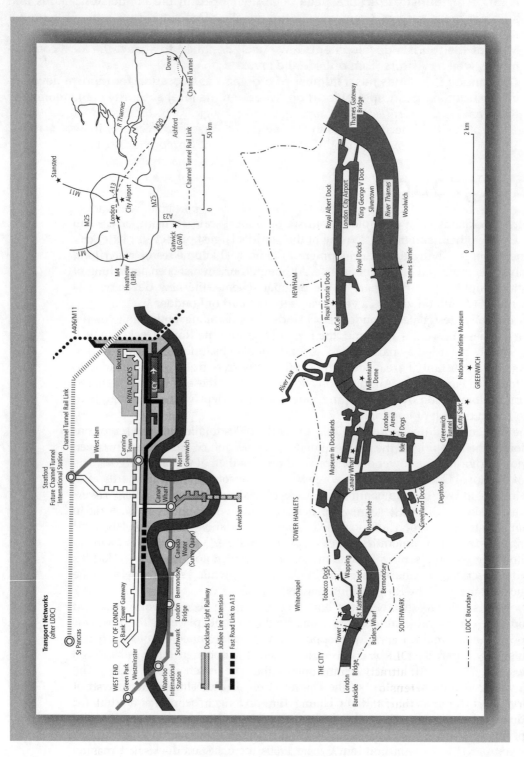

Figure 11.1 London Docklands

As a consequence, the East India, London, St Katherine and Surrey Docks were closed between 1967 and 1970, followed by the West India, Millwall and Royal Docks in 1981. With the loss of an estimated 50 000 jobs, Docklands faced severe social and economic problems. More than 2200 hectares of wet docks, wharves and warehouses now lay derelict, but the private sector was reluctant to invest in redevelopment and the task of urban renewal was clearly beyond the resources of the local authorities for the area – the borough councils of Newham, Southwark and Tower Hamlets.

The Conservative government then in power was ideologically committed to the use of market forces rather than state intervention to reverse the process of inner city decline. Nevertheless, it set up 13 Urban Development Corporations (UDCs) with wide-ranging powers to purchase land, prepare development plans and provide the necessary infrastructure. The sites were then sold or leased to private developers at market value. The London Docklands Development Corporation (LDDC) was the best known of these public agencies. Also of particular relevance to tourism were those UDCs responsible for large-scale redevelopment of inner city and waterfront areas in Bristol, Central Manchester and Liverpool. The LDDC was able to overrule any opposition to the scheme from the Labour-controlled local authorities for the area. Part of the LDDC area was designated by the government as an *Enterprise Zone*, where developers were granted generous tax relief and freedom from planning controls. With substantial financial backing from a Canadian corporation, this became the focus of a massive new office development project, centred on Canary Wharf and the former West India Docks.

Transport

Improved accessibility has been crucial to the success of London Docklands as a tourist destination and business venue. It has involved the following transport initiatives:

- **London City Airport (LCY)** This new airport, financed by the private sector, was designed to meet the needs of business executives, at a location much closer to London's financial district than congested Heathrow. However, the site, between two of the former Royal Docks, is restricted and was originally intended to be a STOL airport. The introduction of longer-range jet aircraft has enabled LCY to serve a growing number of destinations in Europe, while a costly road scheme has improved access to the City of London and the motorway network.
- **The Docklands Light Railway (DLR)** This rapid transit system serving the new developments in Docklands was financed by the LDDC, London Transport (now Transport for London) and the private sector. Elevated above street level, and fully automated, the DLR was a novelty when it was inaugurated in 1987 and soon became a tourist attraction in its own right.
- **The Jubilee Line Extension** This is part of the London Underground system, connecting Canary Wharf to the Channel Tunnel Rail Link terminal at Stratford and Waterloo Station. The Jubilee Line therefore improves the accessibility of Docklands and Greenwich, not only in relation to Central London, but also to the national and Continental rail networks. Canary Wharf Station – itself a masterpiece of civil engineering – is designed to handle 40 000 passengers an hour.

In contrast, the Thames is a neglected resource for transport. Although a variety of craft are used for floating restaurants, corporate entertaining, sightseeing tours and pleasure cruises, regular riverbus services, linking Docklands and Greenwich to the City and Westminster, have had to overcome the following problems:

- It is difficult to find suitable craft, which are fast, manoeuvrable and yet produce the minimum of wash.
- Operating costs per passenger are much higher than for road transport.
- There are restrictions on the use of piers by the Port of London Authority, who control most activities on the river.

In 2004 a new service was inaugurated which for the first time – as part of the Transport for London system – enabled riverbus passengers to use the 'Travelcard' facility. This encourages visitors to use public transport in off-peak times at reduced fares.

Attractions and amenities

London Docklands during the 1980s and 1990s was transformed from an industrial wasteland to a new *city on the water* dominated by ultra-modern business and residential developments. Whereas the old Docklands were a product of the Industrial Revolution, the new Docklands epitomize the 'Information Revolution' based on computer technology. Canary Wharf – boasting London's tallest building (Canada Tower) – is the flagship of the scheme, rivalling Frankfurt as one of Europe's most important financial centres. Not only has 'The City' spread eastwards, but also the newspaper publishing industry, formerly based in Fleet Street, has moved to Wapping and the Isle of Dogs. Many former warehouses of architectural merit have found new roles as restaurants, pubs, shops, artist's studios, apartments and museums. Some of the wet docks have become yacht marinas and provide facilities for a variety of water sports. These areas of open water, amounting to some 160 hectares – together with over 27 kilometres of waterfront now open to public access – are perhaps the most attractive feature of the new Docklands. Some 5000 beds have been added to the capital's accommodation stock, including a new youth hostel at Rotherhithe, and a custom-built 'yacht hotel' at Royal Victoria Dock. However, jobs in the hotel and catering sectors probably account for less than 10 per cent of the employment generated by the various development projects. Not all of these have proved to be successful; for example, Tobacco Wharf in Wapping was promoted as a Docklands version of Covent Garden, but its future as a leisure shopping centre is uncertain.

Most attractions and amenities in Docklands were designed primarily for use by local residents and the business community. Those of most significance to visitors include:

- **Leisure and shopping developments** – such as Hay's Galleria, Butler's Wharf and St Katherine's Dock, which have benefited from their proximity to well-known tourist attractions such as Tower Bridge and the Tower of London.
- **Conference and exhibition venues** are represented by Cabot Hall in the heart of Canary Wharf, and the ExCel Centre, which offers superior facilities to Earls

Court or Olympia. For this reason it was chosen as the venue for the 2002 World Travel Market. However, on opening day large numbers of exhibitors representing the travel and tourism industry suffered lengthy delays getting from their hotels in central London. Transport links need improvement to overcome the disadvantage of a peripheral location, but thanks to ExCel, a business centre is developing in the Royal Docks area that is set to rival Canary Wharf.

- **Heritage attractions** – compared to other areas of Inner London, Docklands has relatively few historic buildings. There are a few eighteenth-century churches, but these are far surpassed in tourist appeal by the riverside pubs in Wapping and Rotherhithe, which have traded on their past associations – real or imagined – with smugglers and pirates. More tangible reminders of the area's maritime heritage are the historic ships moored at the quays in St Katherine's and West India Docks. A former ocean-going liner, converted to a hotel and leisure centre, will boost the visitor appeal of Canary Wharf. The Museum in Docklands brings together materials relating to the development of London's port and its riverside communities from Roman times to the present day.
- **Sport attractions** include the London Arena, which is a major venue for concerts as well as sports events, drawing audiences from all over the capital. The Royal Victoria Dock is set to stage international water sports events, particularly in the light of London's bid for the 2012 Olympic Games.
- Other visitor attractions are proposed for this part of London, including a world-class aquarium at Silvertown.

Critics of the Docklands project allege that it has failed to benefit the local working class communities in terms of job opportunities, as most of these are in the banking and financial sector. The new riverside apartments have been purchased by highly paid City executives and middle-class professionals, while the *gentrification* of the area is also shown by the type of restaurants and shops that have proliferated. The opportunity to re-plan a large part of London on the grand scale has been missed; although there are some interesting examples of modern architecture and engineering, most of the development has been piecemeal and of mediocre design.

Docklands has the following defects as a tourist destination:

- It is too spread out and lacks an overall focus, while the Greenwich Tunnel provides the only river crossing for pedestrians between Tower Bridge and Woolwich.
- Signage for visitors is inadequate.
- Since the demise of the LDDC in 1998, Docklands has been the responsibility of the three local authorities in association with English Partnerships, the government's urban regeneration agency. As a result promotion of the area has been ineffective.
- There is insufficient nightlife for visitors compared to other parts of London – for example, Canary Wharf, a hive of activity by day, is relatively deserted after office hours.

Docklands is likely to appeal to the type of visitor who is more interested in the *new Britain* represented by the Design Museum at Butler's Wharf, than the *theme park Britain* evident in London's more traditional tourist attractions. It is perhaps more realistic to view Docklands as part of a wider area of London, focused on the riverside developments which are taking place along the south bank of the Thames from

Waterloo to the Flood Barrier at Woolwich, and which are now within 15 minutes' travelling time from Canary Wharf:

- To the west of London Bridge lies Bankside, another run-down area which in Shakespeare's time was the entertainment district for London. Attractions here include the reconstructed Globe Theatre, the Tate Modern Gallery and the Vinopolis wine museum.
- Downstream from the former Surrey Docks lies Greenwich, with such well-established tourist attractions as the *Cutty Sark* and the National Maritime Museum, not to mention the effect of the Millennium Dome in regenerating the area.

A consortium of local councils and tourism enterprises has promoted the East End, including the whole of Docklands and Greenwich, as 'Eastside', in a bid to transform the image of the area for the American market. Such re-branding exercises have been tried for other parts of London. However, the future success of Docklands is more likely to depend on transport developments such as *Crossrail*, which would provide a direct connection between East London and Heathrow Airport, and the Channel Tunnel Rail Link. These would act as the catalyst for the regeneration of other run-down areas, namely:

- the 'Thames Gateway' to the south of the river estuary in north Kent
- the Lea Valley to the north, focusing on the major transport node of Stratford.

Reflections on the case

London Docklands is one of the world's most important urban redevelopment projects, located on the edge of what is arguably the world's most popular tourist city. For this reason, the urban regeneration has had a significant tourism component – a component that also appeals to the local population. However, political changes and the geographical situation of the Docklands have acted as a severe constraint on the success of tourism in the area.

Discussion points/assignments

1 Draw up a 'balance sheet' showing the costs and benefits of developing a tourist attraction on a *brownfield* site (one reclaimed from industrial use, such as the Millennium Dome), compared to a previously undeveloped *greenfield* site in the countryside.

2 You work for a tour operator showing American visitors the East End as 'the hidden side of London'. What features of the area would you include in your tour programme?

3 Investigate the advantages and defects of ExCel as a venue for major trade exhibitions such as the Motor Show, compared to Earls Court or the National Exhibition Centre in Birmingham.
4 Debate the pros and cons of holding various events of the 2012 Olympic Games in London Docklands and the Lea Valley.
5 Investigate ways in which the River Thames can be promoted not only as one of London's primary attractions, but also as a major transport artery.

Key sources

Beioley, S., Crookston, M. and Tyrer, B. (1998) London Docklands: the leisure element. *Leisure Management*, 8 (2), 30–31, 33.
Law, C. (2002) *Urban Tourism*. Continuum, London.
Murphy, P. (1997) *Quality Management in Urban Tourism*. Wiley, Chichester.
Page, S. (1994) *Urban Tourism*. Routledge, London.

Website
http://www.visitlondon.com

Case 12

The New Forest: managing tourism in an environmentally sensitive area

Introduction

This case examines the New Forest – an environmentally sensitive area with a unique landscape in Hampshire in the south of England. It is under severe pressure, not only from tourism and recreation, but also from other developments such as housing and transport. On completion of this case you will:

1 Understand the value of the New Forest as a resource for recreation and tourism.
2 Be aware of the components of tourism in the New Forest.
3 Recognize that the impacts of tourism on the New Forest are severe.
4 Understand that there are many stakeholders involved in the management of the New Forest and that there is disagreement over the future priorities for the Forest.
5 Be aware of the main elements of the New Forest's tourism strategy.

Key issues

There are five key issues in this case:

1 The New Forest is a significant natural resource that faces many competing demands. Recreation and tourism create major impacts on both the resource and the local community, although the economy does benefit.
2 The New Forest tourism sector has a number of small attractions, a range of accommodation and road transport is the major means of access.

3 **The New Forest is subject to strict visitor and traffic management regimes to control both visitor volumes and impacts.**
4 **A range of significant stakeholders have interests in managing the New Forest and there is some conflict between their respective objectives.**
5 **In an attempt to resolve conflict over the variety of tourism interests in the New Forest, a series of tourism management plans have been implemented.**

The New Forest

Strictly speaking, the New Forest is neither *new*, nor a *forest*, but an area of open heathland, interspersed with woodland. The sandy soils were infertile and unattractive to early settlers, so that when William the Conqueror set the area aside in 1079 as a private deer hunting reserve, it was sparsely populated. William's 'new' hunting forest was much more extensive than the core area of 230 square kilometres designated as the New Forest Heritage Area, although its status as Crown land has undoubtedly protected the New Forest from development over the centuries. Today, the New Forest's landscape, flora and fauna are conserved under a variety of pieces of legislation which give it national park status in all but name, so that when the government, after a long public inquiry, designated the New Forest National Park in 2004, many stakeholders believed this would bring more problems than benefits. The new national park covers an area of 570 square kilometres, but excludes areas like the Avon Valley and the west coast of Southampton Water that are generally considered to be part of the New Forest region.

The scale of tourism

The New Forest is a very popular destination for both staying and day visitors. Visitor pressure in the Forest arises from the adjacent Bournemouth and Southampton conurbations, and the fact it is easily accessible through the national motorway network. Tourism in the New Forest is estimated to:

• support 3000 jobs in the area
• contribute £70 million annually to the local economy
• attract the equivalent of over 7 million visitor days.

The components of tourism

Attractions

The landscape, flora and fauna is the main attraction for visitors, even though less than half of the New Forest is wooded. There are three main landscape areas:

• the Avon Valley to the west, stretching from Salisbury to Christchurch
• the Forest itself, a mosaic of open heathland, woodland and villages
• the coast, stretching from Christchurch in the west to Southampton Water.

There is a range of visitor attractions in or close to the New Forest:

- Beaulieu – featuring the National Motor Museum, Palace House and Abbey
- Bucklers Hard – a preserved shipbuilding village from the era of the Napoleonic Wars
- Breamore House and gardens
- Paulton's Park – a small theme park close to the Forest
- Gardens like Exbury, Lymington and Everton
- Eling Tide Mill and heritage centre
- Lyndhurst New Forest Museum and Visitor Centre
- Rockbourne Roman Villa
- wildlife attractions such as the Otter, Owl and Wildlife Conservation Park and the New Forest Reptile Centre
- a range of attractions based on farms and farm produce, vineyards, brewing and cider
- attractive villages with traditional thatched cottages, like Emery Down, Burley and Sway
- the annual New Forest Show, which is estimated to attract 100 000 visitors annually.

Transport

A key issue is the management of traffic in the New Forest. Most visitors arrive by car, although the area is well served by the main railway line between Weymouth and London Waterloo. Traffic management includes a 40 mph (65 km/h) speed limit on the unfenced roads of the Forest, and the use of landscaped verges, ditches and ramparts to prevent off-road parking. Visitors are directed instead to over 150 designated parking zones. Until 1999, parking in most of the New Forest was free, but since then visitors pay a car-parking fee. Other forms of transport include the ever-popular horse-riding, cycle hire (although mountain bikes have caused damage in certain areas), horse-drawn wagon rides and regular bus and coach services. These alternatives to the car are coordinated in a series of networks in an attempt to reduce the number of car-borne visitors to the Forest.

Accommodation

Much of the accommodation for visitors to the New Forest is found in the neighbouring resort of Bournemouth. However, the Forest itself has a large number of camping and caravan sites providing over 20 000 bedspaces. Serviced accommodation is in shorter supply, consisting of traditional bed and breakfast and small hotels/inns in the area's towns and villages. Self-catering cottages and apartments provide further bedspaces.

Managing tourism

Managing the growing numbers of visitors is vitally important, given their possible impact on local communities and the sensitive wildlife habitats that visitors find so appealing. The New Forest District Council has regularly carried out visitor surveys and has in place a tourism and visitor management strategy for the Forest entitled *Making New Friends* (NFDC, 1996). This followed a consultation document, controversially entitled *Living with the Enemy*, which mapped out the challenges for the New Forest tourism industry (NFDC, 1994). More recently the Council has provided a kit to assist tourism businesses adopt principles of sustainable operation. Although the National Park now has its own planning authority, a plethora of agencies, committees and other bodies will continue to be involved in the management of the Forest. These include:

- Hampshire County Council – responsible for strategic planning and with a coordinating role.
- New Forest District Council – the local authority with day-to-day responsibility for the management of all elements of the New Forest and its population.
- New Forest Tourism – the local trade association representing over 250 private sector operators.
- The Southern Tourist Board – responsible for promoting tourism in Hampshire and Dorset.
- The Forestry Commission – primarily responsible for managing Britain's woodlands, but with important recreation and tourism interests.
- The Countryside Agency – a government agency charged with protecting the English landscape and managing recreation in rural areas such as the New Forest.
- English Nature – another government agency (whose future is under review) with responsibility for safeguarding the nation's flora and fauna.
- The National Farmers' Union – representing practising farmers in the area.
- The Country Landowners' Association – representing the interests of local landowners.
- The Court of Verderers – which administers the Forest's *commoners* – people who own or rent land and thus have the right to graze animals in the Forest. This ancient land management system means that around 5000 horses and ponies roam the New Forest and are part of its charm, though they are often to be found on unfenced roads and some are killed each year by traffic.

Clearly with so many interested and legitimate stakeholders, managing the New Forest is problematic, but this has been facilitated by the formation of the New Forest Committee to coordinate the management tasks. The local authority recognizes the challenge of balancing everyone's interests in their mission statement:

Our aim is for New Forest District to become a tourism destination where the visitor, tourism industry, local community and environment are in complete harmony, and thus make a significant contribution to improving the quality of life.

This will be achieved by the tourism strategy for the New Forest that aims to:

- target and regulate visitor flow through appropriate marketing
- integrate all tourism and transportation
- research and ensure strategic information is correct and communicated to visitors
- achieve the best quality of service facility and value for money
- involve the local community
- protect and enhance the quality of the environment
- provide the right experience in the right place.

Opponents of the National Park Authority see it as another layer of government bureaucracy and claim that the higher profile implied by national park status will encourage larger numbers of visitors to the New Forest. Supporters allege that the boundaries of the park should be extended to include the Avon Valley and the western shore of Southampton Water, which are now more vulnerable to development than before. Nevertheless national park designation does mean that any major road building scheme in the New Forest is even less likely to succeed.

Reflections on the case

The New Forest is an internationally significant natural resource that attracts large numbers of both recreation and tourism visitors. Whilst tourism and recreation provide jobs and income to the local economy, there is a view that their activities are having a detrimental effect on the resource. As a result, a range of agencies have been involved in complex management schemes in the Forest with a view to reducing both the numbers of visitors and their impacts, a policy likely to be given greater emphasis by the new National Park Authority.

Discussion points/assignments

1 Discuss the advantages and disadvantages of the New Forest's status as a national park, bearing in mind the number of agencies already involved in protecting the area from development. How does the situation here compare with other national parks in England and Wales?

2 As an employee of 'Equus Tours', a UK-based company specializing in holidays for horse-riding enthusiasts, you have been asked to write a report to your manager on ways in which the New Forest can compete with other destinations in Ireland and Continental Europe for the equestrian tourism market.

3 The New Forest National Park is home to 38 000 people. In class, debate the pros and cons of developing tourism in the area and assign roles to members of the class. These roles might include local farmers, newcomers to the area from London, representatives of the Campaign for the Protection of Rural England (CPRE) and the Ramblers Association, the owner of a local visitor attraction, and the business community.

4 With the use of a chart show the roles of public sector, private sector and voluntary organizations in tourism development and conservation in the New Forest.

5 Compare the National Motor Museum at Beaulieu and the New Forest Show as tourist attractions, taking into account their products and services, target markets and 'green' credentials.

Key sources

Climpson, A. (1998) Kitting out tourism businesses. *In Focus*, pp. 6–7.
Demetriadi, J. (2001) Little Acorns protect the Forest. *Hospitality*, October, pp. 14–15.
Font, X. and Tribe, J. (1999) *Forest Tourism and Recreation*. CABI, Wallingford.
New Forest District Council (1994) *Living with the Enemy*. NFDC, Lyndhurst.
New Forest District Council (1996) *Making New Friends*. NFDC, Lyndhurst.

Websites
http://www.forestry.gov.uk/forestry/
http://www.hants.gov.uk/newforest/
http://www.newforest-online.co.uk
http://www.nfdc.gov.uk
http://www.thenewforest.co.uk
http://www.visitsouthernengland.com

Case 13

The Isle of Man: rejuvenating a cold water destination

Introduction

The Isle of Man is an offshore island associated with the UK. As a traditional resort at the end of its life cycle it has repositioned itself away from a typical British seaside destination and is a good example of a rejuvenated destination. On completion of this case you will:

1 Understand how the historic legacy of the Isle of Man's tourism has affected the island's tourism development.
2 Appreciate the significance of the Isle of Man's geographical position.
3 Be aware of the components of tourism in the Isle of Man.
4 Recognize the changing nature of market demand for the Isle of Man.
5 Understand how the Isle of Man has repositioned its tourism product.

Key issues

There are five key issues in this case:

1 Until the last two decades, the Isle of Man was a traditional British seaside destination in the final stage of the life cycle, but supplemented by business tourism from the offshore finance industry.
2 The Isle of Man authorities recognized the need to reposition the island to attract a new tourism market.
3 The island has all the necessary tourism attractions and facilities to succeed in the twenty-first century tourism market.

4 The island's market for tourism has changed since the 1970s both in terms of volume and the characteristics of the visitors.

5 The island has successfully transformed itself into a heritage destination, supplemented by the remnants of the seaside holiday and supported by a strong business tourism market – effectively entering the rejuvenation stage of the life cycle.

The Isle of Man

The Isle of Man – 50 kilometres long and 20 kilometres wide – is situated in the Irish Sea, midway between Ireland, England and Scotland. The island's location is at once both an advantage and a disadvantage. On the one hand it can draw upon the large population catchments of the Midlands and north of England, the Scottish Lowlands and the east coast of Ireland. However, to reach the island involves a short air journey or a sea crossing, often in unpredictable weather, as the island suffers from successive waves of Atlantic fronts passing over the Irish Sea.

The Isle of Man's Celtic legacy is shown by the persistence of the Manx language despite Viking invasions in the ninth century and long periods of Scottish and later English rule. Since the mid-nineteenth century the island has regained its autonomy as a dependency of the British Crown and has its own parliament – Tynwald –, civil administration and postal service.

The island has a long history of tourism, with peak numbers of visitors arriving by steamship in the early years of the twentieth century to enjoy a traditional seaside holiday. However, the Isle of Man's tourism success in the twentieth century has been one of mixed fortunes. There was a surge of visitors immediately following the Second World War, but by the 1950s the island began to experience the beginnings of a constant and sustained decline in visitor numbers. This was caused by the fact that holidaymakers with their changing tastes and aspirations ceased to find the island's traditional holiday formula attractive. Since the 1970s the island has undergone something of a renaissance with a thriving offshore finance industry. This has stimulated business tourism, and quality hotels and restaurants have been developed to serve this market. The island is now used as a setting for film and TV productions, with tours of the locations increasingly available. In 2001 tourism was worth 6 per cent of the island's GDP.

Demand for tourism

Demand for tourism on the Isle of Man was at its height in the late nineteenth and early twentieth centuries when visitors from the north of England, the Midlands and southern Scotland were attracted to the island's traditional seaside product and value-for-money accommodation stock. In the period following the Second World War the island's tourism authorities were slow to respond to changing tastes in holiday taking and the structural shifts taking place in the UK domestic holiday market, and this resulted in falling visitor numbers. However, since the mid-1980s, strong political commitment and support for tourism have seen a rejuvenation of the island's products and facilities (partly driven by the demands of business travellers) and demand has increased to over 300 000 visitors a year. The majority of visitors are from the UK, but the family market in the Republic of Ireland is also an important source. As a result, over half of all visitors arrive by sea.

Supply of tourism

Attractions

- **Douglas and the coastal towns** The main town on the Isle of Man is Douglas, with its sweeping Victorian promenade of guesthouses and terraced hotels. Douglas is the capital and main seaport, featuring the Manx Museum and 'The Story of Mann' exhibition. Douglas represents the main concentration of bed spaces, restaurants and other facilities for the visitor. Indeed, tourism supports many of the shopping and entertainment businesses that are used by residents. These include the restored Victorian Gaiety Theatre, and Summerland – a casino and leisure centre. Other coastal towns, each with a range of small attractions, crafts, galleries and accommodation base, include:
  - Port Erin
  - Peel – where Moore's Traditional Museum showcases the fishing industry and kippers – the Isle of Man's best-known product
  - Ramsey
  - Castletown.
- **Cultural heritage** The island has a rich heritage, including many remains of both Celtic and Norse origin. The key features are:
  - the Laxey Wheel to the north of Douglas, an example of industrial heritage featuring the world's largest working waterwheel
  - historic buildings such as the castle and cathedral at Peel and Castle Rushen at Castletown – the island's former capital
  - the site of the island's first parliament at Tynwald Hill near Peel
  - museums and craft centres, including the Grove Rural Life Museum at Ramsey, the House of Manannan – a newly built heritage centre on the harbourside in Peel, and the Nautical Museum at Castletown
  - Cregneash Folk Village is a recreated rural life museum with original Manx cottages interpreting the crofting way of life of the islanders in the past.
- **Natural heritage** The island has been likened to the landscape of northern England in miniature, as it features all the elements of beaches, fells, valleys and coast, yet within a small area. The natural heritage of the island is interpreted and developed for special interest holidays, and both walking and cycling trails are available – three long distance footpaths have been designated. The key features are:
  - the Point of Ayre – a protected area of dune coast in the north of the island
  - the wetland habitats of the Ballaugh Curraghs with its wildlife park
  - the Calf of Man – a small rocky island which is a wildlife sanctuary to the south
  - a series of 17 mountain and coastal glens managed by the Manx Forestry Department with facilities for recreation
  - the new *Cooil y Ree* (Nook of Kings) gardens in St Johns.

- **Transport heritage** The Isle of Man is famous for a range of transport-based tourist attractions. These include:
  - the annual Tourist Trophy (TT) motorcycle races, dating back to 1904, which takes place on a road circuit around the island and fills the island's bedspaces during 'TT Week'; the circuit is used for other race events throughout the year
  - the electric mountain railway from Laxey up the island's highest peak, Snaefell
  - the horse-drawn *toast-rack* trams that run along Douglas seafront
  - the Manx electric railway between Douglas and Ramsey
  - Groudle Glen steam railway
  - the Manx narrow gauge steam railway from Douglas to Port Erin in the south, with its railway museum at the Port Erin terminus.

Accommodation and transport

The Isle of Man has a varied accommodation base ranging from luxury country house hotels to value-for-money guesthouses. The Manx government has a long-standing scheme to assist the accommodation sector both to adjust to the demands of the contemporary holidaymaker, and also to attract new accommodation stock. The tourism authorities also operate a compulsory registration and grading scheme for accommodation. By 2002 there were almost 7000 bedspaces available on the island, mostly in serviced accommodation.

Traditionally, holidaymakers reached the Isle of Man by steamship, using the Isle of Man Steam Packet Company sailing out of Liverpool, Heysham, Belfast and Dublin. The island is also attempting to break into the cruise stopover market. In recent years fast catamarans have also been introduced, but the success of the island's airline – Manx (now a subsidiary of British Airways) – made it an important carrier for business and leisure passengers. The island's airport, Ronaldsway, has an aviation museum and is served by six airlines with flights to many UK regional airports, as well as to Ireland and the Channel Islands. Of course, as an island, it is very dependent upon its carriers for survival and the Tynwald closely monitors transport policy and scrutinizes applications from new operators serving the route network.

The organization of tourism

The Department of Tourism and Leisure has responsibility for both the promotion and development of tourism on the island as well as leisure and public transport. The department's policy is 'to develop and encourage tourism to optimize economic and social benefits to the Isle of Man'. The department works closely with other agencies that are responsible for heritage and planning. Manx National Heritage and the Manx Nature Conservation Trust are responsible for a number of the island's natural and historic attractions.

The Isle of Man has had to adapt its tourism product to the tastes of twenty-first century holidaymakers. The island's traditional markets sought an English seaside product and while this still forms part of the island's appeal, other elements of the destination mix are now seen as more important in attracting visitors. These include the development of quality accommodation, the encouragement of activity holidays based upon the island's natural and cultural heritage, the attraction of film and TV locations, and the promotion of sport tourism utilizing the island's eight golf courses, excellent fishing and other facilities. It is interesting that this approach also depends upon the provision of good quality, professionally managed tourist accommodation. Traditional establishments in Douglas have struggled to meet these standards and there has been a switch in demand towards, for example, country house hotels in rural parts of the island. The Isle of Man is therefore an excellent example of a destination that has successfully repositioned itself to become more competitive.

Reflections on the case

The Isle of Man is a classic example of the destination area life cycle. Having gone through the full life cycle from exploration to decline by the 1950s, the island authorities made a conscious decision to reposition the island as a heritage destination. This has been highly successful and the island is now entering the rejuvenation stage of the life cycle with new tourism products appealing to new markets.

Discussion points/assignments

1 How far does the history of tourism in the Isle of Man correspond to specific stages of development in Butler's destination life cycle?
2 Describe the steps that have been taken to rejuvenate the island's tourism product and assess their effectiveness in the face of the competition from other resort areas.
3 'Thanks to tourism, the residents of Douglas can enjoy a much greater range of amenities than you might expect for a town of this size.' Discuss the validity of this statement by comparing Douglas with an industrial town of similar population on the mainland of Britain.
4 Investigate the various ways in which the Isle of Man has been promoted for tourism, including 'product placement' in feature films and TV productions.

Key sources

Conlin, M. V. and Baum, T. (1995) *Island Tourism*. Wiley, Chichester.
Cooper, C. (1990) Resorts in decline: the management response. *Tourism Management*, 11 (1), 63–67.
Cooper, C. and Jackson, S. (1989) Destination life cycle: the Isle of Man case study. *Annals of Tourism Research*, 16 (3), 377–398.
Drakakis-Smith, G. and Lockhart, D. (1997) *Island Tourism: Trends and Prospects*. Pinter, London.

Websites
http://www.gov.im/tourism
http://www.isle-of-man.com/

Case 14

Dublin: tourism in a capital city

Introduction

Dublin has developed into an important tourist city on the world stage. This case examines the tourist resources, organization and market of Ireland's capital. On completion of this case you will:

1 Recognize the growing importance of Dublin as a tourist city.
2 Be aware of Dublin's role as the gateway to Ireland.
3 Appreciate the range of tourism resources in Dublin.
4 Be aware of the market for tourism to Dublin.
5 Understand how tourism in Dublin is organized.

Key issues

There are five key issues in this case:

1 Dublin has developed into an important tourist city on the world stage and is the gateway to Ireland.
2 Tourism makes a significant contribution to the economy of the city.
3 Dublin's attractions are focused on its heritage, buildings and institutions of national importance as well as the social life, the food and beverages on offer, and the hospitality of the Irish people.
4 Dublin has a growing level of support facilities for tourism, including good transportation links (although traffic congestion is a problem).
5 Dublin, with the rest of Ireland, has an excellent organization for tourism and has successfully lobbied for European Union funds to develop tourism.

Dublin

Dublin has an attractive setting on the wide Dublin Bay, backed by the Wicklow Mountains. The Dublin area contains over one-third of the Republic of Ireland's 3.8 million population. Dublin has not only become a major tourist city on the world stage, but it is also the most important gateway to Ireland with a major airport and also sea access through the port of Dun Laoghaire. This is reflected in the statistics – the Dublin region has seen the highest growth of visitor numbers in Ireland, such that by 2002 Dublin received 3.3 million overseas visitors and almost a million domestic visits, with tourism supporting 25 000 full-time jobs.

Tourist resources of Dublin

The main tourist resources of Dublin are its history, literary heritage, national institutions and the character of the *old city* with its fine eighteenth-century buildings. This was celebrated in 1991 when Dublin became the 'European City of Culture'. Dublin originated as a Viking settlement in the ninth century, which developed into a medieval walled city, followed by a major period of prosperity and expansion in the eighteenth century, when many of Dublin's finest buildings were erected. Some of the finest examples of Georgian architecture can be seen today along the canals and in the wide streets and spacious squares. The tourist resources of Dublin are focused in a small area, ideal for exploration on foot using the themed trails available. However, this spatial concentration is a controversial issue, and the City Council is attempting to disperse visits away from the core area.

Recent refurbishment and redevelopment schemes have been careful to maintain the traditional street scenes and character of Dublin, while enhancing the townscape for both residents and visitors. This has been aided by the EU-funded Historic Heart of Dublin Project documenting Dublin's building stock in order to regenerate areas of urban decline, social disadvantage and unemployment. The project aims to encourage the economic viability of the heart of Dublin as a truly sustainable city where the heritage is respected and restored, and the economic and social needs of the community are met.

Geographically, the tourist resources of Dublin are focused on two main features – the River Liffey and Trinity College, Ireland's oldest and most famous university.

The River Liffey is well known worldwide as the setting for Dublin's best known product and the Guinness Storehouse has a themed tourism experience. The Liffey also divides the city into the northside and the southside and was the focus for Dublin's city-wide initiatives to celebrate the millennium, including the Millennium Footbridge and a boardwalk along the banks of the river.

On the *southside* of the river, Trinity College houses the Book of Kells and is central to Dublin's emergent tourist zones:

• To the south and south-east of the College lie attractive Georgian squares, rivalling those of Bath and London, such as Fitzwilliam Square. Important national institutions in this area include the National Museum, the National Gallery of Ireland, the National History Museum and the Genealogical Office – an

important resource for the ethnic tourism market, with visitors retracing their Irish roots, and exhibitions of Dublin's history and background – the Dublin Civic Museum, Dublina and the Dublin City Hall multi-media exhibition.
- To the west lies Temple Bar, a newly emerging *left bank* area offering art galleries, shops, pubs, restaurants and street entertainers.
- Beyond Temple Bar is Dublin Castle – the former seat of government under British rule – and the two cathedrals – St Patrick's and Christ Church.

Across the river on the *northside* is one of Ireland's most famous streets – O'Connell Street with the General Post Office, leading to a cluster of attractions that include:

- the Hugh Lane Municipal Gallery of Modern Art in a Georgian mansion in Parnell Square
- Dublin National Museum
- Dublin Writers Museum, featuring the lives and works of Dublin's literary celebrities, such as Joyce, Wilde and Sheridan
- Phoenix Park – Europe's largest enclosed park.

Transport, accommodation and organization of tourism

'Dublin Tourism' is responsible for the promotion and marketing of tourism and is a regional tourism authority affiliated to the national tourist organization, Failte Ireland. Its duties include designing and implementing tourism strategy and action plans, new product development and tourism marketing, as well as operating the tourist information offices. The Dublin Conference Bureau promotes the city for conferences and meetings. There is a wide range of accommodation in and around Dublin, including country houses, castles, hotels, guesthouses, farmhouses, university accommodation, hostels and campsites. Dublin is an important shopping and entertainment centre for both domestic and international visitors. Significant entertainment venues and festivals include:

- the refurbished National Concert Hall, home of the National Symphony Orchestra
- the Abbey Theatre
- the restored Gate Theatre
- the Olympia Theatre
- the Irish Film Centre
- Jury's Cabaret and Doyle's Irish Cabaret
- festivals and events such as the Irish Film Festival, Dublin Theatre Festival and, in 1998, Dublin hosted the start of the Tour de France cycle race, the first start to be held outside France.

The city's one thousand or more pubs also play an important role in advertising Ireland to the rest of the world. Nevertheless, many Dubliners allege that the popularity of areas such as Temple Bar is not altogether beneficial, as pubs are increasingly taken over by rowdy 'hen' and 'stag' parties – mainly groups of young tourists from Britain on weekend 'alcotrips' who are attracted by Ireland's reputation for liberal licensing laws.

Reflections on the case

Dublin is an excellent example of a well-managed and smartly organized tourism destination where all of the key elements for tourism are in place. The city has a range of heritage attractions and institutions of national significance – such as museums and art galleries – as well as world-renowned hospitality in the pubs and restaurants. These key destination elements have been supported by both national and EU funding and add up to a successful tourism destination, and one that reflects Ireland's renaissance as a European nation.

Discussion points/assignments

1 Discuss the influence of the media and the work of Irish writers such as James Joyce in attracting tourists to Dublin.
2 Debate the case for promoting the night-time economy of city centre areas such as Dublin's Temple Bar as against the opinion that serious problems and social costs are a result of the 'all hours' drinking culture.
3 Obtain a map of central Dublin and design a walking tour, taking in a selection of attractions that would appeal to a group of Australian tourists with different backgrounds and interests.
4 One result of Ireland's economic development since the 1970s has been growing traffic congestion in the capital. Investigate the nature of the problem and the measures needed to solve it.

Key sources

Cronin, M. and O'Connor, B. (2003) *Irish Tourism*. Channel View, Clevedon.
Law, C. (2002) *Urban Tourism*. Continuum, London.
Murphy, P. (1997) *Quality Management in Urban Tourism*. Wiley, Chichester.
Page, S. (1994) *Urban Tourism*. Routledge, London.

Websites
http://www.dublincity.ie/dublin/
http://www.visitdublin.com

Case 15

Adventure tourism in Arctic Scandinavia

Introduction

This case introduces two Arctic Scandinavian destinations at the frontier of tourism and certainly in the discovery stages of the destination life cycle. On completion of the case you will:

1 Appreciate that a large part of Scandinavia lies within the Arctic Circle.
2 Be aware of the constraints on tourism development in Arctic Scandinavia.
3 Evaluate the resource base for tourism products in Swedish Lapland.
4 Recognize the safety and development issues of tourism in the Norwegian islands of Svalbard.
5 Be aware of the potential impacts of tourism on the environment and culture of Swedish Lapland.

Key issues

There are five key issues in this case:

1 Around one-third of Scandinavia lies within the Arctic Circle, and while there is potential for tourism in this region, tourism development is characterized by the frontier nature of the region and subject to a series of significant constraints – particularly accessibility and climate.
2 In Swedish Lapland the resource base has allowed winter sports, cultural tourism and ecotourism.
3 In the Norwegian islands of Svalbard tourism is much more constrained and is confined to adventure tourism.

4 The activity of tourism in the region demands that visitors are aware of the severity of the environment as there are significant health and safety issues associated with tourism, particularly in Svalbard. As a result regulations are in place for tour operators.

5 In both these Arctic destinations the development of tourism has to be carefully managed to reduce the impacts on the environment, culture and the local community. However, there are considerable economic benefits to be gained for the region from tourism development.

Swedish Lapland and the Norwegian islands of Svalbard

Approximately one-third of Scandinavia lies within the Arctic Circle, while the Norwegian islands known as Svalbard lie only 1000 kilometres from the North Pole. However, climatic conditions are not as severe as they are in similar latitudes in Greenland, Northern Canada, Alaska and Siberia. The high northerly latitude is compensated to some extent by the warming influence of the North Atlantic Drift, which keeps the seas around the North Cape ice-free all year round, allowing the majority of visitors to Svalbard to arrive by ship rather than by air. In Swedish Lapland summer temperatures compare favourably with those of Scotland, much further south.

Swedish Lapland

Of the two areas in this case study, Swedish Lapland offers much more potential for tourism and other types of economic development. Apart from a warmer climate than Svalbard, it has the following advantages over other Arctic regions:

- It is within easy reach by road, rail and air transport of the major population centres of Sweden and Finland.
- It has been settled by incomers from the south since the sixteenth century, and has a well-developed infrastructure.

Nevertheless, the towns still have a frontier look about them compared to those in southern Sweden. The formerly nomadic Sami people have been assimilated into the mainstream Swedish economy and social structure, without suffering the exploitation, welfare dependency and loss of cultural identity that other indigenous communities in the Arctic have experienced.

Mining is the main economic activity in the region. This is the basis for the prosperity of Kiruna, one of the largest cities north of the Arctic Circle, which is noted for its nightlife throughout Sweden (it also boasts the world's largest iron ore mine). Tourism in the region began in the late nineteenth century, and is growing in importance for the following reasons:

- **Interest in ecotourism and green issues** Swedish Lapland is one of the largest areas of unspoiled wilderness in Europe. It boasts six national parks, of which

Abisko is the best known, extensive forests of pine, spruce and birch, expanses of tundra, lakes and mountain scenery, and fast-flowing, unpolluted rivers. With only 5 per cent of Sweden's population, yet covering 25 per cent of its area, the region is renowned for silence and solitude, especially in winter when the night sky is frequently lit up by displays of the aurora borealis (Northern Lights).

- **Winter sports**   Swedish Lapland is Europe's most northerly developed ski area, offering skiers and snowboarders the novelty of practising their sport until late June under the midnight sun. The area is guaranteed heavy snowfalls, with less risk of avalanches than in the Alpine resorts. However, the season does not start until mid-February, due to the short period of winter daylight. Riksgränsen, situated close to the Norwegian border, on the railway linking Kiruna to Narvik, is the main centre, where Sweden's first ski school was established in 1932. There are extensive cross-country trails for ski-touring and telemarking, but with a vertical descent of only 400 metres, Riksgränsen's slopes have less appeal for downhill skiers. Other winter activities include ice-fishing, snow-scooter safaris and sledging with a team of huskies.

- **Sami (Lapp) culture**   Jukkasjärvi, whose name means 'meeting place' in the Sami language, and Jokkmokk are the traditional centres of Sami culture, where the old ways have continued to flourish, and silver and leather handicrafts are sold to tourists. Here the Sami still wear their brightly coloured leather clothing, and use dog teams for reindeer round-ups, whereas elsewhere they tend to use snowmobiles and mobile phones.

- **The Ice Hotel**   Jukkasjärvi also offers a unique winter attraction – the Ice Hotel – promoted as the world's largest igloo. (It has in fact a North American competitor in Duchesne Park near Quebec, where hot tubs replace the Scandinavian sauna.) Both are interesting examples of sustainable tourism, using renewable natural resources. The rooms and furniture of the hotel are made from 30 000 tons of ice and compacted snow, which is taken each November from the frozen River Torne, and the structure is used until it melts, usually in early May. The temperature inside the hotel is kept at a constant $-7\,°C$, although outside it may fall as low as $-35\,°C$. Bed furnishings are made from reindeer hides and skins, whose insulating properties provide protection from the low temperatures, but needless to say, most tourists prefer to use the adjoining wooden chalet-style huts. There is also an open air theatre modelled on Shakespeare's Globe, but made entirely of ice, and where the plays are performed in the Sami language. The Ice Hotel attracts a variety of clients, from conference groups to Japanese honeymoon couples.

- **Other outdoor activities**   Summer activities include white-water rafting, hiking, mountain climbing and fishing. Swedish Lapland boasts the world's most northerly golf course at Björkliden. Field sports are popular in autumn, while survival training in one of Europe's most rugged environments is available all year round.

The Norwegian islands of Svalbard

Svalbard is situated 1000 kilometres north of the Norwegian mainland but is actually closer to Greenland. Spitzbergen is the name given to the largest island of the group, which is noted for its dramatic landscape of fjords, ice-sculpted mountains and glaciers, as well as for the variety of wildlife that has adapted to an inhospitable environment. Svalbard is in the High Arctic, north of latitude 75°, where winter is characterized by several months of continuous darkness as well as extreme cold. In summer, temperatures rarely rise above $10\,°C$, despite continuous daylight from April to August, and the weather is also highly unpredictable. West Spitzbergen is much more accessible than the rest of the archipelago, which is hemmed in by pack ice for most of the year. Uninhabited at the time of its discovery by the Dutch in the sixteenth century, West Spitzbergen now contains three settlements, two of which are Russian and the third – Longyearbyen – Norwegian. These are based on a coal mining industry that is no longer competitive in world markets. Although the islands are under Norwegian sovereignty, they are regarded as an international zone for commercial activities.

West Spitzbergen was the base for a number of expeditions to the North Pole in the early part of the twentieth century. These played a major role in attracting international interest in the area, with visitors arriving by cruise ship from mainland Norway. Over 20 000 cruise passengers a year currently visit the islands, attracted by the wild Arctic scenery. Longyearbyen offers some tourist facilities, but the main attraction is Magdalen Fjord, with its heritage of the former whaling industry and polar exploration. Some air passengers spend a few days in Longyearbyen and take part in day excursions, whereas others, mainly Norwegian, are attracted by wilderness adventures, which include:

• trekking and mountain climbing
• exploring the coast by kayak or zodiac (inflatable craft with an outboard motor)
• snowmobile 'safaris' and skiing during the spring months
• bird-watching
• survival training and leadership courses.

Most of these activities require months of planning and preparation, and tourists are usually aware of the risk in challenging the wilderness, which includes the possibility of attacks by polar bears (a protected species in Svalbard). Nevertheless, the Norwegian government has imposed a comprehensive system of regulations on tour operators as well as independent travellers, to ensure the protection of the fragile Arctic ecosystems, as well as visitor safety. For example, tour operators must notify the Governor of Svalbard of their activities, and are responsible for their clients' behaviour.

Tourism in Svalbard is far from being a minor activity, as it provides employment for some 10 per cent of the population. Nevertheless, it will have to be considerably expanded if it is to replace coal mining as the mainstay of the economy, but this in turn will increase environmental impacts.

Reflections on the case

This case has demonstrated the issues involved in developing tourism at the discovery stage of the life cycle – effectively at the frontier of tourism, where access and climate are important considerations. In both destinations the products are closely matched to the resource base, particularly in Svalbard with an environment ideally suited to the harder end of adventure tourism. Of course development of tourism in these regions demands careful management and regulation to reduce the impact upon not only the environment and the host community, but also the visitors themselves.

Discussion points/assignments

1 Using the Internet, put together a full tour itinerary for an Arctic cruise including Spitzbergen and the Far North of Russia for a wealthy American tourist. Include all stopovers and transfers, and provide information on ice conditions and the ecology of the islands to be visited.
2 Investigate the impact of tourism on the lifestyle and culture of the Sami people.
3 You have been asked to give a presentation to the local naturalist's society on the ecosystems of Arctic Scandinavia and their potential for a nature-based holiday.
4 With the aid of charts, graphs and tables, compare the climates of Spitzbergen and Swedish Lapland. Give advice on the type of clothing and other equipment needed by independent travellers to these regions.
5 Provide information for a tourist interested in the following:
   • viewing the Northern Lights
   • visiting the North Pole
   • staying at the Ice Hotel.

Key sources

Hall, C. M. and Johnston, M. (1995) *Polar Tourism*. Wiley, Chichester.
West, M. (1997) Polar experience. *Geographical Magazine*, 69 (4), 44–45.

Case 16

Bruges: the impact of tourism in the historic city

Introduction

Bruges is pre-eminent in Belgium's tourism industry and is one of the best-preserved medieval cities of northern Europe. As such it has considerable appeal to both day and staying visitors. This has created a range of issues which are applicable to other historic towns and cities. On completion of this case you will:

1 Be aware of the tourism significance of Bruges.
2 Recognize the tourism attractions and facilities of Bruges.
3 Understand the need for Bruges to achieve a balance between day and staying visitors.
4 Recognize the contribution of tourism to the significant traffic problems of this medieval city.
5 Be aware of the planning and strategy initiatives for tourism in Bruges.

Key issues

There are five key issues for this case:

1 Bruges is a well-preserved and attractive medieval city where tourism plays an important role in the economy.
2 The attractions of Bruges are based upon its heritage buildings, townscape and events, but the city's unique medieval layout creates problems for tourism management.

3 **The tourism market for Bruges comprises both day and staying visitors. This raises the issue of achieving a balance between staying visitors who make a significant contribution to the economy, and day visitors who spend less but do have an impact upon the city.**

4 **The popularity of Bruges as a tourist city has contributed to the significant traffic problems experienced by the historic centre.**

5 **Bruges has developed a strategy to alleviate traffic problems and develop tourism.**

Bruges

Tourism is of major importance to Bruges, supporting an estimated 6500 jobs directly and indirectly in the city and its surrounding area, of which two-thirds are in the hotel and catering sectors. Yet the very popularity of this small city in West Flanders has brought severe traffic problems, threatening its unique heritage. These problems are now well on their way to being resolved through a number of planning and marketing initiatives.

Bruges (or Brugge as it is known in Flemish) is one of the best-preserved medieval cities of northern Europe. For this reason it has become a popular short-break destination as well as a long-established attraction on European touring circuits. It is designated by UNESCO as a World Heritage Site and was selected as the European City of Culture for 2002. Unlike modern conurbations, the townscape of Bruges is on a human scale, a picturesque composition of red-brick gabled buildings, church spires, cobblestone streets and squares and tranquil waterways set in the green Flanders countryside. A map of the city reveals the medieval street pattern threaded by a ribbon of canals which has led to Bruges being described, somewhat misleadingly, as the 'Venice of the North'. Beyond the ring road enclosing the old city lie the new residential and industrial districts, which attract relatively few tourists compared to the historic centre.

There are two squares at the heart of the old city that symbolize its dual role as a trading centre and administrative capital:

- the Markt (market place), and
- the Burg (the site of the fortress of the Counts of Flanders in the early medieval period).

Bruges grew rich in the Middle Ages on the wool trade with England, reaching the peak of its prosperity in the fifteenth century when it was chosen by the Dukes of Burgundy as the capital of their extensive domains in France and the Low Countries. It was then the leading commercial centre of northern Europe, boasting the world's first stock exchange. Most of the important buildings and the art treasures date from this period. Later, Bruges lost wealth and population as the result of the silting up of the Zwin estuary and the shift of international trade to Antwerp. By the early nineteenth century Bruges appeared to be in terminal decline and was described by one popular writer as the 'dead city', but this proved to be its salvation, as the citizens were too poor to replace the old buildings. This was the era of the Romantic Movement in art and literature, and the first tourists were attracted by the timeless atmosphere, encouraging the civic authorities to impose strict conservation measures which remain in force today. At the close of the century Bruges made an economic recovery, establishing a new port on the North Sea coast at Zeebrugge ('Bruges on Sea'). However, tourism continued to grow to become the basis for the city's prosperity.

The tourism resources of Bruges

Attractions

The tourist attractions of the old city include:

- The Belfry, the graceful bell tower which is the iconic landmark of Bruges. Along with the Hallen, a group of former trading halls, it dominates the Markt, and has played a major role in the events that shaped the city's history.
- The Stadhuis (city hall) dominates the Burg, and is another outstanding example of Gothic architecture.
- The medieval churches, of which the most famous is the Onze-Lieve-Vrouwekerk (Church of Our Lady) that boasts a sculpture by Michelangelo.
- The art galleries, which feature paintings by Van Eyck, Memling and other Flemish artists.
- The Begijnhof (beguinage) is the most visited of the medieval almshouses that give Bruges much of its peaceful charm.
- The Minnewater ('lake of love') was the harbour of Bruges in the Middle Ages but is now a romantic backwater.
- Boat trips on the canals are very popular with visitors, some going as far as Damme, a picturesque small town 7 kilometres to the north, which has been designated as 'Bruges in miniature'. Carriage rides in the old city are also popular.
- Event attractions are focused on the medieval period. The most famous example is the 'Procession of the Holy Blood' – one of Belgium's most colourful religious festivals, that has taken place annually since the time of the Crusades. Some purists accuse Bruges of being a 'medieval theme park' and question the authenticity of some of its traditions.
- Apart from these heritage attractions, the city's shops, quality restaurants and markets are popular with visitors. The traditional lace industry would almost certainly have died out were it not for tourism, but is nowadays rarely carried on outside people's homes. Other industries less dependent on tourism are chocolate-making (an art form in Belgium) and brewing.
- Attractions epitomizing the twenty-first century include the Concertgebouw (Concert Hall), which is linked with the European City of Culture project. This is an outstanding modern landmark and asset to the cultural product of Bruges.

Preserving the architectural heritage is not in itself sufficient to give a historic town a unique 'sense of place', if the street scene is cluttered by intrusive modern signs and street lighting which is inappropriate, and where the shopping experience is dominated by the 'big names' in retailing and catering. Bruges has been more successful than most historic towns in retaining its small-scale shops, trades and traditional street furniture, while encouraging public art displays which add colour and interest to city life.

Bruges is promoted jointly with Zeebrugge, which has a lively programme of events and entertainment during the summer. Attractions outside the old city in West Bruges include a theme park and dolphinarium, and a major sports complex, but these have limited international appeal.

Bruges is by no means a 'museum-city' or provincial backwater. Many of its residents commute to Brussels, while the Europacollege is a reminder of the city's important role in the development of the European Union. About 12 per cent of staying visitors are business travellers or conference delegates. Bruges is an important venue for international conferences, offering the Congress Centre and the historic Cloth Hall (where Margaret Thatcher made a famous speech against European federation), while seven of the city's hotels have capacity for the larger meetings with over 100 delegates.

Transport

The city has excellent transport links by road and rail to:

- Brussels Airport
- the ferry terminals at Ostend and Zeebrugge
- Lille on the Eurostar route
- the Channel Tunnel via the E40 motorway
- Paris, using the 'Thalys' fast train service.

Accommodation

Bruges can offer the visitor an extensive range of accommodation. Hotels are the most important category, with over 100 establishments, accounting for 70 per cent of bed capacity and 86 per cent of tourist overnights in 2002. Most hotels are small, with 57 per cent having less than 20 rooms, but there has been a significant increase since the early 1990s in the larger properties with over 80 rooms. The great majority of hotels now offer en-suite facilities and are open for at least ten months of the year, while 80 per cent are in the 3- or 4-star categories. However, they face keen price competition from similar properties in Ghent, Antwerp and Brussels. Over two-thirds of hotel capacity is located in the historic area of Bruges, while cheaper accommodation is generally found towards the outskirts. These include youth hostels (especially popular with young American visitors); campsites; private guest houses, which attract a wide range of independent tourists; and rented holiday homes and apartments catering primarily for the Belgian and Dutch family markets.

The demand for tourism in Bruges

Staying visitors

Bruges attracts visitors from all over the world. Japan was an expanding market in the 1990s, but 9/11 and subsequent crises have had a severe impact, while the USA

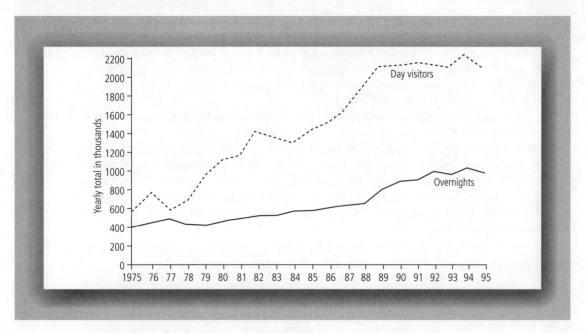

Figure 16.1 Growth of tourism to Bruges
Source: Economic Study Bureau, West Flanders (WES), 1996

has also declined in importance. The majority of hotel guests come from neighbouring countries, with Britain contributing the largest numbers (around 35 per cent) but the lowest spend per capita. Domestic tourists account for only 10 per cent of hotel stays, which is perhaps not surprising given the size of Belgium and the availability of cheaper types of accommodation.

Day visitors

The biggest long-term growth has been in the numbers of day visitors, based mainly in the coastal resorts or cities of Belgium, and this has clear implications for the future direction of Bruges' tourism industry. Between 1975 and 1991, whereas overnight stays by tourists doubled, day visits to Bruges almost quadrupled (see Figure 16.1).

The problems

The majority of visitors arrive by car, and car ownership by Bruges residents is also increasing. The main problem, as in other historic cities all over Europe, is to find a balance between low-volume, high-spend staying tourists, and day visitors whose contribution to the local economy may be offset by their negative impact on the host community and the fabric of the historic town. Table 16.1 summarizes the differences between these two types of tourism in Bruges.

Table 16.1 Characteristics of tourism to Bruges

Characteristic	Staying visitors	Day visitors
Volume		
Trips	616 000	3 050 000
Nights	1 442 000	
Spend (euros)	154 million: high spending – over a half on accommodation, 16% on shopping	100 million: low spending – one-third on shopping
Transport		
Car	43%	57%
Coach	13%	16%
Train	41%	23%
Seasonal distribution	75% of overnight stays in the period Mar–Oct	High concentration in summer months, especially at weekends
Growth pattern	Stable	Booming, but irregular
Orientation	Culture	Recreational shopping is as important as culture
Visitor origin		
Domestic	12%	50% – mainly from Flemish-speaking areas
Neighbouring countries	66%	34%
Other foreign countries	22%	16% (on holiday elsewhere in Belgium)

Source: Economic Study Bureau, West Flanders (WES), 1995, updated to 2002 courtesy of the Director of Tourism Flanders, Wim Vanseveren

As a result of the rapid growth of tourism, Bruges in the early 1990s faced severe traffic problems that threatened to devalue both the tourist experience and the quality of life for local residents. The main problems were:

- The concentration of visitors in a very limited area (430 hectares) of the old city. At peak periods there can be as many as 20 000 day visitors in addition to 8000 or so staying tourists. This is high, given that there are only 20 000 residents in the old city (as compared to a population of 116 000 for Bruges as a whole).
- The large number of tourist coaches impeding traffic flow.
- The inability of the medieval street pattern to cope with the demands of the motor car.

A strategy for tourism

As part of an integrated plan for tourism development, it was necessary to bring together the many small enterprises that make up the private sector in Bruges and the local and regional authorities who formulate planning and marketing policies. To improve the quality of the tourism product, a traffic control plan was implemented in 1992, with the following aims:

- to improve traffic flow within the historic centre
- the diversion of through traffic away from the city centre
- to discourage the use of the private car as the best means of transport to reach the historic centre
- to encourage the use of the bicycle as a 'green' transport mode
- to enable residents to access local services within the city centre.

The main features of the 'mobility plan' are:

- A circulation system consisting of five loops keeps superfluous traffic away from the city centre and diverts it to a number of large underground car parks on the periphery.
- Vehicles have been banned from certain streets and squares such as the Markt, which formerly acted as a traffic hub, and a one-way traffic system imposed elsewhere in the historic centre.
- At the same time, the traffic flow on the ring road has been improved.
- Tourist coaches are directed to parking areas situated just outside the old city.
- Restrictions on car use have gone hand-in-hand with an efficient and frequent bus service. Visitors who use the car parks situated just outside the historic area also get free tickets for the bus into the centre.
- Cyclists are exempt from the one-way street system, and bicycles are available for hire at the railway station and from many hotels.
- Signposting has been improved, and the promotional literature makes it clear to visitors that Bruges is easily accessible by public transport and can easily be explored by bicycle or on foot.

Traffic control is a means to the objective of creating a Bruges where tourism is in balance with the needs of residents and where the emphasis is on quality. This is to be achieved by:

- Restricting the building of new hotels to areas outside the historic centre.
- Encouraging repeat visitors by offering package deals, including public transport, to hotel guests from Belgium and neighbouring countries, who account for most of the demand for hotel accommodation. Of these visitors, half choose Bruges as the sole destination for their trip.
- Promoting seminars and small to medium-sized conferences.

Reflections on the case

This case raises the key issue of how to develop tourism in historic cities whilst still conserving the townscape and delivering a quality experience to the visitor. In Bruges there is the added issue of ensuring that tourism contributes to the economic well-being of the city by ensuring that staying visitors are not displaced by large numbers of day visitors. There is no one right answer to this conundrum as each of these issues requires trade-offs to be made.

Discussion points/assignments

1 You have been asked to plan a three day tour of West Flanders based on Bruges for a group of 20 students from your college. Assess the suitability of each transport mode – road, rail, sea and air – for travel to Bruges, comparing costs and journey times. Provide a route plan from your group's point of departure to their accommodation in Bruges or Zeebrugge, and an itinerary for the three day tour.

2 Compare the ways in which Bruges has managed visitors with other historic towns of similar size and popularity, such as York, UK.

3 In class have a debate on whether a concentration on 'heritage' can result in a 'museum-city' with little to offer young people in the local community. Use Bruges and other historic towns to support the arguments for and against the proposition.

4 Describe the ways in which architects, city planners and the artistic community can give a historic town a unique 'sense of place' and yet enable it to successfully adapt to the demands of the twenty-first century.

Acknowledgement

We are indebted to the Director of Tourism Flanders, Wim Vanseveren, for kindly providing suggestions and updated material for this case study.

Key sources

Ashworth, G. J. and Tunbridge, J. E. (1990) *The Tourist-Historic City*. Belhaven, London.

Drummond, S. and Yeoman, I. (2000) *Quality Issues in Heritage Visitor Attractions*. Elsevier Butterworth-Heinemann, Oxford.

Economic Study Bureau, West Flanders (WES) (1996) *Tourism in Brugge: Socio-Economic Aspects and Influence on City Planning*. WES, Brugge.

Law, C. (2002) *Urban Tourism*. Continuum, London.

Murphy, P. (1997) *Quality Management in Urban Tourism*. Wiley, Chichester.

Page, S. (1994) *Urban Tourism*. Routledge, London.

Richards, G. (2001) *Cultural Attractions and European Tourism*. CABI, Wallingford.

Toerisme Brugge (1999) *Sales and Meeting Guide 1998–1999*. Toerisme Brugge, Bruges.

Vanhove, N. (2002) Tourism policy: between competitiveness and sustainability: the case of Bruges. *Tourism Review* 57 (3), 34–40.

Website

http://www.brugge.be/toerisme/en/index.htm

The impact of winter sports tourism in the Austrian and Swiss Alps

Introduction

The Alps are a major tourism resource and destination on the world scene. This case introduces the development dilemma of tourism in the Alps. On completion of this case you will:

1 Be aware of the attraction of the Alps for tourism development.
2 Understand the potential social impacts of tourism as the Alps move away from an economy based upon agriculture.
3 Recognize the potentially damaging impacts of tourism development upon the Alpine environment.
4 Be aware of the development dilemma faced by the Alpine communities as they attempt to reconcile the economic benefits of tourism with its more negative impacts.
5 Recognize that the decentralized political system of Austria and Switzerland firmly places these development issues within the decision-making powers of local communities.

Key issues

There are five key issues in this case:

1 The Alps are a significant tourism destination on the world scene and tourism makes an important economic contribution to Alpine communities.
2 The development of tourism in the Alps has begun to replace agriculture as the economic mainstay of the region and this is having social consequences in the communities.

3 The development of tourism, particularly winter sports tourism, continues to have significant negative environmental impacts upon the fragile Alpine environment.

4 The key issue for this case is to understand the need for the Alps to develop tourism in such a way as to capitalize upon its economic benefits, whilst also minimizing the negative social and environmental consequences.

5 The decentralized political system of Austria and Switzerland means that tourism development decisions are made by the local communities, making this a classic example of community-based tourism decision taking.

The Alps

The Alps must rank among the world's most visited destinations in terms of spending by international tourists. Other mountain regions can offer similar natural resources but do not have the advantage of a central location and proximity to some of the world's most prosperous cities. Although the landforms are due to differences in geology and the effects of glaciation during the last Ice Age, much of the alpine landscape that tourists find so appealing is the work of mountain farmers over the centuries. The High Alps also provide a refuge for the marmot, the chamois and the edelweiss – symbolic of the fragility of alpine ecosystems. These resources are threatened by large-scale tourism, hydro-electric power generation and not least by road building. The region lies at the heart of Europe's north–south transit system and is faced with the seemingly inexorable growth of motor vehicle traffic, including the movement of vast quantities of freight through routes such as the upper Rhone Valley and the Brenner Pass. Air pollution is a serious problem, aggravated by the frequent temperature inversions that occur in enclosed mountain valleys in the winter months, and forests in some areas have been severely damaged as a result. The impact of tourism is greater in winter than in summer, due to the popularity of snow-based sports, particularly downhill skiing, and the need for high capacity transport systems to convey skiers to the slopes. Over half the Alpine region is contained within Austria, Switzerland and Germany. Together these three countries accounted for about a quarter of the world total of skier visits (including domestic tourists) and the supply of skiing facilities in the late 1990s (Table 17.1).

Social impacts

Many Alpine communities have gradually changed in the course of a century from small farming villages on the margins of national economies to sophisticated ski resorts attracting a wealthy international clientele. Traditionally the local economy was based on a pastoral type of agriculture, with livestock being moved from the valleys to the high alpine pastures above the treeline in summer and back to the villages in autumn. Society was based on the peasant farmer and his extended family, accommodated in substantial farmhouses handed down through the generations. As agriculture yielded only a meagre livelihood, members of farming households supplemented their income with craft industries during the winter months or by

Table 17.1 World distribution of skiing

Destination country	Skier visits (millions)	%	No. of ski lifts	%
Austria	43		3473	
Switzerland	31		1762	
Germany	20		1670	
Sub-total	**94**	**24**	**6905**	**27**
France	56	14	4143	16
Italy	37	9	2854	11
Scandinavia	22	6	1860	7
North America	76	20	3644	14
Japan	75	19	3600	14
Australasia	4	1	203	1
Rest of world	26	7	2605	10
World total	**390**		**25 814**	**100**

Source: Hudson, 2000

temporary migration to find work in the cities. The advent of tourism in the late nineteenth century provided the opportunity to let rooms in the farmhouse to paying guests, and for farmers to work part-time as mountain guides, and later as ski instructors. Since the Second World War, tourism has developed from a profitable sideline to become the basis of most rural economies, to the extent that only 2 per cent of the population now make a living solely from agriculture. The farmhouse has become the family-run guesthouse or hotel. Instead of out-migration from rural communities there are now large numbers of incomers, mostly young people attracted by jobs in the tourism sector.

The ski resort of St Anton in the Austrian Tyrol is an example of this transformation. It has a population of only 2500 but accommodates a million tourist bednights a year, of which 80 per cent take place in the winter season (late December to the beginning of April). The summer season (July and August) is not only shorter but much quieter, with a different type of clientele. There is a division of labour by gender in the tourism sector, with the day-to-day running of the family-owned guesthouse or hotel being the women's responsibility. This involves very long working hours during the winter season and often conflicts with the need for privacy with the family. Men, on the other hand, are much more likely to have jobs that are not centred on the home, are more varied, and with working hours that allow more social contacts. This is particularly true of ski instructors, who have prestige in the community and a glamorous image among foreign tourists. The difference between men's and women's roles in tourism has been blamed for difficulties in marital relationships, alcohol abuse and disruption to family life (McGibbon, 2000).

Environmental impacts

Although tourism has helped to save the rural economy and many aspects of the traditional culture, the growth of winter sports has had a negative environmental impact on many parts of the Alps, in the following ways:

- **Preparation of ski runs** This entails the removal of vegetation and boulders to a depth of 20 centimetres to allow a good accumulation of snow, thus causing damage to ecosystems and leaving unsightly scars on mountainsides, to the dismay of summer tourists once the snow has melted. The deforestation of the lower slopes to create clear runs increases the risk of rockfalls, mudslides and avalanches.
- **Development of lift systems** The earlier lift systems necessitated road building that has caused erosion in formerly remote, unspoiled areas such as the Val d'Anniviers in the Swiss canton of Valais. The use of helicopters to ferry in materials now makes it possible to develop previously inaccessible locations as high altitude ski stations, sometimes with revolving restaurants and other tourist facilities that are inappropriate for their setting. Even glaciers can be used for summer skiing, causing damage to the watersheds of some of Europe's major rivers.
- **Artificial snow-making equipment** Faced with a shorter and less reliable season due to the impact of global warming, ski resort operators increasingly rely on technology to guarantee a supply of snow. Thousands of snow cannons use up vast quantities of water, amounting to 200 000 litres for every hectare of piste (Holden, 2000: 84). The artificial snow melts slowly, reducing the already brief recuperation period for alpine vegetation. For example, due to the rigorous climate alpine grasses have a very slow growth rate, seeding once every seven years. Skiing on shallow snow can cause irreparable damage. Along with a lowering of the water table and noise pollution, there is the problem of soil contamination, caused by the chemicals used to speed up the process of crystallization that results in artificial snow.
- **Growth of motor vehicle traffic** Although Switzerland was the first European country to impose strict exhaust emission standards, it has little control over the millions of foreign vehicles that pass through the Alps each year, so that pollution remains a serious problem in a region once renowned for the purity of its air and water. Some ski resorts – notably Zermatt – have banned cars altogether in favour of 'green' modes of transport, but this still means that long-stay car parks have to be provided for visitors and residents further down the valleys.
- **Off-piste skiing** More than half the world's avalanches occur in the Alps, and the problem is increasing as skiers and snowboarders push deeper into the mountains, away from the crowds and relative safety of the prepared ski runs. Vibrations can trigger the displacement of the snowpack from the unstable cornices overhanging smooth leeward slopes. Although communities have lived with the hazard they call 'the white death' for centuries, they have been protected to a large extent by the forests on the lower mountain slopes. The avalanche that overwhelmed the Austrian resort of Galtur in 1999 demonstrated the destructive power of masses of snow in motion, no longer checked by these natural defences. Concrete barriers and rows of steel fences on the mountainsides are expensive, intrusive and a poor substitute for healthy forests, but they are often the only option available.

The development dilemma

The decentralization of planning in Austria and Switzerland means that decisions are made, not by central government or outside business interests, but by local communities, who can vote for large-scale development for winter and summer tourism (as in the case of Crans-Montana and Verbier), or perhaps shun the industry altogether. Only a small part of the Austrian and Swiss Alps has national park status, giving a full measure of state protection, while conservation bodies such as the Swiss League for the Protection of Nature lack the resources of their British equivalent, the National Trust. Ownership of the facilities in a typical Alpine resort may be divided between a dozen farmers, with the outcome of competing and non-integrated services, in contrast to the situation in North America where development is in the hands of large corporations who exercise uniform control. With the large number of resorts available, skiers are unlikely to tolerate lengthy queues at ski lifts as they can choose to go elsewhere. The decision to opt for large-scale expansion involves heavy capital investment in lift systems and the associated facilities, and the risk of financial disaster for the community in the event of a poor season. Moreover, if the lift system is expanded, more skiers will be attracted, and more hotels will be needed to accommodate them. This will further reduce the area available for the traditional farming activities that give the alpine landscape its appeal for summer tourists. The prospect of a shorter winter season may persuade the community to diversify into summer sports tourism, which inevitably means more investment in facilities such as golf courses and mountain bike trails, and further environmental damage.

Hiking and other 'green' activities are an alternative to ski resort expansion. Although some erosion would result from the widening of existing trails, summer tourism has a minimal impact on the Alps compared to the winter sports industry. Alternative tourism is now being promoted through an agreement between the seven countries that share the Alps, designating an international system of hiking trails that highlight the natural and cultural attractions of the region under the banner of 'Via Alpina' (the Alpine Way). The work of pressure groups such as Alp Action is also important in persuading local communities to aim for more sustainable forms of development.

Reflections on the case

The Alps pose the classic development dilemma – how to develop tourism to capitalize upon its economic benefits whilst at the same time paying heed to the potential negative social and environmental consequences. In the Alps, this issue is heightened by the fact that decision making is devolved to the local communities who are left to wrestle with this complex issue, raising the question of whether it is wise to devolve internationally significant tourism development issues to community based forums.

Discussion points/assignments

1 With the use of diagrams, describe the topography and facilities of two resorts at different altitudes in the Austrian or Swiss Alps, so that your client can make an informed choice on the best place to ski.

2 Select a resort in either Austria or Switzerland for a Canadian couple with two teenage children. They want to do 'some serious sightseeing' and visit a number of cultural attractions, as well as participating in winter sports. You should include the following considerations in your choice of resort:
   - accessibility to major cities and historic towns
   - altitude and topography, including slopes suitable for skiers with a range of abilities
   - natural attractions such as lakes and waterfalls
   - the transport infrastructure, including scenic highways, mountain railways, and the different types of lift systems – namely cable cars, gondola lifts, chairlifts and drag lifts
   - the type of accommodation available, recreation facilities for non-skiers, and *après ski* nightlife.
3 Describe the changes that have taken place in a typical alpine village since the nineteenth century, and discuss whether tourism has improved the 'quality of life' for the inhabitants along with living standards.
4 In class hold a debate about the pros and cons of going for large-scale development of winter sports tourism in a small alpine community, and assign roles to members of the class. These roles might include the local mayor, farmers, business people, school teachers and other members of the local community.
5 Assess the risk from avalanches and landslides in particular resorts in the Austrian and Swiss Alps, and evaluate the measures that have been carried out to minimize the danger to residents and visitors.

Key sources

Barker, M. L. (1994) Strategic tourism planning and limits to growth in the Alps. *Tourism Recreation Research*, 19 (2), 43–49.

Fuchs, M., Peters, M. and Weiermair, K. (2002) Tourism sustainability through destination benchmarking indicator systems: the case of alpine tourism. *Tourism Recreation Research*, 27 (3), 21–33.

Galvani, A. (1993) Mountain tourism in Cortina d'Ampezzo: sustainability and saturation. *Tourism Recreation Research*, 18 (1), 27–32.

Goddie, P., Price, M. and Zimmerman, F. M. (1999) *Tourism and Development in Mountain Regions*. CABI, Wallingford.

Holden, A. (2000) *Environment and Tourism*. Routledge, London.

Hudson, S. (2000) *Snow Business*. Cassell, London.

Juelg, F. (1993) Tourism product life cycles in the Central Eastern Alps: a case study of Heiligenblut on the Grossglockner. *Tourism Recreation Research*, 18 (1), 20–26.

Koenig, U. and Begg, B. (1997) Impacts of climate change on winter tourism in the Swiss Alps. *Journal of Sustainable Tourism*, 5 (1), 46–58.

McGibbon, J. (2000) Family business: commercial hospitality and the domestic realm in an international ski resort in the Tirolean Alps, in M. Robinson (ed.), *Reflections in International Tourism: Expressions of Identity, Culture and Meaning*. Sheffield Hallam University, pp. 167–181.

Mose, J. (1993) Hohe Tauern National Park: test case for 'soft' tourism in the eastern Alps. *Tourism Recreation Research*, 18 (1), 11–19.

Pechlaner, H. and Raich, M. (2002) The role of information technology in the information process for cultural products and services in tourism destinations. *Information Technology and Tourism*, 4 (2), 91–106.

Pechlaner, H. and Saverwein, E. (2002) Strategy implementation in the alpine tourism industry. *International Journal of Contemporary Hospitality Management*, 14 (4), 157–168.

Socher, K. (1997) The influence of tourism on the quality of life in the evaluation of the inhabitants of the Alps. *Tourist Review*, 2 (April/June), pp. 17–21.

Case 18

Berlin: the revitalization of a European capital

Introduction

Since the reunification of Germany in 1990, Berlin has begun to develop into one of the world's major tourist cities. This case examines the role of tourism in this development. On completion of the case you will:

1 Understand the background to the reunification of Germany and some of the issues involved.
2 Recognize how the tourism development of Berlin has been influenced by the contrasts between the former East and West Berlin.
3 Understand the development dilemmas surrounding the redevelopment of some of the historic features of Berlin.
4 Recognize that Berlin is competing with successful European capitals and tourist cities and that the ambitions of Berlin have not always been fulfilled.
5 Be aware of the economic issues involved in rebuilding the former East Germany and the impact that this has had on developing tourism in Berlin.

Key issues

There are four key issues in this case:

1 Berlin is beginning to develop as a significant European capital and tourist city in Europe; however, it is finding it difficult to compete with other, more established tourist cities.
2 Berlin's attractions are primarily based upon its history, heritage and the institutions of a capital city. The reminders of the Second World War in particular create a tourism development dilemma, in terms of the appropriate level of attention and interpretation to be provided to these 'dark tourism' resources.

3 **The former East and West Berlin developed in very different ways and this legacy has been transmitted into the tourism developments of today.**
4 **The rebuilding of the former East Germany is a drain upon Germany's economy and this has affected the tourism development of Berlin.**

The historical background

The reunification of Germany in 1990 brought together two major cities – East and West Berlin – that had evolved for almost half a century under the two very different political and economic systems of East Germany (officially the German Democratic Republic or DDR) and West Germany (officially the Federal Republic of Germany or BRD). A year earlier the Berlin Wall, which since 1962 had prevented free movement between East and West, ceased to exist except as a resource for souvenir-hunters from all over the world. At the time of the fall of the Berlin Wall the population of East Berlin was estimated to be 1.3 million, whereas West Berlin had a population of over 2 million. During the 1990s both the administrative functions of the German federal government and embassies were gradually moved from Bonn to Berlin, which had been the capital of a united Germany from 1871 to 1945. The process of reinstatement was symbolized by the opening of the new Reichstag (Parliament Building) in 1998, as part of a huge government complex on the eastern edge of the Tiergarten – Berlin's central park, which also includes the new Chancellery. Another landmark event was the ending of the four-power military occupation of the city by the wartime allies (the USA, Britain, France and Russia) in 1994. This allowed Lufthansa to operate flights to Berlin's Tegel Airport for the first time since Germany's defeat in 1945. The city now has its own regional airline, Air-Berlin.

During the period of the Cold War, East and West Berlin used the medium of tourism to deliberately promote themselves as showcases for the achievements of socialism and Western democracy by the governments of East and West Germany.

- In East Berlin the Alexanderplatz was chosen as the centre of the DDR, the 350 metre high Television Tower symbolizing the power of the Communist state. Before 1945 this impressive square had been the power centre of the Kingdom of Prussia and later of the Third Reich, and the East German regime was determined to obliterate this legacy of the past. East Berlin also contained what had been the most fashionable street of the pre-war capital – the *Unter den Linden* – which had suffered massive destruction as a result of Allied bombing in the Second World War. The majority of Berlin's cultural attractions – its great museums, cathedrals, universities, palaces and art galleries – were likewise in the Communist zone.
- In contrast, West Berlin focused on the Kurfurstendamm, which had been a secondary centre in the pre-war capital. This became noted for its shops, restaurants, cabarets and hotels, while West Berlin as a whole generated cultural dynamism and prosperity under a free market economy, aided by generous subventions from the federal government in Bonn. The Europa Centre epitomized this commercial success in contrast to the greyness and the restricted shopping and nightlife of East Berlin. West Berlin was also multicultural, not only in comparison to

East Berlin, but also to the rest of the Federal Republic, attracting immigrants from all over Europe. It was also a major tourist centre, whereas East Berlin placed restrictions on Western tourists.

West Berlin was a detached part of West Germany, an enclave or 'island of democracy' completely surrounded by the Soviet-controlled DDR throughout the Cold War period. This made the city a vulnerable target for economic blockade since its surface transport links could be cut at any time. When in 1948 Stalin tried to starve the city into submission, the Western allies responded with the Berlin Airlift (which indirectly led to the rise of the air charter entrepreneurs, using the surplus aircraft, once that crisis was over). The need for NATO military protection also made West Berlin a potential flashpoint in any dispute between the two superpowers – the USA and the Soviet Union.

The heart of pre-war Berlin – the Potsdamerplatz – remained a wasteland throughout the Cold War period due to its location on the border between East and West. Since the late 1990s this area has become the focus of one of the world's greatest urban rebuilding projects, with the aim of making Berlin the European metropolis of the twenty-first century. The Potsdamerplatz is a new commercial centre, with a mix of theatres, hotels, shopping malls and restaurants. Most of the projects are taking place in the former East Berlin – specifically in the historic area of the city known as Mitte lying to the east of the Friedrichstrasse. This contains what little is left of the medieval nucleus of Berlin and the elegant baroque city, centred on the Unter den Linden, laid out by Frederick the Great and other kings of Prussia in the eighteenth century.

The rebuilding programme is controversial in that it raises questions as to which elements of the city's heritage should be preserved or restored. Here ideological considerations play a major part, given Berlin's role in shaping European history during the twentieth century. For example:

- Of Hitler's Chancellery and wartime Bunker, no trace remains, and even the sites are left unmarked, to avoid the possibility of them becoming neo-Nazi shrines. In contrast, a museum to the Jewish Holocaust has been opened in the locality.
- Similarly, many Germans would like to see the monuments of the East German regime removed. In 2002 the Reichstag voted to demolish the Palace of the People (the DDR Parliament). This had been built on the site of the Stadtschloss, the former palace of Kaiser Wilhelm II and the kings of Prussia, which is to be reconstructed as a heritage attraction.
- The Communist regime neglected the baroque heritage of East Berlin for many years, but in the 1970s initiated a massive restoration programme following a re-appraisal of the role of Frederick the Great as a national leader. Since reunification there has been controversy around the restoration of Berlin's most well-known landmark – the Brandenburg Gate – as the Prussian Eagle and Iron Cross were regarded by many as symbols of the old militaristic Germany.
- The medieval nucleus of Berlin is unlikely to be restored on an intimate scale, given the high cost of land in the city centre and the need to yield economic returns.

The new Berlin has become a centre for fashion, music and the performing arts, boasting one of the world's largest street parties – the annual 'Love Parade'. This recalls the avant-garde role of Berlin cabaret during the era of the Weimar Republic

(1919–33), and as a short-break destination the city exerts a special fascination because of its recent history. It is also a green city, with a great deal of recreational space in the form of parkland, woods, lakes and canals.

Transport facilities are excellent, and it is worth noting that the U-bahn and S-bahn networks, which functioned efficiently even during the Cold War division of the city, have now been extended. A shortlist of Berlin's attractions might include:

- **The Berlin Wall** Only a segment remains of the original 160 kilometre-long Wall, but this is now the world's largest open-air art gallery. Near the site of Checkpoint Charlie on Friedrichstrasse (the former entry point to East Berlin for Western visitors) a museum now commemorates the attempts made by East Berliners to escape to freedom in the West.
- **Museum Island** This historic area of East Berlin has some of Europe's finest museums and art galleries, the most famous being the Pergamon Museum, which is a collection of art objects from the ancient civilizations of the Middle East, the most spectacular being the Ishtar Gate from Babylon.
- **The Egyptian Museum** This is the equivalent collection of antiquities in West Berlin, containing the three-thousand-year-old bust of Nefertiti.
- **The Charlottenburg Palace** This was a favourite residence of Frederick the Great, along with his ornate summer palace at Sans Souci, in the western suburb of Potsdam.

Nevertheless, the new Berlin is only partially a success story. The downturn in the German economy has made it difficult to justify building costs that ran well over budget, resulting in a massive deficit in the city's finances. There is an oversupply of hotel accommodation, as the growth of business and conference tourism to the new capital has been less than anticipated. The building boom of the 1990s has not yet led to an economic revival, but rather to a number of business failures; moreover the population stood at 3.5 million in 2002, much lower than the expected 5 million. This is because Berlin has to compete against a number of well-established regional capitals, and the city is no longer eligible for generous subsidies from the federal government to attract and retain businesses.

Reflections on the case

Berlin is unique as a tourism city in that it is re-creating itself after decades of division between East and West. Tourism is playing an important role in this re-creation, but there are issues surrounding the very different natures of the former East and West Berlin, and also the appropriate redevelopment of features associated with previous regimes. At the same time, the rebuilding of Berlin is affected by the cost of developing the economy of the former East Germany. Berlin is also finding the competitive environment difficult as other capital cities in Europe are making significant tourism investments.

Discussion points/assignments

1 Explain the appeal of Berlin for art and music lovers.
2 You work for a tour operator which is proposing to add Berlin to its city breaks programme aimed at the 20 to 35 age group. Which aspects of Berlin would you include in the brochure and why?
3 Define what is meant by 'dark tourism', and discuss the ethics of including places associated with disaster and human suffering under the Nazi and Communist regimes in a tour programme.
4 Unlike London and Paris, Berlin has a number of serious rivals as the nation's primary city. Find out the reasons for this, and discuss ways in which Berlin can deal with the competition from Munich, Hamburg and Frankfurt.
5 Describe one of Berlin's site or event attractions in detail, and relate this attraction to a particular market.

Key sources

Irving, C. (1998) The new metropolis. *Condé Nast Traveler*, November, 96–108, 174–178.
Page, S. (1994) *Urban Tourism*. Routledge, London.

Websites
http://travel.yahoo.com/p-travelguide-1230601-berlin attractions-i
http://tripadvisor.com/Attractions-g187323-Activities-Berlin.html
http://www.berlin.world-guides.com/attractions.html

Case 19

The French Riviera: fashion as an influence on resort development

Introduction

The French Riviera is one of the world's best known and most fashionable resort areas. This case examines the influence of fashion upon the development of the destination. On completion of the case you will:

1 Understand the historical evolution of tourism on the Riviera.
2 Understand that the Riviera has been the home to a number of different types of tourism since the nineteenth century.
3 Be aware of the influence of fashion upon the evolution of tourism on the Riviera.
4 Recognize the key tourist attractions of the Riviera.
5 Be aware of the impacts of tourism development on the Riviera.

Key issues

There are three key issues in this case:

1 As a destination, the Riviera has a long history which reflects the influence of fashion upon its products, from exclusive winter health tourism to mass beach tourism.
2 The Riviera has an impressive range of attractions and tourism facilities to support these products.
3 The development of tourism on the Riviera has, however, brought with it a number of negative impacts.

The evolution of tourism on the Riviera

One of the world's best known and most fashionable resort areas, the French Riviera is the name given to the stretch of Mediterranean coast extending almost 200 kilometres from Toulon to the Italian border, while the Côte d'Azur is usually defined as the section east of Cannes. It is a spectacularly beautiful coastline – east of Nice the mountains of the Maritime Alps almost reach the sea. Three scenic highways, known as *corniches*, hug the contours of the cliffs. The mountains also shelter this south-facing coast from the blustery *Mistral*. Well endowed with natural attractions, the Riviera is easily accessible by road, rail and air communications and offers a full range of amenities. The region has experienced several stages of development in response to changing fashions in tourism, namely:

- **Exclusive winter health tourism** From the mid-nineteenth century to the outbreak of the First World War, the Riviera was exclusively a winter destination. Wealthy British tourists began the vogue for winter holidays on the Mediterranean coast, a fact commemorated by the *Promenade des Anglais* (sea front promenade) at Nice. In 1886 a French poet named the coastline the *Côte d'Azur* ('the azure coast') – an early example of resort promotion. By this time the coast between Cannes and Menton was already well established as a destination for the rich, well connected and famous throughout Europe, including Russian aristocrats, whose legacy is still evident in Nice. Queen Victoria made several visits, confirming the Riviera's exclusive status. Grand hotels such as the Carlton in Cannes, and the Negresco in Nice were built to accommodate these visitors, while casinos and racecourses were provided to keep them entertained. The world-famous casino in Monte Carlo opened in 1863, an initiative which almost overnight made the fortunes of the principality of Monaco and its ruling Grimaldi family.
- **Exclusive summer beach tourism** Until the 1920s, the elite had shunned the Mediterranean in the summer months. This changed when celebrities such as the French fashion designer Coco Chanel and the American writer Scott Fitzgerald made sunbathing fashionable. Juan-les-Pins was the Riviera's first summer resort, attracting a new moneyed clientele of writers, artists and entertainers who were quite different from the European aristocracy, whose fortunes had declined as a result of wars and revolutions. The region's accessibility improved with the construction of a new coastal highway – the *moyenne corniche* – and the inauguration of the *Train Bleu* (the Calais–Mediterranean express) which provided luxury travel to the resorts. The coast's mediocre beaches were also improved, sometimes by importing sand from elsewhere.
- **Popular tourism** After the 1950s, the Riviera considerably widened its appeal, catering for a much larger domestic market. This had been foreshadowed by the French government's decision in 1936 to introduce holidays with pay and encourage cheap rail travel to the resorts, but the Second World War set back the process of democratization. Campgrounds and a sprawl of holiday villas developed along the western Riviera, while many luxury hotels were converted into apartments. On the other hand, new resorts – such as the former fishing village of Saint-Tropez – strove to maintain exclusivity along with some of the established centres. Fashion innovations such as the bikini ensured that the Riviera remained the focus of international attention.

Attractions

The Riviera offers a diversity of tourism products, and has to a large extent adapted to changing fashions. It retains its stylish image as a result of pricing and the types of facilities offered – marinas, often combined with luxury accommodation, as in the purpose-built resort of Port Grimaud, beach clubs, casinos and grand hotels. The resorts also vary considerably in character, from the exclusive hideaways of the very rich – Cap Ferrat near Nice is a good example – to unpretentious places catering for the French family market such as Saint Maxime and Saint Raphael. Market segmentation was evident as early as the 1920s, when an advertising slogan for Cannes claimed that

Menton's dowdy, Monte's brass, Nice is rowdy, Cannes is class

This had an element of truth, in that Menton had a reputation for attracting elderly invalids, whereas Monte Carlo appealed to the *nouveaux riches*. Nowadays, Menton, with its pink stucco villas set amid lemon groves, is the most old-fashioned of the resorts. Most of its visitors still tend to be elderly, in contrast to Juan-les-Pins, which attracts hordes of young French holidaymakers to its bars and discotheques. The main resorts and tourist areas of the Riviera are:

- **Monte Carlo**, which has always gone for the 'big money'. However, the principality of Monaco is less dependent on gambling revenues than in the past, having diversified into hosting international sports events and exhibitions as well as the business sector – many of its 27 000 residents are wealthy tax exiles. With an area of only 195 hectares, space in this tiny state is at a premium, resulting in a 'mini-Manhattan' of high rise buildings. Nevertheless, the old town of Monaco perched above the yacht harbour retains some of its traditional atmosphere in contrast to Monte Carlo, which developed around the Casino. The principality's attractions include:
  ○ the Oceanographical Museum – associated with the undersea explorer Jacques Cousteau
  ○ the Jardin Exotique – a world-famous collection of cacti, made possible by the favourable micro-climate.
- **Nice** is less of a resort and more a large commercial city and major port, with a population approaching half a million. It has a range of accommodation to suit most budgets, while its airport handles not only a large volume of holiday traffic – much of it on 'no frills' airlines – but also a substantial amount of business travel attracted by the growing information technology industries which have developed in this part of France. Nice is a major cultural centre, with a history going back to the times of Ancient Greece and a recent association with some of the greatest modern artists; as a result, it boasts almost as many museums and art galleries as Paris.
- **Cannes** has retained its style and exclusive image to a greater extent than the other major resorts of the Côte d'Azur. The crescent-shaped *Croisette* beach of imported golden sand is backed by a promenade lined with palms and grand hotels. Designer boutiques line the streets of the new town, which contrasts with the old quarter overlooking the harbour. The Film Festival is the best known of the event attractions that bring in considerable revenue and publicity.

- The **Western Riviera** between Cannes and Hyères is generally less exclusive than the Côte d'Azur and less heavily developed. Hotel and restaurant prices are lower (except in Saint-Tropez), while the beaches on the other hand are more attractive and in many cases open to the public. Inland, the Esterel and Maures mountains are less spectacular than the Maritime Alps, but give rise to some striking scenery. Saint-Tropez is the leading resort of the Western Riviera, with a setting on a beautiful bay, a fashion scene that attracts celebrities, and a multitude wishing 'to see and be seen'. As a result, more than 10 000 cars arrive each day in Saint-Tropez during the tourist season, stretching the town's resources to the limit.
- **Provence**   The hinterland of Provence offers a contrast to the sophisticated resorts of the Riviera, but this is changing since the rural villages are increasingly drawn into the tourism industry, providing accommodation, for example, as pressures on the coast increase. The cultivation of flowers for the perfume industry at Grasse, and of fruit and early vegetables for the Paris markets, still remain important to the local economy. The numerous hilltop villages – the so-called *villes perchés* – are a reminder of former times when the coast was menaced by Saracen pirates from North Africa rather than tourists. Some of these villages – notably Eze and Saint Paul de Vence – have become artist's colonies and specialize in a variety of craft industries aimed primarily at the tourist market.

The impacts of tourism

The Riviera's popularity as a tourist destination has resulted in a number of problems, including:

- **Seasonality**   The reluctance of the French to stagger their holidays leads to overcrowding in the peak months of July and August. Traffic congestion is acute, hotels increase their tariffs by 40 per cent, while spaces in campsites are at a premium. Water shortages are also a major problem due to excessive demands on supplies.
- **Appropriation of land for development**   Of the 5500 kilometres of French coastline, 1000 kilometres are said to be densely urbanized and another 2000 kilometres are characterized by 'dispersed development'. Pressures are greatest on the Côte d'Azur where 90 per cent of the coastline is already built up. These pressures result from a rapidly growing population combined with the burgeoning demand for second or retirement homes. Not only is there an almost continuous linear development of apartments and villas along the coast, but dispersed development in the hinterland threatens to engulf the rural communities.
- **Pollution and environmental degradation**   Pollution from industrial effluents and untreated sewage has closed beaches, while fires – many started deliberately to clear land for development – have devastated large areas of pine forest and *maquis* scrubland.
- **Crime**   Drug-related crime, emanating from Marseilles and Nice, is an increasing threat to tourist security on the Riviera.
- **An outdated image**   The Riviera is also finding it difficult to adjust to new forms of holidaymaking that have an emphasis on self-catering, and is vulnerable to competition from Spain and Italy.

Reflections on the case

This case has shown the influence of fashion on the development of tourism on the Riviera as it has moved from being a nineteenth-century winter health resort through to the mass beach tourism of today. However, whilst the Riviera is perceived as a successful tourism destination and has adjusted its products to fashion, tourism has brought with it a number of negative impacts.

Discussion points/assignments

1 Draw up a list (with brief biographical details) of the twentieth-century writers, artists, film stars and sporting celebrities that have been associated at various times with specific places on the Riviera.
2 As a tourism consultant, draft a plan that will transform the Riviera's 'tired image' and attract new markets.
3 Investigate the importance for tourism of event attractions such as the Nice Carnival, and draw up a 'balance sheet' of the costs and benefits to the local community of staging such events.
4 Suggest alternative ways of travel for a young couple from London who wish to spend their honeymoon in Monte Carlo. In your comparison of the various transport options available by air, rail, road and sea include considerations such as comfort, safety and convenience as well as cost and journey times. Also provide a route plan from London to Monaco for your clients.

Key sources

Bailey, M. (2000) Nice. *City Reports*, 1, 67–74.
Ring, J. (2004) *Riviera: The Rise and Rise of the Côte d'Azur*. John Murray, London.
Rudney, R. (1980) The Development of Tourism on the Côte d'Azur: An Historical Perspective, in D. Hawkins (ed.) *Tourism Planning and Development Issues*. George Washington University, 213–224.

Website
http://www.maison-de-la-France.com

Case 20

Payback time for tourism: the Balearic Islands' eco-tax

Introduction

This case examines the 'polluter pays' principle as applied to tourism, using a Spanish example – the *ecotasa* or environmental tax which was briefly imposed by the regional government of the Balearic Islands between May 2002 and October 2003. On completion of this case you will:

1 Be aware of the massive growth in tourism to Mallorca and Ibiza since the 1950s, and the environmental and social impacts of mass tourism to these islands.
2 Recognize the need for sustainable tourism in an area as threatened by pollution and over-development as the Balearic Islands.
3 Understand the part played by tour operators, hoteliers, political parties, regional and national governments in determining tourism policy in the islands.
4 Appreciate that the eco-tax is one of a number of measures that governments and local authorities can adopt to finance conservation and improvements to the environment of tourist areas.
5 Understand the reasons for the strong opposition to the eco-tax.

Key issues

There are five key issues in this case:

1 The eco-tax puts the responsibility for protecting the environment and the 'quality of life' of the host community on the tourist and the tourism sector. This should encourage both tourists and local communities to make a positive contribution to maintain the resources on which tourism depends.

2 **More than most holiday destinations, the Balearic Islands have experienced the negative impacts of mass tourism, and compensation for this has long been overdue.**
3 **The image of the islands is one of hedonism and beach tourism, but Mallorca, Minorca, Ibiza and Formentera each has a distinct character, with cultural and natural attractions that can appeal to other market segments.**
4 **The eco-tax was a political issue. It was supported by most of the islands' population and the proponents of sustainable tourism, but was opposed by most of the tourism industry.**
5 **The eco-tax as actually implemented was basically flawed, and was widely seen as being unfair and discriminatory. Nevertheless it established a useful precedent for other destinations to follow.**

The Balearic Islands

The Balearic Islands lie in the western Mediterranean some 200 kilometres from mainland Spain. They include four holiday destinations; Mallorca (better known in the UK as Majorca), Minorca, Ibiza (known as Eivissa in the regional Catalan language) and Formentera. Mallorca and Ibiza are nowadays associated with the excesses of mass tourism, with an image based on the five Ss (sun, sand, sea, sex and sangria). In fact, Mallorca, which is by far the largest of the islands, seemingly has the physical capacity to absorb most of the 11 million tourist arrivals a year received by the Balearics. Mass tourism – the 'Majorca' of popular legend in northern Europe – is largely confined to a few mega-resorts around the Bay of Palma and the northeast of the island, while 'the other Mallorca' continues to attract wealthy celebrities and the more upmarket tour operators. Tourism in Mallorca is not a new phenomenon – a tourist board was established in Palma in 1905 – whereas it came to Ibiza much later and was grafted on to a poorer, less sophisticated society. In the years prior to the Spanish Civil War (1936–39), the island's mild climate and beautiful landscapes attracted wealthy tourists and artists such as Joan Miró, while the poet-novelist Robert Graves did much to publicize the island from his home in the mountain village of Deia. In the early 1950s Mallorca was promoted by the newly created Spanish Ministry of Tourism as a honeymoon destination, 'the isle of love', an image guaranteed to appeal to the countries of northern Europe that were still recovering from the Second World War. Large-scale tourism followed and soon spread to the other islands. This was made possible by developments in air transport and tour operation, while government controls over hotel tariffs ensured that the Balearics remained a low-cost destination. The authoritarian regime of General Franco saw tourism as the engine of economic growth that would lift Spain and its people out of poverty, but the regional culture of the islands was largely suppressed. In a few decades the Balearic Islands were transformed from being one of the poorest regions of Spain, with a high rate of emigration and an economy based on agriculture and fishing, to one of the wealthiest, boasting one of the highest rates of car ownership in Europe.

Most of this tourism development was poorly planned, and largely unregulated by the local authorities. Although the islands gained a measure of self-determination in

1978 as an autonomous region as part of the post-Franco democratization of Spain, it was not until the 1990s that serious efforts were made to control tourism development. By this time there was an oversupply of accommodation, particularly at the cheaper end of the market, and a spiral of decline in the quality of tourism, in terms of spending per capita, which is proving difficult to reverse. The economy of the islands is precariously dependent on tourism, which accounts for 50 per cent of the regional domestic product. Moreover two countries dominate the market – Germany and the UK – with domestic tourists accounting for less than 10 per cent of arrivals. Much of the employment in tourism is seasonal and badly paid compared to other sectors of the economy in Spain. The negative impacts of tourism include:

- A coastline damaged by badly planned development.
- Pollution resulting from emissions of carbon dioxide from tourist coaches and hired cars, and inadequate waste disposal systems. Moreover, it is estimated that 100 000 tonnes of litter are left behind by tourists each year. Even the secluded beaches of Formentera are under threat from pollution.
- A great strain on infrastructure that may be used for only part of the year owing to the seasonal nature of tourism demand.
- Problems of water supply. The islands are of limestone formation and largely depend on ground water resources. Excessive demands have caused a lowering of the water table and penetration of the aquifer by sea water. Tourists during the peak season – which corresponds to the dry summer months – consume the equivalent of 440 litres of water daily, reaching 800 litres for those staying in luxury hotels. In Mallorca water has to be brought in to Palma by tanker on a daily basis.
- The outnumbering of the 800 000 inhabitants of the Balearic Islands by tourists. In Magaluf, pubs such as *Benny Hill's*, fast food eateries and tawdry souvenir shops cater for a downmarket British clientele, while the *bierkellers* of Arenal provide a similar 'home from home' for the Germans. This, and the growth of second home ownership by the more affluent tourists, has led to a loss of cultural identity and the feeling among many islanders that they have been taken over by foreigners.
- Some of the youth element in mass tourism, known to the Spanish as *hooligans*, are notorious for anti-social behaviour.

The eco-tax as a solution

The idea of a tax specifically for environmental improvement came about as a result of pressure from local communities, while many foreign visitors were also unhappy with the effects of mass tourism and runaway development. Unlike other forms of taxation, the public would know how much money was collected and how much would be allocated to various environmental projects. In 1999 the idea was taken up by an alliance of left of centre political parties in the regional parliament in Palma; this included the Balearic Islands Socialist Party (PSIB), the Spanish Socialist Workers Party (PSOE) and the environmentalist Green Party. The tax was opposed by most of the islands' hoteliers and the right-of-centre Popular Party, who were in power in Madrid until their defeat by the PSOE in the national elections of March 2004. These politicians feared that the eco-tax would be adopted by other holiday regions of Spain. Outside Spain, opposition came from British and German tour operators such as JMC/Thomas Cook and TUI, which between them provide most of the inclusive tour market to the Balearic Islands. The Association of British Travel Agents (ABTA) later claimed it was not against the eco-tax in principle, but the way in which it was to be applied without sufficient notice to their clients. It even threatened to break with a 30-year tradition by holding its annual convention at a venue other than Palma.

In April 2001 the central government in Madrid argued that the tax was 'unconstitutional' to the Spanish Supreme Court, which nevertheless ruled in favour of the regional government. The tax did not come into force until May 2002, not long before the defeat of the alliance by the Popular Party in the regional elections, and then as a watered-down compromise. The regional government was unable to collect the tax, as originally proposed, from all tourists on arrival at the airports and seaports of the islands, as these were controlled by the powers in Madrid. Instead the tax was applied principally to hotels, which then had to collect it from their guests. The tax amounted to an average of 1 euro per tourist per day, ranging from 0.25 to 2 euros according to the official category of the accommodation.

The proceeds of the tax, amounting to 36.7 million euros in 2002 and 48 million euros in 2003, have been allocated to the following types of project:

- The renovation and refurbishment of the major resorts. This includes a clean-up of the beachfront at Playa de Palma, and the encouragement of energy and water-saving programmes in the hotels.
- The acquisition of areas of natural beauty in the countryside, with the aims of conservation and improving public access. One such example in Mallorca is the *finca* (country estate) of Son Real near Alcudia; this offers a unique dune ecosystem and a number of *talayots*, prehistoric stone monuments of archaeological significance. In Minorca an interpretation centre was proposed to publicize the island's status as a World Biosphere Reserve. In Ibiza an area of wasteland is to be restored to productivity with irrigation techniques first used by the Moors centuries ago during their occupation of the islands.
- The improvement of facilities in existing nature parks and reserves.
- The promotion of 'green' routes for hiking and cycling.
- The preservation of the rich cultural heritage of the islands. This includes museums and heritage trails as well as the restoration of historic buildings.
- The revitalization of agriculture. The growth of tourism has been accompanied by a decline in traditional farming practices, such as the maintenance of the elaborate terraces that conserve soil and water, and which form a vital component of the landscape of the Balearic Islands.

Critics of the eco-tax claim that it has aggravated the tourism crisis the islands faced before its introduction, and that it is unfair. It is true that the number of tourist arrivals has fallen since 2001, but this is probably due to competition from 'new' destinations such as Bulgaria, Croatia, Tunisia and Turkey that can offer a similar beach product but at lower prices. With more than 95 per cent of tourists arriving by air, the impact of 9/11 also has to be considered. The economic situation in Germany has had an adverse effect, particularly on tourism to Mallorca. As far as the UK is concerned the eco-tax may have deterred some low-budget holidaymakers, but Spanish commentators believe this could improve the image of the islands in the long run.

Much more significant is the supposed unfairness of the tax, since it fell on tourists staying in hotels, *pensiones*, rural guest houses and campsites. It is estimated that up to 2 million tourists did not pay the tax, because they were staying in second homes, apartments, luxury yachts and unregistered accommodation. In effect most of these were from the higher income groups. Golf courses and dispersed development, consisting mainly of villas in the countryside, each with its garden and private swimming pool, may look more attractive than the high-rise resorts, but they place much greater demands on land, water and power resources. The use of four-wheel-drive vehicles further compounds the problem. This is hardly compatible with a strategy for sustainable development.

Reflections on the case

The Balearic Islands provide some of the most striking examples of the impact of mass tourism on some of the Mediterranean's most attractive coastal environments. A rural, traditional society has been transformed within the space of a generation to a service-oriented, consumer lifestyle, with the economic benefits of tourism being accompanied by a loss of cultural identity. However, regional autonomy has given the islanders the means to put right the damage resulting from decades of unregulated tourism. The eco-tax has provided the funding for a large number of small-scale projects, and although it has been flawed in its implementation, has set a useful precedent for other small island destinations.

Discussion points/assignments

1 **In large-scale tourism development there are often 'winners' and 'losers' among the host community. Suggest ways in which the benefits of tourism can be more widely distributed in your own country or home region to compensate the less fortunate sections of the community.**
2 **The eco-tax in the Balearic Islands was criticized for being unfair. To what extent was this criticism justified? Draw up your own guidelines for implementing an eco-tax that will persuade the international tourism industry to support it, as well as local communities.**
3 **Debate the concept of voluntary 'visitor payback' as an alternative to taxation for the funding of conservation projects.**
4 **Design a 'mini-guide' for Ibiza or Minorca that focuses on the island's cultural and natural resources, and encourages sustainable forms of tourism.**

Key sources

Brook, E. (2003) Taking the paving from paradise. *Tourism in Focus*, 46, 10–11.
Morgan, H. (2000) A taxing time. *Tourism in Focus*, 36, 6–7.

Presley, J. W. (2000) 'Frizzling in the sun': Robert Graves and the development of mass tourism in the Balearic Islands, in M. Robinson (ed.), *Reflections on International Tourism: Expressions of Culture, Identity and Meaning in Tourism.* Sheffield Hallam University, pp. 231–244.

Santamarta, J. (2001) La ecotasa de Baleares, un paso hacia el turismo sostenible. *World Watch* (Spanish edition), 11 (4), 1–5.

Van den Berg, E. (2003) Ecotasa: un impuesto medioambiental. *National Geographic* (Spain edition), 13 (3) special report.

Websites

www.tourism-watch.org
www.amics-terra.org

Case 21

Venice: heritage in danger

Introduction

Venice is a unique tourist city. This case examines the development of tourism in Venice and focuses on the challenges facing the city in the twenty-first century. On completion of the case you will:

1 Understand the significance of Venice as a tourist city.
2 Be aware of the attraction of Venice and its tourism resources.
3 Recognize the consequences for the community and the environment of developing tourism.
4 Understand that many of the challenges facing Venice are due to its low-lying location and are outside the control of the tourism sector.
5 Recognize the urgency of planning and managing for the future of the city if it is to be preserved.

Key issues

There are five key issues in this case:

1 Venice is a unique tourist city due to its low-lying location, canals and its art and architectural treasures.
2 The development of tourism in Venice has to be achieved sensitively and is highly constrained by the site of the city.
3 The scale of tourism in Venice has brought about negative social and environmental impacts, with a massive growth in the number of motor vessels.
4 The survival of Venice is threatened by its low-lying location and a range of engineering and pollution issues.
5 Urgent planning and management solutions are needed if Venice is to survive.

Venice: the tourist city

Venice is truly unique – an irreplaceable resource. Here we see a city without the problems of the motor car; this is due largely to the city's location on a cluster of low-lying islands in the middle of an extensive shallow lagoon. Venice has few rivals in its wealth of historic buildings and art treasures. However, it is not so much individual attractions that define this city's appeal, as its waterland setting and townscape which have changed remarkably little over the centuries. We need to remember that Venice is not just this historic island-city, but also includes a sprawl of industrial suburbs on the mainland, and it is here that most Venetians actually live and work.

Attractions

The best-known tourist attractions of Venice are to be found in and around the Piazza di San Marco (St Marks Square), one of Europe's finest meeting places. Like the rest of this city it has evolved over the centuries without formal planning, but somehow seems of a piece. Here you can see the Basilica of St Marks, which is architecturally quite unlike any other cathedral, and the Doge's Palace, which was the seat of government for the powerful Venetian Republic. The palace is lavishly decorated with paintings by Titian and other famous artists, and is connected by 'The Bridge of Sighs' to the former prisons. Venice's other well-known bridge is the Rialto, which dates from medieval times. Many of the 200 or so palaces lining the Grand Canal were built by rich merchants between the thirteenth and sixteenth centuries, when Venice controlled the Eastern Mediterranean and the trade in luxuries such as silk and spices from Asia. By the eighteenth century Venice had declined as a business centre, but had found a new role as a resort for gamblers and pleasure-seekers from all over Europe. The Venice Carnival, when people dress up in elaborate masks and costumes, is a reminder of this period. It is during Carnival that the timeless quality of this city can best be appreciated, long after the hordes of summer tourists have departed.

To escape the crowds you can visit the other islands in the Lagoon. These include:

- Murano – famous for its glass industry based on traditional craftsmanship and exclusive design.
- Burano – noted for lace making.
- Lido di Venezia (Venice Lido) – Venice's own beach resort, built on a sand spit (lido) separating the Lagoon from the Adriatic Sea. Venice Lido is famous for its casino and international film festival.

Transport

On the mainland between Mestre and Treviso, Venice has its international airport, named after Marco Polo, the famous Venetian merchant-adventurer. Relatively few tourists arrive by sea, other than cruise passengers, although Venice ranks as Italy's fifth largest port. You can also reach the city by road or rail. The most stylish way to arrive is by the Orient Express, where the standards of service and the decor of the carriages recall the 'golden age of travel' before the Second World War. But whatever your mode of transport, once you have crossed the causeway linking the island-city to the mainland, and arrived at the bus terminal or car park in the Piazzale Roma, or the Santa Lucia rail terminus, all onward travel to your destination must be on foot or by boat. Confronting you is a maze of narrow streets and alleys, sometimes opening onto a small square or *campo*, and superimposed on an intricate network of canals. The S-shaped Grand Canal, four kilometres in length, is the main artery of Venice, bisecting the city and crossed by only three bridges. The *vaporetto* (waterbus) and water taxi are the usual means of transport. The traditional gondola is expensive and nowadays used by Venetians only on special occasions, yet gondoliers are very much part of the city's romantic image, and their expertise as guides is appreciated by tourists.

Accommodation

Accommodation is expensive everywhere in Venice, so that many visitors prefer to stay at Lido di Jesolo, the principal resort of the 'Venetian Riviera', 30 kilometres to the north.

The problems

As a destination Venice has many strengths but it also has weaknesses. Opportunities for developing the tourism product are strictly limited, and the unique qualities of the resource are under threat for a number of reasons.

The social impact of tourism

Venice's popularity is itself a major problem. More than 50 000 visitors arrive in the historic city each day during the summer. The great majority are excursionists or tourists on a tight budget, whose contribution to the city's economy may be minimal while adding to its costs in litter disposal, policing etc. Venice is in danger of becoming a 'museum-city' for tourists. Venetians allege that the regional culture is being neglected in favour of Neapolitan music, which foreign tourists regard as more 'typically Italian'. The resident population of the historic city is now less than 80 000, half what it was in the 1950s (or the sixteenth century for that matter), and the decline is accelerating as Venice's environmental problems increase. The social composition of the population is also becoming less balanced. Middle income families continue to move to Mestre on the mainland, where most of the job opportunities outside tourism are to be found. This leaves the historic city to the wealthy, who can afford the upkeep of expensive palazzo-apartments, the elderly and those on low incomes, who are unable to leave.

The City Council has given serious consideration to imposing a quota on the number of day visitors. In 1989, they tried to ban backpackers from sleeping rough in the city's few public open spaces, but later revoked the law when it proved unworkable.

The threat of flooding and subsidence

Venice is built on foundations consisting of billions of timber pilings driven many centuries ago into the mud of the Lagoon, and these pilings are slowly eroding.

Venice has always been subject to flooding, but the problem is getting worse due to the rise in sea level brought about by global warming. The combination of high tides and storm surges in the Adriatic has led to St Marks Square being flooded much more frequently than was the case in the 1950s. Although Venetians have coped with the flood risk by, in effect, abandoning the lower floors of their dwellings, great damage has already been done to the fabric of many buildings, which are slowly sinking into the Lagoon.

The 1966 flood disaster alerted the world to the possibility that the city would have to be abandoned. The *Venice in Peril Fund* was set up to coordinate international efforts in the work of restoration and salvage, and to galvanize the authorities into action. The Italian government's response has been to propose the construction of huge movable floodgates across the three entrances to the Lagoon, saving Venice by closing it off from the Adriatic during periods of exceptionally high tides. This has attracted widespread criticism as a 'quick-fix' solution because:

- The project is not cost-effective, as the savings in the costs of flood damage do not justify the vast expense.
- It would disrupt navigation into the port of Venice. Considerable investment has taken place to improve port facilities, including the dredging of a deep-water channel for oil tankers (which itself has upset the balance between salt and fresh water in the Lagoon). The scheme would accelerate the silting up of the shipping channels.
- It would aggravate the build-up of pollution in the Lagoon.

The impact of pollution on the Lagoon ecosystem

The Venetian Lagoon is a fragile ecosystem. It is a patchwork of marshes, small islands, slow-flowing rivers and sandbanks, acting as a sponge-like barrier between the city and the Adriatic Sea. Pollution is the most deadly and insidious threat to Venice. Venetians have, for centuries, been aware of the need to protect their water resources and the Magisterio alla Acqua, financed by the city government, is probably the world's oldest environmental protection agency, with regulatory powers over the canal system and the Lagoon. The scale of the problem is probably much greater now than in the past, with pollution coming from the following sources:

- Waste from the city's households, hotels and restaurants – Venice has no sewers and domestic sewage is simply dumped in the canals. Regulations that hotels and restaurants should install biological water treatment works have been largely ignored. Sewage treatment works around the Lagoon have themselves contributed to the problem and a city-wide system of sewage disposal is required.
- Discharges of effluents from industrial plant on the mainland at Porto Marghera – factories were built here in the early 1900s to solve Venice's unemployment problem, but they were sited in the wrong place, far from the cleansing action of the tides. Pollutants include concentrations of heavy metals and ammonia. Limits for discharges are set by the Magisterio alla Acqua, but penalties for non-compliance are limited to a fine. Industrialists prefer to pay this rather than install waste treatment facilities; in effect a polluter's charter. This is also true of Murano's glassworks, which emit arsenic; here the individual enterprises are much smaller than on the mainland and they are financially unable to carry out the treatment required.

- The drainage into the Lagoon of pesticides and fertilizer from agriculture, much of it taking place on reclaimed land – an excess of nitrates and phosphates has contaminated fish and shellfish resources, to the extent that fishing is now prohibited over wide areas of the Lagoon. These conditions favour the spread of algae, which in turn decompose. With the absence of natural predators, swarms of *chironomides* (insects similar to mosquitoes) have become a plague, at times even threatening to disrupt air and rail communications. No effective solution has been implemented, partly because it is difficult to track down the polluters. A long-term solution would be for farmland to revert to marsh, restoring the original ecosystem.

The future

These problems are not just the concern of the environmentalists, but clearly threaten the viability of Venice as a tourist destination, unless both the private and public sectors can agree on drastic anti-pollution measures. In the public sector, closer cooperation is needed between the three levels of government – the city of Venice, the region of Veneto and the Italian State, to formulate a policy of sustainable development for the area.

Reflections on the case

The simple fact that Venice is a unique city draws millions of visitors every year. Whilst these visitors themselves create a range of problems for the local community, it is 'bigger picture' problems that threaten the survival of the city, including subsidence, flooding and pollution. Unless these can be addressed then the city may not survive the twenty-first century.

Discussion points/assignments

1 Draw up a chart that identifies the stakeholders in Venice's tourism industry and shows the different ways in which they are involved.
2 Obtain a large-scale map of Venice and locate a selection of major and lesser known attractions. Identify three special interest tourism markets (for example, food and wine lovers, opera-goers). Suggest alternative tourist routes for each of your markets.
3 Discuss the practical measures that could be implemented to protect the more popular attractions and art treasures of Venice from the pressure of excessive numbers of visitors.

4 Design a holiday brochure for cultural tourists that focuses on the life and work of famous Venetians such as Vivaldi and Titian, and the buildings or sites in Venice and the Veneto region that are associated with them.

5 Debate what modern cities can learn from the Venetian experience in dealing with transport and environmental issues.

Key sources

Ashworth, G. J. and Tunbridge, J. E. (1990) *The Tourist-Historic City*. Belhaven, London.

Bevilacqua, E. and Casti, E. (1989) The structure and impact of international tourism in the Veneto region, Italy. *Geojournal*, 19 (3), 285–287.

Canestrelli, E. and Costa, P. (1991) Tourist carrying capacity: a fuzzy approach. *Annals of Tourism Research*, 18 (2), 295–311.

Dove, J. (1991) Venice: the environmental challenge. *Geography Review*, 5 (2), 10–14.

Drummond, S. and Yeoman, I. (2000) *Quality Issues in Heritage Visitor Attractions*. Elsevier Butterworth-Heinemann, Oxford.

Law, C. (2002) *Urban Tourism*. Continuum, London.

Murphy, P. (1997) *Quality Management in Urban Tourism*. Wiley, Chichester.

Page, S. (1994) *Urban Tourism*. Routledge, London.

Richards, G. (2001) *Cultural Attractions and European Tourism*. CABI, Wallingford.

Russo, A. P. (2002) The 'Vicious Circle' of tourism development in heritage cities. *Annals of Tourism Research*, 29 (1), 165–182.

Van der Borg, J. (1992) Tourism and urban development: the case of Venice, Italy. *Tourism Recreation Research*, 17 (2), 46–56.

Van der Borg, J. and Costa, P. (1993) The management of tourism in cities of art. *Tourist Review*, 48 (2), 2–10.

Case 22

A SWOT analysis of tourism in Greece

Introduction

Greece is one of the world's oldest tourism destinations, yet it has a number of issues relating to the tourism sector. In this case we examine these issues in the form of a Strengths, Weaknesses, Opportunities and Threats analysis (SWOT). On completion of this case you will:

1 Be aware that the strengths of tourism in Greece include the heritage attractions and Greek hospitality.
2 Understand that Greek tourism suffers from a dominance of small businesses and a poorly organized public sector.
3 Recognize that tourism in Greece has a range of opportunities, including having staged the 2004 Olympic Games and quality products.
4 Be aware that the threats to Greek tourism stem from competition from other countries.
5 Understand the need for effective planning and management for a strategy for Greek tourism in the future.

Key issues

There are four key issues in this case:

1 Greece is one of the oldest tourism destinations, but suffers from a lack of organization and vision, making it less competitive than it could be.
2 Greece has the strengths of its heritage products and hospitality, and the opportunities provided by having staged the Olympic Games in 2004.
3 However, Greece also suffers from a poorly organized tourism sector and the lack of a strategic vision which leaves it vulnerable to future developments elsewhere.
4 Greece needs to develop an effective strategy for tourism.

Background

There is no doubt that Greece is one of the leading destinations in the world, and has a long pedigree in the tourism sector based upon its unique heritage, natural resources and unparalleled hospitality since ancient times. At the same time, however, the country is also suffering from a range of factors relating to tourism which may act to prevent the Greek tourism sector fulfilling its true potential and thus contributing more fully to national welfare. In particular these issues focus upon the country's lack of coordination, poor planning and thus an inability to deliver the type and quality of tourism products that will be demanded in the twenty-first century. This case study provides a SWOT analysis of tourism in Greece in order to demonstrate these issues.

Strengths

Greece can offer tourism resources that have few rivals elsewhere in the world, and a tradition of hospitality. In addition it has:

- a long involvement in tourism
- excellent heritage, natural and cultural products
- a flexible private sector able to design and deliver tourism products tailored to customers' needs, so achieving high levels of repeat business
- a high level of entrepreneurial involvement in tourism with strong labour loyalty and low labour turnover, partly due to the many family-run enterprises
- a broad tourism sector with the ability to support a wide range of tourism products and activities
- the strong local flavour of Greek hospitality and products.

Weaknesses

However, Greece does suffer from a number of weaknesses inherent in a traditional tourism sector with a long pedigree:

- Amateur tourism enterprises in terms of strategy, finance and marketing; in addition these enterprises are not re-investing in their businesses.
- Domination by small enterprises run by families with little formal training in tourism; this leads to poor levels of management and marketing in the creation and delivery of tourism products.
- Domination by foreign tour operators who pay low prices for products and services.
- Inconsistent and uncoordinated political intervention by government based upon emotional and subjective judgements.
- Lack of visibility in global distribution systems which leads to both over-dependence on tour operators to supply the Greek market, and also to an overall reduction in the arrivals of independent, higher-spending tourists.

- Infrastructure and tourism plant of poor quality, which fails to satisfy higher spending and emergent market sectors and therefore handicaps attempts to diversify markets.
- Lack of coordinated tourism planning.
- Inadequate levels of education/training in tourism.
- Poor levels of understanding of information technology.
- Seasonality of demand, particularly for coastal tourism.
- Substantial leakages in tourism earnings owing to the peripheral coastal areas and islands having to import many of the goods needed to supply tourists.
- Poor levels of quality assurance and regulation of the tourism sector.
- Lack of information and interpretation of the cultural product for the visitor.
- Inadequate research in the tourism sector.

Opportunities

Fortunately, it is possible to identify a range of real opportunities which could allow Greece to overcome these weaknesses:

- European Union support for tourism in Greece, particularly in terms of cultural products, environmental improvements, information technology and aid to small businesses. Infrastructure will also benefit from European assistance.
- Growth of demand for Greece combined with trends in demand that will support the country's cultural and environmental products.
- Emergence of a new breed of tourism enterprise utilizing contemporary management approaches, run by professionals and setting a benchmark for future operations. In part this has been caused by consolidation of companies in the domestic sector.
- New organizational focus on quality by agencies such as the Association of Greek Tourism Enterprises.
- Emergence of cooperation at regional and local levels to coordinate tourism.
- Increasing penetration of the use of the Internet and other information technology in the operation and marketing of tourism enterprises.
- Emergence of a new professional breed of human resources in the sector as a result of formal tourism education both in Greece and overseas, which will allow Greece to capitalize upon good practice in the tourism sector globally.

Threats

Yet Greece must be vigilant if it is to counter a range of threats to its tourism sector:

- Concentration of tourism initiatives into larger companies through globalization, which could marginalize smaller enterprises in the distribution channel.
- Environmental degradation of the Greek product, through poor environmental management, leading to reduced demand.
- Oversupply in the tourism sector is increasing, leading to price competition.
- Over-dependence upon traditional beach products.

- The Single European market opening up Greek enterprises to take-overs from larger European firms.
- Competition from low-priced exotic long-haul products in the inclusive tour market.
- Geographical proximity to regions where war and terrorism may impact upon demand, namely the Balkans and the Middle East. This led to massive expenditure on security for the 2004 Olympic Games, amounting to as much as 20 per cent of the total budget.

The way forward

Buhalis (1998) sums up the implications of these issues:

As a result, Greece fails to attract the desired *high quality, high expenditure* tourists as it is increasingly unable to satisfy their requirements. The deterioration of the tourism product and the image leads to a lower willingness-to-pay by consumers which consequently, leads to a further drop in quality, as the industry attempts to attract customers with lower prices.

Clearly the issues identified above demonstrate the need to closely link tourism products with demand, and in particular to safeguard the unique environmental and cultural assets which form the basis of the tourism sector in Greece. What is needed is a coordinated public/private sector strategy that addresses these problems and recognizes that the tourism marketplace is changing. This approach would allow the Greek tourism sector to take advantage of its unique environmental and cultural resources, as well as its unparalleled heritage.

Reflections on the case

Despite the fact that Greece is one of the world's oldest tourism destinations, it currently has a poorly organized tourism sector that lacks the strategic vision to capitalize upon its strengths. For Greece to be a competitive destination in the twenty-first century it will need to develop a strategic vision for tourism.

Discussion points/assignments

1 Discuss the impact of feature films such as *Troy* in drawing attention to the legacy of ancient Greece in art and literature, and raising the profile of cultural tourism to Greece.

2 Draw up a 'balance sheet' of the costs and benefits of the 2004 Olympics, not just to the economy of Greece but also to the people of Athens and the nation as a whole.

3 Indicate ways in which the tourism product of the Greek islands could become more self-sufficient and sustainable.

4 Since 2000 international tourism has slumped in Greece, despite the global publicity generated by the Olympic Games, and massive investment in transport infrastructure. Suggest possible reasons for this decline.

Acknowledgement

This case study is based upon the work of Dimitrios Buhalis. See Buhalis, D. (1998) *Tourism in Greece: Strategic Analysis and Challenges for the New Millennium*. Studies and Reports, Planning and Development Series Volume 18, International Centre for Research and Studies in Tourism, Aix en Provence.

Key source

Buhalis, D. (2000) Athens. *City Reports*, 4, 5–22.

Case 23

Tourism as an agent of economic restructuring in Eastern Europe

Introduction

In the former Communist countries of Eastern Europe tourism is central to the process of economic restructuring. This case study examines the issues surrounding the use of tourism as a development agent in the region. On completion of the case you will:

1 Understand the constraints on tourism development in the former Eastern bloc.
2 Be aware of the role of tourism in the general process of economic restructuring of the region.
3 Understand the role of tourism in the evolution of command economies to market economies.
4 Recognize that the administration of tourism in the region is changing from a centralized structure to public–private partnerships.
5 Understand the environmental issues associated with the region and their implications for tourism.

Key issues

There are five key issues in this case:

1 Tourism in the former Eastern bloc was transformed with the fall of the Berlin Wall in 1989; having been built on a socialist model in the years following the Second World War, this changed to a market economy during the 1990s.

2 The legacy of tourism in the former Eastern bloc has been problematic and there are a range of obstacles to its successful development.
3 Tourism is being used in the region to assist in economic restructuring particularly through privatization and the changing role of the former public sector tourism administrations.
4 There are severe environmental problems in the region, a legacy of socialist regimes, which have implications for the development of tourism.
5 Tourism experts have found that the economic restructuring approach is as much a political process as it is a developmental one.

Background

In the former Communist countries of Eastern Europe tourism is seen to be central to the process of economic restructuring as it cuts across a variety of economic sectors and is primarily comprised of small and medium-sized enterprises (SMEs). The transformation of economic, political and social frameworks in the region, allied to the curiosity factor and deregulation of international travel constraints, has actively encouraged tourist development. However, there are very real practical difficulties and issues surrounding the use of tourism as a medium of change since the political events of 1988/1989 moved the region towards a market economy. In particular there is a need to ensure that tourism developments are sustainable and do not threaten the already vulnerable environmental resources in the region. Also, there is the need to win hearts and minds in the host population by motivating enthusiastic entrepreneurs and explaining the relevance of 'Western' concepts of business management – the progress towards a market economy is as much a political process as an economic one. The incorporation of the region into the international tourism industry has not therefore been easy. For example, the European Commission has identified 25 key issues that the industry is faced with if tourism is to be successful in the region (Table 23.1).

We can examine the role of tourism as an agent of change under four key headings:

• economic restructuring
• tourism administration
• environmental concerns
• tourism infrastructure.

Economic restructuring

Communism as the political and economic model has had a profound effect on tourism in the region. Following the political events of the late 1980s, the former countries of Eastern Europe are moving from a centralized command economy to one based on private enterprise and the free market, and from a totalitarian,

Table 23.1 Development obstacles to tourism in Eastern Europe

- Insufficient buying power in domestic tourism markets
- Difficult political environment to operate in
- Lack of understanding of the nature of tourism
- Lack of economic incentives for tourism development
- Lack of a clearly defined tourism image
- Lack of funds for tourism promotion
- Lack of regional tourist boards
- Lack of local tourist boards
- Overcrowded honey-pots such as Prague
- Insufficient transport facilities
- Insufficient accommodation at some levels
- Unreliable catering standards
- Poor entertainment facilities
- Inadequate tourism services – such as information and interpretation
- Poor telecommunications
- Poor facilities for currency exchange
- Difficult border crossings and lack of good border facilitation
- A slow privatization process
- War, terrorism and organized crime in some parts of the region
- Lack of tourism product innovation
- Lack of tourism market research
- Insufficient knowledge of tourism marketing
- Insufficient sources of funds for local tourism investment

Source: Adapted from the European Commission, 1992

one-party system towards a pluralist democracy. In the case of countries such as Hungary, this transition is proceeding relatively smoothly. Elsewhere in the region, the change is more complex, particularly in those countries where the regimes had developed a highly centralized economy. For these countries, the economy is going through a series of stages:

1 **the 'hiatus' period**, which rejects the Communist past, while institutions and structures seriously debilitated by past misuse begin to recover
2 **the transition stage**, where tourism is seen as playing an important role in the process, and finally
3 **a market economy**.

Tourism contributes to this process in a variety of ways:

- privatization of state monopolies exposes organizations to competition and efficiency measures
- private sector entrepreneurs are encouraged as tourism is often used to demonstrate 'Western' business practice
- exposure to international tourism competition often demands the imposition of universally recognized standards – such as hotel classification.

Tourism administration

These economic and political changes have had a profound effect on tourism administration. In the past, the state tourist organizations, which were in effect tour operators and travel agencies operating at national, regional and local level, had a monopoly position. Many were set up on the lines of the Soviet Union's INTOURIST, and their inflexibility, standardization of approach and lack of competition meant that they were unable to respond to the demands of Western tourists. The old state agencies have now lost their monopolies and a range of new organizations is emerging, from the purely private, through cooperatives, to state-run concerns. Here, tourism is acting as a medium for a change of attitudes in the public sector, towards, for example, concepts such as marketing.

Environmental concerns

Economic problems in the region render governments less able to deal effectively with the environmental problems and degradation that is the legacy of Communist rule. However, unless these problems are tackled the growth of tourism experienced in the 1990s will not be sustained. A particular concern is the lack of understanding of these issues by those involved in tourism:

- For example, hunting is still common in some countries, yet this is a practice which demands sensitive handling – some tourists will be attracted by the activity, whilst others will be deterred.
- Also, in countries dominated by almost fifty years of centralization, the idea of 'bottom-up' planning and the involvement of host communities in decision taking still requires some adjustment of attitudes.
- Encouragement of SMEs may also be problematic, as this is not a sector that traditionally has the will, the expertise, or the resources to respond to environmental initiatives.

Already tourist sites are suffering. In Hungary, for example, there are high levels of pollution in many leading tourist centres; the historic buildings in Budapest are eroding; and Lake Balaton is heavily polluted. Clearly tourism must act as an agent of change in terms of both environmental attitudes and the demonstration of good environmental practice.

Tourism infrastructure and facilities

The low and variable quality of visitor attractions, facilities and service standards in the past have created a poor image of tourism. Training of tourism staff is under way to adapt the workforce to new approaches and the priorities of customer service. Initiatives to upgrade the industry include assistance with catering, computerization and ticketing, through to the redevelopment of transport systems.

Transport systems are struggling to cope with a market orientation as public subsidies are removed and investment fails to keep pace with increased tourism numbers. The ability of international carriers in the region to compete with the rest of the world is also in question, particularly as the region is experiencing increased demand from the West and Vienna emerges as the regional hub.

Accommodation is in short supply in some categories. In the budget category of accommodation, the emergent class of entrepreneurs now acts as providers, but in the four- and five-star categories there is a need for partnerships with international companies. Joint ventures are a useful way to stimulate the accommodation industry, not only by exposing the region to international good practice but also by putting into place the quality mechanisms needed (and expected by Western tourists) and to act as a catalyst for other businesses to adopt these practices in a competitive market environment. However, over-reliance on foreign investment and joint ventures may lead to reduced economic benefits for the host country. Elsewhere in the accommodation sector state-run hotel chains have been sold, franchise agreements and management contracts are operating and loan agreements are making capital available in the sector.

Reflections on the case

This case has shown how tourism can be used as an agent of restructuring in the former Eastern bloc. Tourism is a useful medium of development because it is dominantly made up of small enterprises and can quickly transform a region's command economy into a market-based one. Nonetheless there are many obstacles to the successful implementation of this strategy, not the least being that the process is as much political as economic.

Discussion points/assignments

1 Draw up a chart comparing the characteristics of tourism under the command economies of the pre-1990 Communist regimes of Eastern Europe with those that have developed under a free market economy.

2 Discuss the extent to which poor service standards are continuing to hold back the development of inbound tourism in the countries of Eastern Europe and the former Soviet Union.

3 Describe the impact of pollution on the architectural and natural heritage of a number of East European countries. Why is pollution such a pervasive problem in Eastern Europe, and what measures should be undertaken by the public and private sectors to control pollution?

4 Prepare a detailed itinerary for a group of students interested in the art, architecture and music of the Czech Republic, Slovakia, Hungary, Poland and Lithuania. Describe the cultural attractions of the historic towns and cities that would be visited on the tour, and also include some of the relics of the recent Communist past.

Key sources

Hall, D. (1991) *Tourism and Economic Development in Eastern Europe and the Soviet Union*. Belhaven, London.

Williams, A. M. and Shaw, G. J. (1991) *Tourism and Economic Development: Western European Experiences*. Belhaven, London.

3.2
The Middle East and Africa

Case 24
Tourism issues in Yemen

Introduction

Yemen is one of the world's poorest countries and has a complex history. This case examines the issues surrounding the development of tourism in Yemen. On completion of this case you will:

1 Understand Yemen's historical and social background.
2 Recognize that Yemen was a divided country until recently, and that this is reflected in its tourism development with security concerns as a major issue.
3 Be aware of Yemen's tourism resources and facilities.
4 Appreciate the constraints on tourism development posed by the country's cultural and religious traditions.
5 Recognize that Yemen is a country in the early stages of the tourist area life cycle, and that planning and management are needed to sustain its archaeological resources.

Key issues

There are five key issues in this case:

1 Yemen is a country in the early stages of the tourist area life cycle.
2 Yemen has significant archaeological attractions, as well as cultural resources that attract the more adventurous visitor.
3 As one of the poorer countries in the world, Yemen needs the economic benefits of tourism, but there are significant social and cultural constraints on tourism development.
4 Yemen's political background and incidents of attacks on tourists mean that safety and security issues act as a further constraint on its tourism development.
5 Yemen must plan for the sustainable management of its major tourist attractions – particularly the unique archaeological resources.

Background

Yemen occupies the south-west of the Arabian Peninsula with a coastline along the Red Sea and the Gulf of Aden. High mountains offer a cooler climate and provide the country with a more abundant water supply than the rest of Arabia. In ancient times this supported the Sabaean (Sheba) civilization which grew rich on the trade in frankincense and myrrh. However, Yemen nowadays is classified by the UN as one of the world's poorest countries. It is an example of a complex tribal society that is slowly opening up to Western investment and tourism. In this respect the kidnappings and deaths of tourists in the late 1990s and the association of Yemen with terrorism were a major setback for the fledgling tourism industry. The fascination of the country for Westerners is that it still retains the lifestyles of bygone centuries and a feeling of isolation from the rest of the world.

The situation for tourism development is complicated by the fact that until 1990 there were two Yemens reflecting wider Cold War divisions, and we can identify two distinct approaches to tourism development as a result:

- The **People's Republic of South Yemen** came into being when the British protectorate based in Aden ended in 1967. South Yemen was a hard-line Marxist–Leninist regime supported by the Soviet Union, whereas
- The **Yemen Arab Republic** based in Sana'a in the north remained a deeply traditional and strongly Islamic tribal country after centuries of despotic rule.

Unification as the **Republic of Yemen** with a population approaching 12 million failed to reconcile two very different political and economic systems, resulting in civil war in 1994. It was not until the return to a more stable political situation that tourism could be seriously considered.

Tourism is in the very early stages of development in Yemen – a good example of the involvement stage of the tourist area life cycle. Although a small amount of business travel took place during the colonial era in Aden, due to its role as a staging point on the British P&O shipping route to India, organized international tourism did not begin until the 1970s. Two international hotels were built in the 1980s; yet even at the beginning of the twenty-first century volumes of tourism remain small, fluctuating considerably according to the levels of security in tribal areas – where the writ of the central government does not always run – and the political situation in Sana'a and Aden.

Tourism demand

The majority of visitors either arrive in organized groups to see the antiquities and the lifestyle of the Yemeni people, or are on oil-related business trips. Before the widely publicized kidnappings in 1998 (resulting in the deaths of four tourists in a shoot-out between government troops and the hostage-takers), Yemen received around 60 000 international visitors a year with a spend of US$39 million. Since then the situation has scarcely improved, following the suicide bombing of an American warship in Aden harbour and the heightened tensions post-9/11, when Yemen was suspected of harbouring Al-Quaeda terrorists.

The gateways are the international airports at Sana'a and Aden. Leisure tourism to Yemen has the following characteristics:

- The focus is on north Yemen, based on Sana'a where touring circuits for the antiquities/heritage sites have been developed.
- Visitors stay on average 4 or 5 days.
- West Europeans dominate the market.
- Most visits are by organized groups, often with a military escort for security reasons.
- Demand is highly seasonal, concentrated in the cooler months of December to March.

Domestic tourism is important, contributing between one-half and two-thirds of bednights in Yemen. Apart from visits to friends and relatives it includes adventure excursions to the desert. Here there is a contrast with international tourism as domestic trips are less seasonal and tend to focus on the south of the country.

Tourism supply

Tourism resources

These are based on the culture and lifestyle of the people, and the unique architectural heritage. Apart from cultural tours and trekking, Yemen offers the potential for snorkelling and scuba diving off the Red Sea coast and also ecotourism on the remote outlying island of Socotra in the Indian Ocean. However, cultural attitudes mean that beach tourism is not really an option, in contrast to the situation in Dubai.

The traditional culture and lifestyle is all-pervasive, as shown by the *souks* of Sana'a which sell all manner of merchandise, including *qat* – a narcotic widely used in Yemen – and the highly decorated daggers worn by Yemeni tribesmen. Yet it is strangely difficult for the international visitor to access. In contrast, the architecture is accessible and is of international significance – for example, the central area of the capital, Old Sana'a, which is a World Heritage Site. The impressive tower houses made of mud-brick, featuring stained glass windows and alabaster decorations, give many of the towns and villages a medieval atmosphere. That so much remains from previous centuries is due to Yemen's poverty, in contrast to the situation in the Gulf states where the traditional architecture has been swept away as a result of the oil boom. However, lack of funding also means that many buildings are in a poor state of repair and some are being lost, while the illicit trade in artefacts from archaeological sites further endangers the country's heritage.

The archaeological resources are found mainly to the north-east of Sana'a, at Marib – site of a spectacular irrigation dam built by the ancient Sabaeans – and at Baraqish. Although there are many ground handlers in Yemen designing tourist circuits, two companies dominate the market. The circuits are mainly in north Yemen, in the triangle between Sana'a, Hudaydah and Ta'izz, although unification has allowed tour operators to include the Hadramaut Valley in the south-east, focusing on Shibam – another World Heritage Site. However, the infrastructure to support tours is primitive, the roads are dusty and in poor repair, and this has led the tour operators to invest in hotels and other facilities en-route.

Organization of tourism

Overall, the Ministry of Tourism coordinates tourism, with the General Tourist Authority (GTA) as the implementing agency. These public bodies are assisted by:

- the Higher Tourism Council with an oversight of strategy and policy
- the Yemen Tourism Promotion Board.

Tourism priorities for Yemen are as follows:

- developing sustainable tourism for the benefit of the community
- enhancing and preserving Yemen's cultural, historic and natural assets
- promoting the unified Yemen internationally
- facilitating tourism and removing constraints
- assisting in the construction and upgrading of the accommodation sector
- improving the level and output of tourism training.

In addition to these priorities, there is a need to address the regional imbalance between the former North Yemen – which receives the bulk of international tourism – and the former South Yemen. In part international assistance will achieve these aims through two master plans carried out since unification. However, tourists' fears regarding their safety and security may render these plans meaningless.

Accommodation

In the past, the state has intervened in the accommodation sector; in the former South Yemen the government owned and operated hotels, whereas in North Yemen government incentives were provided. A number of projects demonstrated how historic buildings could be converted and managed as hotels. Since unification, the government has leased its own hotels to the private sector. This means that the accommodation sector remains dominated by locally owned small hotels and *funduks* (traditional-style inns, often with outdoor sleeping quarters for the very hot summers) at the lower end of the market. This situation is slowly being addressed as a number of international chains – namely Movenpick, Sheraton and Taj – have shown interest in the hotel sector. At the beginning of the twenty-first century there were around 12 000 bedspaces in Yemen.

Reflections on the case

Yemen is a complex country. In one of the world's poorest countries tourism has the potential to make a significant contribution to the national economy and improve the quality of life for the average Yemeni. Yet the development of tourism in Yemen is far from straightforward, as there are issues of religion and culture, as well as security concerns stemming from the uncertain political situation. In addition, Yemen's unique archaeological resources are in danger of being lost unless effective planning and management is put into place.

Discussion points/assignments

1 Investigate why Western-style beach tourism is not really an option for development in Yemen and most of the Middle East region, whereas it has been successfully developed in Dubai.
2 Give possible reasons why Western visitors find it difficult to access the lifestyle and culture of the Yemeni people.
3 Explain why it is so important to protect the architectural heritage of Yemen, and the difficulties facing those responsible for carrying out conservation measures.
4 Describe the challenges desert travellers face from the climate and terrain, and the type of equipment needed for trekking and other types of adventure tourism in Yemen.

Key sources

Burns, P. and Cooper, C. (1997) Yemen. *Tourism Management*, 18 (8), 555–563.
Kia, B. and Williams, V. C. (1989) Saving Sana'a. *Geographical Magazine*, 61 (5), 32–36.
Kopp, H. (1989) Tourism and recreation in Northern Yemen. *Tourism Recreation Research*, 14 (2), 11–15.
Thomas, K. (2002) High hopes: conservation in Yemen. *Geographical*, 74 (8), 30–35.

Website
www.yementourism.com

Case 25

Managing Nile cruise tourism

Introduction

The Nile is the world's longest river, and Nile cruises are one of Egypt's best-known tourism products. This case outlines the Nile cruise product and identifies some of the issues surrounding Nile cruises. On completion of the case you will:

1 Understand the history and development of Nile cruises.
2 Recognize the characteristics of the Nile cruise.
3 Be aware of some of the problems surrounding the organization of the Nile cruise sector.
4 Recognize that Nile cruises are dependent on the overall health of the tourism sector and the political situation in Egypt and the Middle East generally.

Key issues

There are four key issues in this case:

1 Nile cruises are an easily recognized tourism product, based on the resource of this famous river, and allowing visitors to access a variety of ancient Egyptian sites from the comfort of a 'floating hotel'.
2 Nile cruises have a number of distinctive characteristics that make their management and organization difficult.
3 The Nile cruise industry faces a number of challenges, not the least of which are the overcrowding and chaotic organization at the landing sites.
4 The Nile cruise industry faces a number of challenges in the future including safety/security issues and problems relating to water levels and pollution in the Nile.

The Nile

The Nile is the world's longest river at 6700 kilometres, and Nile cruises are probably Egypt's best-known tourism product. A cruise is a romantic way of seeing many of Egypt's best-known 'antiquities' – the sites of its ancient civilizations – which include the temples at Luxor and Karnak, the Colossi of Memnon, Tutankhamun's Tomb and the Valley of the Kings. Cruising has the advantage of providing an accommodation base in a floating hotel, avoiding the often arduous journeys by road or rail otherwise involved in sightseeing.

The Nile is synonymous with Egypt and for thousands of years it has been a vital resource and the transport lifeline between the north and south of the country. Until recently, the river used to flood extensive areas regularly between July and October, following the rains at the source of the Blue Nile in the highlands of Ethiopia. These floods renewed the fertility of the soil by depositing a layer of silt on the fields. With the construction of the Aswan High Dam in 1971, a gain of 20 per cent in the area of cultivatable land and a boost to power supplies has been offset by ecological changes and a reduction in water levels, which has impeded cruise operations. When Thomas Cook inaugurated steamship services on the Nile in 1869, thus opening up Egypt to modern tourism, the river was navigable upstream to Aswan throughout the year. Since the early 1990s, cruises no longer operate on the lower Nile between Cairo and Luxor, as silt has built up in the river, aggravating the problem of low water levels during the winter months.

The development of Nile cruises

Since the days of Thomas Cook, tourism on the Nile has grown steadily. Initially, small groups of independent, adventurous tourists were attracted, and the Agatha Christie novel *Death on the Nile* exemplified the upper class, predominantly British, image of Nile cruising before the Second World War. More recently, larger groups on inclusive tours, drawn from a wider range of countries and socio-economic groups have become the norm. Many Nile cruisers are young couples in their twenties, although the over-fifty age group is also well represented. All-inclusive packages are now common, bringing the price of a Nile cruise within reach of budget travellers. The international hotel chains have entered the cruise market; Hilton, for example, began operating five-star cruise vessels in 1988, while Sheraton and Marriott soon followed. The number of vessels grew considerably during the early 1990s from a total of 55 in 1990 to over 200 by 1995. This probably represents the Nile cruise industry at its peak (see Table 25.1). Since then, terrorism by Muslim fundamentalists has drastically reduced both the numbers of visitors to Egypt and the number of cruise operators.

Table 25.1 clearly shows that on average the higher quality 'floating hotels' are much larger than the two-star vessels, with three times as many cabins. The majority of cabins have two berths, indicating the importance of the 'couples' market. Most of the vessels have air conditioning and water purification systems. On-board

Table 25.1 Floating hotels on the Nile, 1995

Rating	Units	Cabins	Beds
5 star	82	5186	10312
4 star	40	1831	3642
3 star	20	607	1209
2 star	13	249	488
Under classification	51	2859	5267
Total	206	10732	20918

facilities for those in the higher price range include a sundeck with bar, games area and small swimming pool, entertainment lounge, restaurant and boutiques.

Characteristics of Nile cruises

- Nile cruises are a unique product, using shallow-draft four-deck vessels. Most are of a standardized 'shoebox' design, but some have been modelled on the paddle steamers used in Cook's time. The emphasis is on comfort and sightseeing rather than speed. The newest vessels can cruise at 16 km/h upstream against the Nile current, and 22 km/h downstream.
- The major cruising stretch of the Nile is between the Valley of the Kings (the site of ancient Thebes), Luxor and Karnak in the north, and Aswan to the south. En-route, passengers visit the temples at Edfu before arriving at Aswan to see the 3 kilometre long High Dam and the Temple of Philae.
- To the south of Aswan, another cruising area has been opened up as a result of the High Dam, which created the 500 kilometre long Lake Nasser. Known locally as the 'Nubian Sea', the attractions of this vast artificial lake are less well known, with the exception of the temples of Abu Simbel, which were rescued from inundation by UNESCO.
- Most cruises have a duration of between 3 and 11 nights. In the shorter version clients cruise from Luxor to Aswan in one direction only, with domestic flights based on Cairo forming the other 'legs' of the trip. Longer cruises allow more quality time for sightseeing with short excursions on both banks of the Nile. Sometimes, tour operators offer 'cruise and stay' arrangements with one or more nights in a hotel at Luxor and/or Aswan, adding an extra dimension to the holiday.
- The high season for cruising is from October to April when the climate is ideal for sightseeing. The vessels also operate in the summer low season, when the heat can be extreme, at considerably reduced prices.
- Crews tend to be recruited locally, with the length of training varying from a few weeks to a few months according to the job description.
- Ground-handling of cruise passengers at the sites tends to be organized by Egyptian travel agencies who provide transport and guides for the visiting groups, often under contract to the larger inbound tour operators.

- The base for the Nile cruise industry is at Luxor, which has a long history as an international tourist centre. It was made world famous by Howard Carter's discovery of the tomb and treasures of the boy-pharaoh Tutankhamun in 1922. Until recently Luxor was difficult to reach except by boat. The construction of a new road to the Valley of the Kings in 1995, followed by a bridge linking Luxor to the west bank of the Nile two years later has improved access considerably. The floating hotels moored on the east bank complement other accommodation in and around Luxor.

The problems affecting tourism

- **Overcrowding** The Nile cruise industry is poorly organized and visits to the sites when a vessel has berthed can be chaotic, with guides, taxi drivers and traders vying for the attentions of tourists. At Luxor, for example, most guided tours are arranged to meet tour buses and the arrival of cruise ships at certain times of the day, resulting in considerable congestion as visitors and vehicles converge. There is a case for phased visits and good visitor management as this focusing of visitor pressure is threatening the integrity of the sites. Some idea of the pressures can be gauged from the average daily numbers of visitors at the key sites in December, shown in Table 25.2.
- **Terrorism** The Egyptian government has stepped up security in the Luxor area, since the terrorist attacks in November 1997 at the Temple of Hatshepset received wide international publicity. This led to a severe downturn in the number of visitors, particularly from European countries, with hotel occupancy rates in Luxor falling to 25 per cent during most of 1998. In response, the Egyptian government has launched an initiative to encourage Egyptians to visit the antiquities in greater numbers, but the success of this campaign adds to congestion at the sites.
- **Port facilities** The main overnight berthing points for cruise vessels are Luxor, Esna, Kom Ombo and Aswan, where docks and other facilities are of a poor standard. Travel agents and cruise operators are developing their own quays in the absence of official provision. For example, at any one time there can be between 30 to 80 vessels moored at the dock on the east bank at Luxor, with as many as

Table 25.2 Average daily numbers of visitors at the key sites in the Nile Valley in December

Site	Average daily number of visitors
Valley of the Kings	9297
Karnak Temple	2647
Luxor Temple	2426
Deir El Bahri	1074
Tomb of Tutankhamun	848
Valley of the Queens	743

Source: Supreme Council of Antiquities, Luxor

seven moored side by side. This means that passengers have to cross from vessel to vessel to reach the shore, at some risk and inconvenience to themselves.

- **Pollution** The vessels are mainly diesel powered, causing pollution of the Nile and corrosive fumes at the sites.
- **Low water levels** Low water levels in the Nile can disrupt cruise schedules at certain times of the year. This is nowadays due to controls by the authorities on the amount of water leaving Lake Nasser through the Aswan High Dam. A more insidious problem is the run-off of the fertilizers that farmers are forced to use, now that the annual cycle of Nile floods has been disrupted. This encourages the growth of algae and weeds that not only upsets the ecological balance of the river, but causes damage to the propellers of the vessels.

Reflections on the case

This case has shown that Nile cruises have a long pedigree and are a significant part of the Egyptian tourism sector. As such they are viewed as a romantic way to view the Nile and the antiquities of the region. However, the Nile cruise industry suffers from poor organization, particularly at the landing points and this detracts from the tourism experience. In addition the cruise sector is vulnerable to changes related to water levels and pollution in the Nile, as well as security issues in Egypt and the Middle East region as a whole.

Discussion points/assignments

1 Investigate the impact of the 1997 terrorist attack at Luxor on Egypt's tourism industry. How effective were the measures undertaken by the authorities to restore confidence among foreign visitors after the crisis?

2 Account for the deficiencies in organization and traffic management at the Nile landing sites. Suggest practical ways in which the situation could be improved for the benefit of cruise passengers, and for the people who depend on cruise tourism for a livelihood.

3 Describe a number of world-class heritage attractions that can be visited by cruise tourists on the Upper Nile, and explain why the civilization of ancient Egypt continues to fascinate people worldwide.

4 Nile cruises since the late 1990s have faced a fall in demand, in contrast to the market for sea/ocean cruises which has shown considerable growth. Explain to the rest of your class how you would go about creating more awareness of the Nile cruise product to the 35–54 age group.

Key sources

Fawzy, A. (2001) The potential for corporate meetings on Nile cruises. *Hospitality Review*, 3 (3), 52–55.

Pakkala, L. J. (1990) Egyptian tourism: cruising for growth. *The Cornell Hotel and Restaurant Association Quarterly*, 31 (2), 56–59.

Rivers, J. (1998) Thebes (Luxor, Egypt) traffic and visitor flow management in the West Bank of the Necropolis, in M. Shackley (2000) *Visitor Management: Case Studies from World Heritage Sites*. Elsevier Butterworth-Heinemann, pp. 161–181.

Website

http://www.idsc.gov.eg

Case 26

CAMPFIRE: local community involvement in safari tourism

Introduction

This case study introduces an innovative tourism programme that involves the management of wildlife by local communities in Africa so that they can benefit directly from tourism. On completion of this case you will:

1 Be aware of some of the wildlife management issues in Africa.
2 Understand the principles of the management of wildlife by local communities under the CAMPFIRE programme.
3 Be aware that the key elements of the programme involve hunting and safari tourism.
4 Understand that there is opposition to the programme from those that oppose hunting.
5 Recognize that the CAMPFIRE project is a good example of community-based tourism.

Key issues

There are five key issues in this case:

1 Tourism in Africa faces a number of challenges, two of which are the imperative for sustainable wildlife management and the need to deliver the benefits of tourism to the local community.

2 **The CAMPFIRE programme is focused upon hunting and safari tourism.**
3 **The CAMPFIRE programme is a partnership between local authorities, African communities and the tourism sector to allow local people to manage game reserves and thus benefit from the exploitation of wildlife by tourists.**
4 **There is opposition to the CAMPFIRE programme from those who oppose hunting in the West.**
5 **The CAMPFIRE programme is a classic example of successful community-based tourism.**

CAMPFIRE

CAMPFIRE (Communal Areas Management Programme for Indigenous Resources) was founded in the 1980s in Zimbabwe and has since spread to other countries in Southern Africa. It involves the management of wildlife resources by local African communities to earn money from tourism. Wildlife conservation is no longer an end in itself – it must be seen to pay its way.

The rural areas of Zimbabwe, as elsewhere in Africa, are experiencing the following problems:

- a demographic crisis, with the population in some areas doubling every 20 years
- a fall in real incomes
- a decline in investment
- climatic change, with droughts becoming more frequent – this particularly hits subsistence farmers who make up more than 80 per cent of the population.

At the same time wildlife habitats are dwindling. This causes:

- environmental degradation in the existing game reserves through overgrazing
- damage to African farms outside the reserves; for example, by elephants trampling crops, or predators killing livestock.

Traditionally, wildlife in Zimbabwe had been utilized by the African tribes as a community resource controlled by the chief and his council. Under British colonial rule, wildlife in what was then Rhodesia was declared the property of the state and hunting was reserved for the white settlers, who were also granted the best agricultural lands. The marginal areas were allocated to the tribal groups as 'Communal Lands'. The designation of the Hwange and Gonorezhou National Parks in the 1950s and 1960s involved the eviction of thousands of villagers of the Shangaan tribe from their lands without compensation. When the coming to power of the ZANU government in 1980 brought no improvement to their situation, the Shangaan reacted with a poaching campaign directed against the national park system. The government responded by transferring ownership of wildlife from the state to the local community. The CAMPFIRE programme is a partnership between the district councils – representing the local communities – and the private sector in tourism.

Although a few CAMPFIRE communities are involved with white-water rafting companies operating on the Zambezi, and in managing luxury camps for eco-tourists, the bulk of their income is from hunting safaris, in the following ways:

- Safari companies pay rent for the use of communal lands, and employ local people as trackers, for example.
- Hunters pay hunting and trophy fees, amounting to approximately $10 000 for a mature elephant, the most sought-after game. While the hunter retains the trophies, the meat is shared out amongst the villagers, whose everyday diet lacks protein.

The district council decides on an annual quota of animals to be killed, with the advice of the World Wide Fund for Nature as to sustainability. The revenue is distributed to the local villages, each of which has a CAMPFIRE committee that decides how the money should be spent.

From an African viewpoint CAMPFIRE is justified for the following reasons:

- It encourages high income, low volume tourism. Although fees are high there is no shortage of wealthy clients. Hunting tourism has arguably less environmental impact than the type of wildlife tourism practised in Kenya, for example, which involves fleets of Land Rovers carrying tourists on photo-safaris, and it also brings in much more foreign exchange per capita.
- Big game hunting is beneficial for the conservation of wildlife, as numbers are kept within the ecological capacity of the area by selective culling. Elephant numbers have actually increased in CAMPFIRE managed areas, as poachers can no longer count on tacit support from the local community.
- Hides and ivory are valuable wildlife resources in marginal areas where little else can be produced. The lifting of the 1989 ban on the export of ivory by CITES (the UN Convention on International Trade in Endangered Species) would earn Zimbabwe as much as $50 million a year in revenue from countries like Japan. This ivory would be from legally culled elephants.
- Hunting benefits the local community, bringing in revenue for much-needed schools, clinics and infrastructure. It encourages enterprise and involvement by local people. The revenue from sport hunting is four times more profitable per hectare than raising cattle on the same land. Not surprisingly, one-third of all land in Zimbabwe is now given over to wildlife conservation, including privately owned game reserves and game ranches, as well as the state-controlled national parks.

Opposition to the CAMPFIRE programme in Southern Africa has come mainly from environmentalists in the USA. The powerful animal rights lobby – the Humane Society – opposes hunting in principle. The future of this type of tourism hangs in the balance because the CAMPFIRE project is funded as part of the package of foreign aid that has to be approved each year by the US Congress. Big game hunting is also seen by many in Africa and elsewhere as a form of 'neo-colonialism'. The continuing success of CAMPFIRE in Zimbabwe itself is problematic in view of the deteriorating economic and political situation in the early years of the twenty-first century.

Reflections on the case

This case has demonstrated a successful example of community-based tourism. The CAMPFIRE programme succeeds in the twin aims of delivering tourism benefits to indigenous communities whilst at the same time contributing to the sustainable management of Africa's wildlife resources. CAMPFIRE has shown that local communities can become more self-reliant on this basis. Whilst it is criticized by those who oppose recreational hunting, there is no doubt that the African tourism sector needs more of these types of initiative.

Discussion points/assignments

1 Discuss whether the Western world is justified in imposing its own value systems regarding wildlife conservation on African communities.
2 Debate the ethics of hunting and safari tourism in Southern Africa from the viewpoints of the various stakeholders involved. These might include representatives of African rural communities, NGOs (non-governmental organizations) working in the region, tour organizers, the pro-animal welfare lobbyists, and the tourists themselves.
3 Design publicity material for distribution at 'grass roots' level that would convince African villagers of the case for regarding wildlife as an asset to be conserved, rather than as a liability.
4 Explain why, despite initiatives such as CAMPFIRE, the future of wildlife in Southern Africa remains under threat.
5 Investigate the methods of transport and the types of accommodation used by tourists visiting the game reserves of Southern Africa, and suggest ways in which the safari experience could be made more sustainable.

Key sources

Dieke, P. (2000) *The Political Economy of Tourism Development in Africa*. Cognizant, New York.
Gamble, W. P. (1989) *Tourism and Development in Africa*. John Murray, London.

Websites

http://www.panda.org/about_wwf/what_we_do/policy/indigenous_people/on_the_ground/zimbabwe.cfm
http://www.unsystem.org/ngls/documents/publications.en/voices.africa/number6/vfa6.08.htm
http://wildnetafrica.co.za/bushcraft/articles/document_campfire.html
http://www.worldbank.org/wbi/sourcebook/sbxc05.htm

3.3
Asia and the Pacific

Case 27

Adventure tourism in Nepal

Introduction

Nepal offers an attractive environment for Western tourists seeking wilderness adventure, and has built upon its legendary mountain climbing legacy. This case analyses the organization and impacts of adventure tourism in Nepal. On completion of this case you will:

1 Appreciate the tourism resources of Nepal and their use as a basis for adventure tourism.
2 Understand the organization and management of trekking in Nepal.
3 Be aware of the economic benefits of adventure tourism in Nepal.
4 Recognize the significant impacts of tourism upon the Nepalese environment and communities.
5 Be aware of strategies to manage the impacts of adventure tourism in Nepal.

Key issues

There are four key issues in this case:

1 Nepal offers an ideal resource base for adventure tourism products such as mountain climbing, trekking, mountain biking and river running.
2 Trekking is a major industry in Nepal and along with other adventure tourism products contributes to the Nepalese economy.
3 However, adventure tourism across Nepal has brought with it significant negative impacts to both the environment and the host community.
4 There have been a number of initiatives to alleviate these impacts including the Annapurna Conservation Area project.

Adventure tourism in Nepal

The Hindu kingdom of Nepal is sandwiched between India and Chinese-occupied Tibet. It forms part of the central Himalayas and boasts the majority of the world's highest summits, over 8000 metres. Nepal offers an attractive environment for Western tourists seeking wilderness adventure. In fact, surprisingly little of this mountainous but quite densely populated country is uninhabited wilderness in the North American sense. Adventure tourism includes the following related activities:

- **Mountain climbing** The expedition to climb Annapurna was the first group of Western visitors allowed into Nepal. It was followed three years later by Hillary and Tenzing's successful ascent of Mount Everest in 1953, which attracted world-wide attention. Climbing the Himalayas is exceptionally hazardous, because of the extreme weather conditions and the lack of oxygen at high altitudes; even the base of a mountain like Annapurna is at a higher level than any summit in the Alps. In view of these conditions, most expeditions have been organized on a lavish scale, involving teams of climbers, sophisticated equipment and a small army of Sherpa guides and porters to provide logistical support. While some climbers are adopting the minimalist approach, pioneered by Reinhold Messner, who proved it was possible to climb peaks at over 8000 metres without the use of supplementary oxygen, others rely on an infrastructure of ropes and ladders put in place by the experts. Some peaks are so popular in fact that they need to be 'booked' years in advance, and are increasingly the focus of publicity stunts. Moreover the accumulated waste left by successive expeditions – particularly on Everest – continues to be an environmental disgrace, necessitating a major clean-up operation.
- **River running** Nepal's fast-flowing rivers, including the Trisuli, Sun Kosi and Karnali, offer ideal conditions for white-water rafting and kayaking, particularly the first two, which are more accessible from Kathmandu (see Figure 27.1).
- **Mountain biking** Like river running, this is often combined with trekking by younger Western tourists, and takes place at relatively low altitudes.
- **Trekking** which provides the main focus of this case study.

Introduction

Trekking is the most popular tourist activity in the Himalayan zone of Nepal. During the late 1990s trekkers accounted for over a quarter of all visitors. Trekking originally developed as a separate activity from climbing in the 1960s, and the treks were based on the approach routes used by the Everest and Annapurna expeditions. Trekking is a way of visiting locations 'off the beaten track', but differs from hiking in a number of ways. Trekkers usually walk in organized groups escorted by a *sirdar* (guide), with a back-up team of cooks and porters who carry food supplies and equipment between the stopping places on the route. Although itineraries can be tailor-made to meet the requirements of small groups of clients, most treks differ little in organization from other types of inclusive tour. Western-based tour operators carry out the marketing, bring together the clients in their country of origin and arrange for the trekking permits, which for independent travellers involves

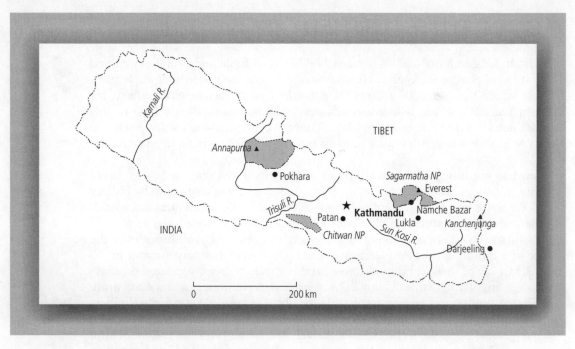

Figure 27.1 Map of Nepal

a time-consuming hassle with Nepalese bureaucracy. Like other tour operators, they may opt for consolidation if there is not enough demand for a particular trek. Some tourism experts allege that trekking is not a truly sustainable type of tourism, and as we shall see, there is some evidence to support this view.

The organization of trekking

Nepal offers a great variety of trekking opportunities, including some of the world's most spectacular scenery, the different ethnic groups who have modified this landscape over the centuries, and a wide selection of routes and types of trek to suit most clients:

• The longer treks, such as the Annapurna Circuit, take up to three weeks and involve tackling steep gradients at altitudes ranging from 1000 to over 5000 metres above sea level. These require a high standard of fitness, and *hypoxia* (altitude sickness) is a risk at the higher levels even for experienced hikers and climbers.
• On the other hand, short treks lasting three days or so are available at lower altitudes on less rugged terrain.

The trails – based on established trading routes – are well maintained and trekkers are rarely far from a village. Moreover, large numbers of lodges providing overnight accommodation, and *tea houses* offering basic catering facilities, have sprung up along most routes to meet their needs.

However, trekking in Nepal shows a high degree of seasonality. Climatic conditions largely dictate that the majority of treks take place between October and December (before snow blocks the high mountain passes) and from March to May, prior to the monsoon rains.

Although new areas are being opened up to meet the demand, the north-west of Nepal is too remote and is the region most affected by the activities of Maoist insurgents. Trekking therefore shows a high degree of concentration in particular areas of central and eastern Nepal, including:

- The Annapurna region west of Pokhara, with its well-developed infrastructure of trails and lodges, is the most popular with trekkers and tour operators. It includes among its attractions the Kali Gandaki Valley, reputed to be the world's deepest gorge, and the Annapurna Sanctuary wildlife reserve. The region is particularly rich in plant and animal species, including more than 100 species of orchid and the endangered snow leopard.
- The Everest route, from Lukha to the base camp at the foot of Mount Everest, is more demanding for trekkers than the Annapurna circuit and acclimatization to high altitudes is even more essential. It includes the Khumba region with its Sherpa villages, the famous Thyangboche monastery, and the Khumbu glacier that marks the approach to the world's highest mountain. Most of the region has been designated as the Sagarmatha National Park.

The impacts of trekking

Economic impacts

Trekking is estimated to provide about 24 000 full-time jobs and another 20 000 on a part-time basis. In the Annapurna region, 60 per cent of the population rely on tourism for a livelihood. Here the Thakali ethnic group has been particularly successful in taking advantage of the trekking boom, since they run most of the lodges on the Annapurna Circuit. Nevertheless the local economy is too poorly developed to supply most of the goods and services needed by Western tourists, so these have to be imported, often from India. As a result, only an estimated 20 cents out of the 3 dollars spent daily by the average trekker actually contributes to the local village economies, while for Nepal as a whole almost 60 per cent of tourism revenue flows out of the country as import leakages. Nevertheless, in the Khumba region, one of the least fertile and highest areas of Nepal, the Sherpa lifestyle has changed within a generation, from subsistence pastoralism based on the yak to a cash economy. With a long tradition as traders over the high mountain passes into Tibet, the Sherpas are very much in demand as guides and porters for at least part of the year. Others work in tea houses, shops selling local handicrafts and tourist lodges. Income from tourism, allied to Sir Edmund Hillary's fundraising from international donors, has provided schools and basic infrastructure. These impacts are most apparent in Namche Bazar, once a small hamlet and now an important tourist centre, where almost every other building is a hotel or curio shop.

On the other hand, Tourism Concern has highlighted the fact that some tour operators have exploited the porter workforce on which trekkers depend. Contrary to popular belief, most porters are recruited from villages in the sub-tropical foothills, and unlike the Sherpas they are not acclimatized for carrying loads weighing 60 kg at high altitudes. Like trekkers, they are vulnerable to altitude sickness, and with inadequate footwear and clothing they are at risk from frostbite and cold-related illness.

Social/cultural impacts

The economic opportunities presented by trekkers and mountaineering expeditions have stemmed the previously high rates of out-migration from Himalayan villages, while improved medical care and greater prosperity have encouraged a high rate of population growth. Nevertheless, as in other Third World countries, the contrasts between the lifestyles and attitudes of affluent Western tourists and the poverty of the village communities has resulted in a number of impacts, including:

- the breakdown of traditional social structures due to the differentiation of earning power between those involved in the tourism sector as compared to agriculture
- the demonstration effect as younger Nepalis strive to emulate Western lifestyles
- the high incidence of begging from tourists, particularly by young children
- the loss of the cultural heritage – this can be direct, as in the desecration of religious artefacts that are stolen and sold on the international art market, or indirect, through craftsmen adapting their designs to suit the preferences of Western tourists, for example in the sale of *thankas*, Buddhist temple scrolls, which are highly decorative.

Environmental impacts

Although national parks and other protected areas demonstrate Nepal's commitment to conservation, the country's forest resources were already dwindling before trekking arrived on the scene to make matters worse. In a country without cheap renewable sources of energy, firewood is used by villages for fuel and cooking. Forest clearance on steep slopes means accelerated soil erosion. In Nepal, 400 000 hectares of forest are cleared each year, resulting in devastating floods and landslides. Trekkers have contributed to Nepal's environmental problems in the following ways:

- The lodges along the major trek routes demand firewood for heating, often from virgin rhododendron forest which is slow to regenerate at high altitudes.
- Large quantities of litter are discarded by trekkers, including plastic water bottles and a trail of toilet paper.
- Water sources are contaminated by human waste from trek campsites.

On the other hand, strict conservation measures, as applied in the Sagarmatha National Park, may put additional strains on traditional agricultural systems already under threat from tourism.

Trekking, perhaps more than other forms of tourism, is characterized by an insatiable demand for new 'unspoiled' locations, which may well be in countries other than Nepal. There is already competition from Ladakh in the western Himalayas and other mountain regions of India, while Bhutan has imposed strict controls on tourism to protect its natural and cultural resources. Trekking destinations outside the Indian sub-continent include the Andes of South America and some of the desert and mountain regions of Africa. Despite tourism's impact on the culture and environment of the host community, there is little to show for it in economic terms, as Nepal remains one of the world's poorest countries.

The Annapurna Conservation Area Project

Measures involving local communities would appear to provide one solution to the problem, as in the Annapurna Conservation Area Project. This is a partnership between tour operators and local entrepreneurs to encourage sustainable development and prevent ecological disaster along Nepal's most popular trekking routes. The project covers an area of 2600 square kilometres. Its conservation strategy includes:

- The levy of a permit fee on each visitor which goes towards conservation projects.
- The substitution of solar power or kerosene as alternative fuels to firewood, and the development of small-scale hydro-electricity power projects.
- A programme of re-afforestation, and forest management that allows local villagers sustainable use of these resources.
- The raising of environmental awareness among visitors and the local communities.

Reflections on the case

This case has demonstrated how the resources and mountain climbing legacy of Nepal have been developed to support a range of adventure tourism products. However, despite the positive economic benefits to the Nepalese economy, adventure tourism is having a number of significant social and environmental impacts. These have raised international concern and have become the focus for 'clean-up' tourism and conservation projects such as that for Annapurna.

Discussion points/assignments

1 Investigate ways in which trekking could become more sustainable, such as the recycling of discarded materials.
2 Draw up a code of conduct for tour organizers that will respect porters' rights and improve their working conditions, taking into account the economic and social realities of life in Nepal.
3 Differentiate between 'soft and 'hard' adventure. Account for the growth in demand for activities such as trekking, climbing and river-running in developed Western countries. Which particular groups in Western society generate most of the demand?
4 Using the Internet and a range of holiday brochures, select suitable trekking routes and give appropriate advice to (i) a group of college students who have experience of the 'great outdoors', but who have never visited an Asian country; and (ii) a retired bank manager with a family history of heart and pulmonary illnesses.

Key sources

Adams, V. (1992) Tourism and sherpas: Nepal: reconstruction of reciprocity. *Annals of Tourism Research*, 19 (3), 534–554.

Baumgartner, R. (1988) Tourism and socio-economic change: the case of the Rolwaling Valley in Eastern Nepal. *Tourism Recreation Research*, 13 (1), 17–26.

Cockerell, N. (1997) Nepal. *International Tourism Reports*, 1, 40–57.

Deegan, P. (2003) Appetite for destruction. *Geographical*, 75 (3), 32–36.

Goddie, P., Price, M. and Zimmerman, F. M. (1999) *Tourism and Development in Mountain Regions*. CABI, Wallingford.

Godwin, S. (2003). Trekking into trouble. *Geographical*, 75 (3), 22–27.

Guha, S. (2001) An altitude problem. *Tourism in Focus*, 37, 4–6.

Gurung, C. and De Coursey, M. (1994) The Annapurna Conservation Area Project: a pioneering example of sustainable tourism, in E. Cater and G. Lowman (eds), *Ecotourism: A Sustainable Option?* New York, John Wiley and Sons.

Holden, A. and Sparrowhawk, J. (2002) Understanding the motivations of eco-tourists: the case of trekkers in Annapurna, Nepal. *International Journal of Tourism Research*, 4 (6), 435–446.

Nepal, S. K. (2000) Tourism in protected areas: the Nepalese Himalayas. *Annals of Tourism Research*, 27 (3), 661–681.

Shackley, M. (1994) The land of Lo, Nepal: the first 8 months of tourism. *Tourism Management*, 15 (1), 17–26.

Shackley, M. (1995) Lo revisited: the next 18 months. *Tourism Management*, 16 (2), 150–151.

Sharma, J. (1997) Nepal: too many tourists build a mountain of problems. *Contours*, 7 (11/12), 11–12.

Case 28

The Maldives: tourism in an island nation

Introduction

The Maldives are a pristine marine environment in the Indian Ocean. This case study examines the nature of tourism in the Maldives and the associated development issues. On completion of the case you will:

1 Understand the characteristics of the Maldives and the scale of tourism.
2 Be aware of the fragility of the Maldives' marine environment and its value for tourism.
3 Be aware of the tourist resources and facilities of the Maldives.
4 Be sensitive to the religious and cultural character of the islands and the implications for tourism.
5 Understand the issues surrounding the development and marketing of resorts on the Maldives.

Key issues

There are five key issues in this case:

1 The islands of the Maldives are set in a pristine marine environment over a large expanse of the Indian Ocean, which causes both access and logistical problems for tourism.
2 The main tourism resource of the Maldives is the marine environment of coral atolls, although the culture of the Maldives is also an attraction.
3 Tourism development is sensitive to the cultural and religious traditions of the islands.
4 The Maldives find themselves in the classic dilemma of gauging how much tourism development to allow in order to ensure the conservation of the marine environment.
5 The Maldives authorities have drafted development and marketing plans to control the development of tourism and to ensure that the Maldives attract upper income tourists.

The Maldives

The Maldives is an independent republic located in the Indian Ocean, south-west of the Indian sub-continent. Geographically, the Maldives is a unique collection of 26 coral atolls, containing almost 1200 coral islands and hundreds of small sandbanks. The Maldives was formed by volcanic eruptions millions of years ago, leaving behind coral reefs as the volcanic cones subsided. All the islands are low lying, on average less than 2 metres above sea level, making them vulnerable to long-term changes in sea level. The islands are scattered over a large expanse of the Indian Ocean, more than 800 kilometres from north to south and 130 kilometres from east to west. This makes transfer to the tourist resorts a logistical problem – indeed in the early days of tourism experts recommended that the distances involved made tourism development impossible. The climate is hot and humid, with a rainy season between May and October and sea temperatures between 25 and 29 °C, perfect for beach tourism, diving and the marine life.

Resorts have only been developed on islands not inhabited by the local people. This has the following advantages:

- the privacy of visitors is assured
- it minimizes negative impacts on the culture of the islanders
- it minimizes competition for scarce resources between the tourism industry and other sectors.

The islanders are strict Muslims and no alcohol is allowed except in the resorts. Mosques are found on many islands and visitors are expected to respect the traditions of Islam in terms of modest dress when visiting the capital, Male. English is the second language to the local *Dhivehi* tongue.

Apart from tourism, the Maldives also have an important fishing industry. However, tourism is the driving force in the economy as it:

- supports 45 per cent of the jobs in the islands
- brings the islanders an enhanced quality of life
- provides amenities and facilities both for tourists and locals alike through the taxes levied on tourists (there is both a bed tax and an airport tax)
- contributes 56 per cent of the gross domestic product
- represents almost a quarter of capital investment.

Tourism demand

The Maldives receive around 300 000 international visitors annually, predominantly from Europe (Germany, Italy and the UK), but other important source markets are Japan, Australia, India and South Africa. The North American market is in its infancy for the Maldives but holds considerable potential. Growth of demand was steady through the 1990s and expected to increase in line with greater bed capacity to the year 2005.

Tourism resources

- **The marine environment**   The prime tourism resource of the islands is the pristine marine environment where the quality of the coral reefs and marine life is unrivalled anywhere in the world. The majority of visitors arrive in the Maldives to experience this marine environment and also for water sports. Each of the resort islands (many of which are very small) has a diving base and the resort 'house reef' is commonly within wading or swimming distance from the accommodation. Scuba diving and snorkelling (night dives and drift dives are a speciality), fishing, underwater photography and a variety of water sports are popular and many resorts have both indoor and outdoor sports facilities, swimming pools and other activities to supplement the attractions of the reef. However, this does raise the question as to whether air conditioning, swimming pools, gyms etc. are compatible in terms of their energy use, with truly sustainable tourism.
- **Male**   The capital, Male, is a small town with a few shops and restaurants, but little to attract the visitor, although it contains two-thirds of the population of the Maldives. Moreover it is the gateway to the islands through Hulhule International Airport.
- **Resorts and safari vessels**   Tourism is a relatively recent development in the Maldives, with the first resort opening as recently as 1972. By the late 1990s, tourism was developed on 73 islands. Tourists have the choice of either basing themselves on one of the resort islands or using 'safari vessels' with 'floating beds'. In the late 1990s, the resorts had almost 12 000 bedspaces, and the safari vessels a further 1500 bedspaces. The resort islands are self-contained, tending to import all the produce for visitors, although a few are experimenting with growing their own vegetables. Water is desalinated and each resort island has its own fleet of boats. Staff tend to work on the islands for short intensive periods before returning to Male for a few days to be with their families. This highlights the isolation of each of the resort islands – visitors are effectively trapped on the island of their choice for the duration of their stay unless they opt for an 'island-hopping' excursion for a day. There are two trends in the accommodation sector:
  - the growing popularity of 'all inclusive resorts'
  - a number of international hotel companies are now active in this area (namely Hilton, Four Seasons and Club Mediterranée), although most of the accommodation is leased by local resort operators from the Government of the Maldives, which retains ownership of the islands.

Transport

As with all island destinations, air access is the key to success or failure. The Maldives are a difficult destination to reach. There are charter flights from Europe (the UK and Germany), and scheduled services include

- Air Lanka
- Emirates

- Lauda Air
- Air Maldives (part government owned)
- Singapore Airlines.

However, scheduled services are routed through the respective hub of the airline, so that there are no direct scheduled flights to the Maldives from its main generating markets.

The main gateway to the islands is Hulhule International Airport, which is a short speedboat or *dhoni* journey from Male. Each resort island or safari vessel has to be reached by transfer from the airport. These transfers are sometimes lengthy and thus expensive, as many resorts are over 120 kilometres from Male. Transfers are by:

- traditional sailboat or *dhoni* (slow and rarely used)
- speedboat (becoming less popular as reaching some resorts from Hulhule involves a journey of up to three hours)
- seaplane (more commonly used today because of the distances involved).

In the early 1990s, Russian-built helicopters were used for transfers but safety issues led to them being withdrawn from service. Two companies – Maldivian Air Taxis and Hummingbird – operate seaplane transfers. However, seaplanes cannot land at night, so visitors arriving or departing on night flights have to spend one night in a hotel in Male before being transferred in the daylight hours. For the remoter islands, regional airstrips are being developed to allow landing at night, as well as to stimulate investment.

Tourism policy and organization

It is imperative that tourism development in the Maldives does not threaten the marine environment. Although global warming and rising sea temperatures have affected the coral, these events are outside the control of the islands themselves. In the islands there are marine reserves and tourism codes of conduct. Tourism development is being used as a regional development tool for the remoter islands, although this does mean visitors have to undergo long transfers from Male.

The Ministry of Tourism oversees tourism development and regulates the resorts. In the late 1990s the Maldives Tourism Promotion Board was created to market the islands internationally. The islands were the subject of a tourism master plan in the mid-1990s and also have rolling marketing plans. These plans and policies will determine the future direction of tourism in the following ways:

- **Marketing** The islands are attempting to position themselves as the premium ecotourism destination in the world, and to diversify their markets.
- **Development** For tourism development in the Maldives the key phrase is *the highly managed expansion of tourism*. The target is to have around 15 000 bedspaces in resorts by the year 2005. This will be achieved on a geographical basis as follows:
  - the Central Region, consisting of Male and Ari atolls, involving the consolidation and upgrading of accommodation
  - expansion of development to the north and to the south of Male and Ari atolls to add between 20 and 30 new resorts

○ in the Southern Region, the development of Vilingili Island
○ in the remoter atolls, the development of regional airport gateways to stimulate investment.

Reflections on the case

This case has shown how the Maldives are having to balance the demands for tourism development on the islands, with the imperative to conserve the pristine marine environment – which is after all why the tourists visit the islands. The tourism product of the islands is one of high quality and has been developed with the social and religious traditions of the islands in mind.

Discussion points/assignments

1 Describe the main threats to the marine environment of the Maldives and the measures that are being undertaken to protect these resources.
2 Debate the pros and cons of the policy of limiting tourism development to islands away from local communities; after all one justification for tourism is that it encourages understanding between different cultures, but on the other hand there is the need to preserve the integrity of indigenous communities.
3 Diving is a major component of recreational tourism in most warm-water destinations, and particularly in the Maldives. Describe the various organizations and enterprises in your country that serve and supply divers, and the facilities that are available in the islands.
4 Put together a full tour itinerary for a holiday in the Maldives for a family with two young children living in Wellington, New Zealand. Include all transfers and stopovers, and give a detailed description of the resort island you have chosen for your clients.

Key sources

Anon. (1999) On the beach. *Economist*, 350 (8101), 65.
Fisher, B. (2000) The Maldives. *Country Reports*, 4, 45–64.
Garrod, B. and Wilson, J. (2003) *Marine Ecotourism*. Channel View, Clevedon.
Lambert, J. (2001) Making tourism sustainable in the Maldives. *Hospitality Review*, 3 (2), 22–29.
Sathiendrakumar, R. and Tisdell, C. (1989) Tourism and the economic development of the Maldives. *Annals of Tourism Research*, 16 (2), 254–269.

Website
http://www.visitmaldives.com/intro.html

Case 29
Bali: tourism in crisis

Introduction

In 2002 the bombing of nightclubs in Bali had a devastating effect on the island's tourism. The case study examines tourism on Bali and the neighbouring island of Lombok with this crisis in mind. On completion of this case you will:

1 Be aware of the scale of tourism development on Bali and Lombok.
2 Recognize the key tourism attractions and facilities of the islands.
3 Understand the key geographical features of the islands and their relevance for tourism.
4 Be aware of the impacts of tourism on the islands.
5 Recognize the importance of the Australian market, and understand the impact of the 2002 bombings on tourism demand and Bali's economy.

Key issues

There are four key issues in this case:

1 Bali and Lombok show contrasting styles and levels of tourism development, but are probably the most developed islands of Indonesia for tourism.
2 Bali and Lombok have considerable natural and cultural tourism resources and these have become the basis for their appeal.
3 Tourism has caused significant impacts upon the life of the local communities as well as the environment, although the economic benefits of tourism were considerable before 'Black October' (the nightclub bombings in the resort of Kuta on 12 October 2002).
4 The 'Black October' crisis has had a devastating impact on Bali's tourism industry.

Bali and Lombok

Bali and Lombok are the best known of the holiday islands of Indonesia, and are readily accessible from Australia and Japan, their principal tourism markets. Bali is separated from Java to the west by only a narrow stretch of water, whereas Lombok to the east is more remote and less developed. Bali has a long-established reputation as a 'tropical paradise', where a seemingly gentle, artistic people live in harmony with their environment. However, with tourist arrivals exceeding 2 million a year in the late 1990s – compared to less than 30 000 in 1969 – it has become difficult to sustain this image. Unlike most of Indonesia, the two islands were relatively unaffected by the turmoil that followed the Asian financial crisis of 1997–98 and the troubles in East Timor. In fact, the fall in value of the *rupiah* against Western currencies meant that Bali became a value-for-money destination for many tourists. Lombok has benefited from Bali's popularity, and tourism development has been rapid since the mid-1980s.

The events of 'Black October' 2002 dealt a severe blow to the Balinese economy, which had become over-dependent on tourism. Matters were made worse by the reaction of some Western governments to the threat of terrorism; Britain's Foreign and Commonwealth Office, for example, issued an advisory against travel to the island, which was not lifted until June 2004. In the meantime, hundreds of craft workshops and other small tourism-related businesses had closed down through lack of orders, while hotel occupancy rates slumped far below the 50 per cent needed to cover operating costs. Many Balinese were forced to return to their farming villages in the face of widespread unemployment in the tourism sector. Australians were the main victims of the bombings, and not surprisingly the fall in demand was greatest in the inclusive tour market catering for middle income Australians. The Japanese market was more resilient; this accounts for the largest number of tourist arrivals, but with a short length of stay averaging less than a week. Young Japanese tourists find the relaxed lifestyle of Bali a welcome escape from the social conventions and conformity prevailing in their own country. The backpacking youth travel market, and what might be called 'five star' tourism at the other extreme, already seem to be recovering from the crisis of 2002. Domestic tourism has increased, with the encouragement of the Indonesian government.

Bali: physical and cultural resources

Bali is densely populated, with some 3 million people living in a small mountainous island only 5600 square kilometres in area. The northern part of the island is dominated by a chain of volcanoes – some still active – rising to over 2000 metres. Rich volcanic soils, monsoon rains and a complex irrigation system support the agricultural village communities that make up 80 per cent of the population. Bali's appeal is based on the photogenic quality of its land and people, with physical and cultural resources that include:

- A favourable tropical climate, with a dry season lasting from May to October. This coincides with the winter months in Australia to the south.

- A spectacular landscape, featuring emerald-green rice terraces carved out of the hills, mountains clothed in lush vegetation, and crater lakes.
- Balinese art and culture. Throughout their history the Balinese have adopted cultural traits from other peoples – the Hindu religion and dance dramas from India, for example – and made them part of their own distinctive lifestyle. Art and religious ritual are part of everyday life in this 'island of the gods', and Hindu temples are a feature of every village. Along with the strong sense of community encouraged by the *banjars* or village councils, this has helped to preserve Balinese culture amid the world's largest Muslim country and in the face of a mass invasion by international tourists.
- The colourful festivals, that integrate art, *gamelan* music, drama and dance. The graceful *legong* dancers have become the island's best-known tourist icon. The Balinese do not deem to mind the presence of outsiders at their religious ceremonies – even the elaborate cremations have become tourist attractions.
- Balinese painting and sculpture first became a means of personal expression and a commercial activity in the 1930s with the encouragement of Dutch and other Western expatriate artists, who introduced new techniques and a much greater range of styles. Tourism has led to the development of new art forms and the revival of some traditional handicrafts.

Recreational resources

The most well-known of Bali's recreational resources are the surfing beaches and the coral reefs offshore for scuba diving. There is some spa tourism utilizing mineral springs. Other activities have been introduced as a result of tourist demand. For example, golf courses have been developed, primarily for the Japanese market, while adventure sports, such as bungee-jumping and rafting, appeal to the international youth market.

Accommodation and transport

Bali offers a range of accommodation – from luxury five-star hotels – concentrated in Nusa Dua – to simple beach bungalows. Small hotels and guesthouses, known as *losmen* or 'homestays', provide inexpensive, informal accommodation throughout Bali for backpackers and independent tourists. Often built in the style of a traditional Balinese village compound, with rooms opening off an inner courtyard, they allow visitors to sample the Balinese way of life. As they are usually run by local families, a much higher proportion of the visitor spend is retained within the local community than is the case with the larger hotels, owned by companies based in Java or outside Indonesia.

Most foreign visitors to Bali, and a high proportion of domestic tourists from the major cities of Indonesia – Jakarta, Yogyakarta and Surabaya – arrive by air. The opening of the Ngurah Rai International Airport at Denpasar (DPS) in 1968 was the catalyst for the large-scale expansion of tourism in Bali. Denpasar is served by scheduled and charter air services from Australia, Japan, Western Europe and the USA. Internal transport is by road, using a variety of vehicles such as *bemos* (mini-buses) and pick-up trucks as well as cars, coaches and taxis.

The impacts of tourism

Although the Balinese had little say in determining the Indonesian government's policy of developing tourism in their island, they have experienced some of its economic benefits. Before the 2002 crisis, tourism provided jobs for more than 20 per cent of the adult population. It is a supplementary source of income for rice farmers who can let rooms to backpackers, and ensures a ready market for handicrafts as well as a textile industry geared to producing beachwear. As a result of tourism average incomes are twice those of Java. The Balinese have been able to market their culture, which has proved remarkably resilient compared to those of other tropical islands. However, the high rate of tourism growth, and the modernization this inevitably entails, is putting a heavy strain on limited land and water resources, and is threatening the integrity of Balinese cultural traditions. For example, the need to provide electricity for luxury hotels has led to a controversial decision to build a power station on a mountain held sacred by the Balinese. The negative impacts of tourism include:

- The annual loss of some 1000 hectares of rice fields to development, so that Bali no longer produces enough rice to meet its needs.
- Coastal erosion, due to sand dredging and the drainage of mangrove swamps for development.
- Damage to coral reefs.
- Untreated waste disposal, causing marine pollution.
- Problems of water supply, with priority given to luxury hotels and golf course developments rather than local communities.
- Air and noise pollution from cars and motor cycles.
- Leakages of tourism income. As inclusive tours dominate the industry, most of the income goes to the international tour operators and hotel chains.
- The 'packaging' of Balinese traditional culture for Western consumption in the big international hotels. For example, the *kechak* dance dramas, which typically last for several hours, have been drastically abbreviated for tourist audiences.
- Prostitution and drug-taking.
- A spatial imbalance in the distribution of the benefits of tourism. Most tourist activity is concentrated in the south of the island, although development is spreading to the interior and the north coast.

The tourist regions of Bali

South Bali

Once a relatively poor area in agricultural terms, this part of Bali has experienced considerable economic and population growth since the 1960s as a result of the tourist boom. Denpasar, the island's capital, is now a major city with a population approaching 400 000. It offers a number of attractions including the Bali Museum, which showcases Balinese dance, paintings and handicrafts. The south includes the major resorts of the island, which have developed along some of Bali's best beaches within easy reach of the international airport. The following resorts exemplify different approaches to tourism:

- **Sanur**   This small fishing village attracted Western artists and intellectuals in the 1930s, giving it wide publicity that eventually resulted in large-scale development along the seafront in the 1960s. Sanur is a mix of large hotels and smaller bungalow developments, interspersed with shops and restaurants. It attracts visitors from Europe, Australia, Japan and the USA.
- **Kuta Beach**   Kuta has acquired a downmarket image, having developed in the 1970s as a resort for Australian surfers, who were attracted by its broad sloping beach, breakers and offshore breezes. Some 18 000 bedspaces are available, accounting for almost a third of Bali's capacity. Much of the accommodation is both informal and small in scale, resulting in a low rise sprawl of bungalows, small hotels, restaurants and shops, which extends northwards to Legian. A variety of traders compete to provide goods and services – which include 'beach massage'. In some respects, Kuta is to Australians what some Spanish resorts are to young British holidaymakers; a tourism experience based on 'sun and fun', fast food, bars and discotheques rather than any appreciation of the local culture. Kuta also illustrates the complexity of relationships between hosts and guests in a Third World country. Young Balinese men have adopted Western 'surf culture', and the surf-board has become yet another art form. The 'topless' female 'sun-worshippers' from Australia and other Western countries have become an 'attraction' (or distraction) for domestic tourists from Java. This is ironic, given that when Indonesia gained its independence from colonial rule, Balinese women were persuaded to dress modestly by the new government in the name of progress.
- **Nusa Dua** is definitely upmarket. Land in Sanur was in short supply by the late 1970s, leading to the development of a purpose-built resort on the Bukit Peninsula just south of the airport. The site had the following advantages:
  - It was a dry limestone plateau of little value for agriculture and thinly populated.
  - The cultural impact of tourism could be minimized by physical separation.
  - The beaches are protected by a coral reef and are thus suitable for bathing.

  Nusa Dua was designed and built as a World Bank project and is managed by the Bali Tourist Development Corporation. It is a beautifully planned and landscaped resort area, with its own water filtration plant, and accommodation is restricted to luxury hotels. The development has aroused controversy – some say that it is an excellent example of 'enclave tourism', while others argue that little of the culture of Bali, or contact with local people, is to be found there – in other words, Nusa Dua is a 'tourist ghetto', like so many other luxury resorts in the Third World.

Central Bali

The central region of Bali is well known for its cultural traditions, with villages specializing in particular handicrafts. They include:

- Batubulan – famous for its stone carvings. Other attractions include traditional dancers performing for tourists and the Pura Puseh Temple.
- Celuk – noted for gold and silver filigree.
- Sukawati – celebrated for its puppeteers.
- Batuan – a centre for traditional textile weaving.
- Mas – famous for wood-carvings and masks.
- Ubud – often regarded as the cultural centre of Bali with a great number of artist's studios and galleries.

North and east Bali

This region was formerly isolated from the rest of Bali until the Dutch colonial authorities built a road across the central spine of mountains in the 1920s. The north-west is still relatively undeveloped and a large area of forest is protected as a national park. There are a number of attractions of volcanic origin; of these Lake Batur is the most spectacular – a 20 kilometre-wide caldera with villages sited along the rim of the former crater. Lake Bratan is a peaceful backwater, where picturesque pagodas blend harmoniously with the natural landscape. Tourism is mainly focused on the emerging beach resort of Candi Dusa. The port of Pudang Bai is visited by cruise ships and has ferry services to Lombok.

Lombok

Lombok has been the main beneficiary of government policy to spread tourism away from Bali. The two islands are roughly the same size and are superficially similar – indeed Lombok is often regarded as a less developed version of Bali. However, there are a number of important differences:

- The climate is drier. This is a disadvantage for agriculture – Lombok is one of the poorest regions of Indonesia – but a 'plus' for tourism.
- Lombok has better beaches than Bali. The scenery of the interior is less spectacular, although there are some high mountains – Rinjani, for example – in the north of the island.
- Their ecosystems are different, due to the barrier presented by the deep Lombok Strait. The Wallace Line, which separates Asian species of plants and animals from those typical of Australasia, runs between the two islands.
- They are culturally distinct. The Sasak people of Lombok are Muslims, and so tend to be less tolerant of immodest behaviour by Western tourists.
- Lombok has a less developed feel. There is less of the 'hard-sell' approach to tourism and merchandising evident in Bali.
- Lombok has a policy for upmarket tourism development, further differentiating its product from Bali.

Lombok is, therefore, focusing on five-star hotels and resorts, with associated infrastructure development, including a new international airport and improvements to ferry services, port facilities and the road network. The Lombok Tourism Development Corporation has purchased land fronting beaches in the south and west of the island, and is proposing joint ventures with the big accommodation developers. It is alleged that local small enterprises, catering for backpackers and other lower-spending visitors, are being squeezed out, with the tourism industry becoming dominated by Javanese and foreign interests.

Much of the development has taken place on the west coast of Lombok, which has safe sandy beaches, excellent coral reefs for diving, and facilities for sailing and other water sports. The main resort here is Senggigi Beach, a few kilometres north of Mataram, the island's capital, while the Gili Islands are also attracting developers.

Although Lombok has a number of villages noted for handicrafts such as weaving, basketwork and pottery, there is less emphasis on the decorative arts, and fewer cultural attractions than in Bali. Most of these are located near the capital and include:

- Cakranegara – the former royal capital, which contains the Pura Meru Temple
- the Narmada Gardens
- the Surranadi Temple.

Reflections on the case

Bali and Lombok show contrasting levels and types of tourism development. Both have cultural and natural attractions, although in the past tourism has caused considerable impacts. This case has also demonstrated how a single terrorist act can devastate the tourism sector of a destination. Before the 'Black October' bombings in 2002 Bali was one of the most popular holiday islands in the East Asia–Pacific region. Bali's uniqueness is due to its people and landscapes, and these assets should ensure a rapid recovery from that crisis, but in the future tourism should be carefully managed for the benefit of local communities. However, much depends on the return of political stability to Indonesia as a whole and the effectiveness of security measures against the terrorist threat.

Discussion points/assignments

1 Describe the various ways in which tourism and exposure to Western values has affected the lifestyle and artistic traditions of the Balinese.
2 'Backpackers have played an important role in the development of tourism in Bali, but they have not always respected the culture of the host community.' Discuss this statement, and give appropriate advice to young British tourists visiting Bali as part of their gap year.
3 Debate the pros and cons of government advisories on travel to countries in crisis, using the Bali bombings as one of your examples. Be aware of the continuing threat of terrorism to other parts of South-East Asia.
4 Compare the role of Bali as a holiday destination for Australians with that of a specific Mediterranean island popular with British tourists. Take into account the differences in culture, lifestyle and income levels between 'hosts' and 'guests' in each island.
5 Compare the prospects for tourism in East Timor (which gained independence from Indonesia in 1999) with those of Bali following 'Black October'. To what extent are the pro-poor tourism policies described in a previous case study applicable to both islands?

Key sources

Brace, M. (2003) The road back to Bali. *Geographical*, 75 (10), 26–34.

Dhune, S. (2002) Grounded in paradise. *Far Eastern Economic Review* (31 October), 62–65.

Eber, S. (2003) *FCO Travel Advisories: The Case for Transparency and Balance*. Tourism Concern, London.

Hall, C. M. and Page, S. (2000) *Tourism in South East Asia: Issues and Cases*. Elsevier Butterworth-Heinemann, Oxford.

Hitchcock, M. (2000) Bali: a paradise globalised. *Pacific Tourism Review*, 4 (2/3), 63–73.

Hitchcock, M., King, V. T. and Parnwell, J. G. (1993) *Tourism in South East Asia*. Routledge, London.

Long, V. and Wall, G. (1996) Successful tourism in Nusa Lembongan, Indonesia? *Tourism Management*, 17 (1), 43–50.

Picard, M. (1998) *Bali: Cultural Tourism and Touristic Culture*. Tuttle Publishing, Boston, MA.

Shaw, B. J. and Shaw, G. (1999) 'Sun, sand and sales': enclave tourism and local entrepreneurship in Indonesia. *Current Issues in Tourism*, 2 (1), 68–81.

Sutjipta, N. (2000) The dilemma of tourism in Bali: tourism destroying tourism. *Contours*, 10 (3), 4–12.

Vickers, A. (1998) *Bali: A Paradise Created*. Tuttle Publishing, Boston, MA.

Wall, G. (1992) Bali: sustainable development project. *Annals of Tourism Research*, 19 (3), 569–571.

Wall, G. (1993) International collaboration in the search for sustainable tourism in Bali, Indonesia. *Journal of Sustainable Tourism*, 1 (1), 38–47.

Wall, G. (1999) Research report: mechanisms in support of research efforts: the Bali sustainable development project, a multidisciplinary and collaborative activity. *Tourism Geographies*, 1 (2), 183–191.

Wall, G. and Dibnah, S. (1992) The changing status of tourism in Bali, Indonesia. *Progress in Tourism, Recreation and Hospitality Management*, 4, 120–130.

Website

http://tourismindonesia.com

Case 30

Kangaroo Island: debating tourism development

Introduction

Kangaroo Island is the third largest of Australia's offshore islands, and, as an important wildlife site, tourist destination and home to local communities, it has become a classic case study in the debate about the future development of tourism. On completion of this case you will:

1 Understand the location of and characteristics of Kangaroo Island.
2 Be aware of the natural resource base of Kangaroo Island.
3 Understand the organization of tourism on Kangaroo Island.
4 Recognize the potential conflict between nature conservation and tourism development.
5 Understand the innovative planning approach taken on Kangaroo Island.

Key issues

There are five key issues in this case:

1 Kangaroo Island is situated off the southern coast of Australia and is rich in flora and fauna which have been designated as nature reserves.
2 The island has become a classic example of the development dilemma between tourism, the local community and nature conservationists.
3 The island's natural resources have been developed as tourism products in a number of cases.
4 The island's market is changing with improved access from the mainland of South Australia, with more overseas visitors arriving and considerable numbers of day visitors.
5 Kangaroo Island has approached its development dilemma by implementing an innovative planning regime, the Tourism Optimization Model (TOMM) that is a model for other communities.

Kangaroo Island

Kangaroo Island is situated off the coast of South Australia, 150 kilometres from the capital Adelaide. Its main feature is a low plateau rising to 300 metres resulting in a spectacular coastline. It is thinly populated even by Australian standards, with only 4200 inhabitants occupying an area of 4350 square kilometres (roughly the size of Long Island). Most of these live in the coastal towns of Kingscote and Penneshaw, and inland around Parndana. From the 1980s visitor arrivals steadily increased, so that the island has become a significant tourist destination in South Australia, second only to Adelaide. In the early years of the twenty-first century tourism has become the major contributor to the island's economy, which was based on sheep and cattle raising, and the local farmers have benefited from the additional income gained by developing farm-stays, bed and breakfast, camping and sales of local produce. The authorities and the community therefore have to meet the challenge of sensitively developing tourism in a fragile environment. As part of the South Australia tourism region, the island is committed to sustainable tourism development.

Tourism resources

Kangaroo Island's tourist appeal is based upon its rural lifestyle and the fact that, although the island gives the impression of isolation, it provides easier access to Australia's wildlife resources than the Outback of the continental interior. Although only a narrow stretch of water separates it from the mainland, this has been sufficient to protect the native animals from introduced species such as the dingo, fox and rabbit. The wildlife includes a range of marsupials as well as marine species representative of the Southern Ocean, such as penguins, seals and sea lions. The main attractions are the Flinders Chase National Park, a wilderness area of *mallee* scrub and woodland, and the Seal Bay Conservation Park, both receiving over 100 000 visitors annually. Other tourism resources include:

- the dramatic coastal scenery, featuring natural attractions such as Remarkable Rocks, Cape Coudic, Admiral's Arch, and sea caves
- the opportunities for sailing, scuba diving and surfing; fishing charters are available from the north coast
- bird watching
- the natural bushland is ideal for nature retreats, wildlife viewing and *'bush walking'* (hiking)
- an interesting heritage, including historic lighthouses and shipwreck sites
- niche agricultural products, local gastronomy and wine
- an expanding events programme – including horse races and local markets.

Transport and accommodation

- Kangaroo Island is easily accessible from Adelaide by fast ferry
- Kangaroo Island is also served by a vehicle ferry from Cape Jervis, the nearest point on the South Australia mainland
- small plane services are available.

Touring on the island is mainly by coach, or more tailor-made tours using four-wheel-drive vehicles. At Penneshaw, the island's gateway visitor centre acts as an orientation and interpretation point for newly arriving visitors.

Accommodation is mainly in the form of apartments, small motels and hotels and ranges from informal camping sites, through farm stays and holiday houses, to low impact holiday villages and 'heritage house accommodation' (historic cottages) in the Flinders Chase National Park. In many cases the accommodation stock is in need of rejuvenation, requiring upgrades and new development. In part this is due to the small-scale nature of the sector and the lack of appropriate management expertise, but it has become a constraint for the development of high-yield tours.

Other problems facing further tourism development are the limited water resources and the fire risk to the native vegetation.

Demand

Most visitors arrive in the summer months and during school holidays. Visitor numbers approached 150 000 in the early years of the twenty-first century. Around 20 per cent are day-trippers as the island is accessible from Adelaide and the main touring circuits can be completed in one day. The majority of visitors therefore come from Adelaide but there are a growing number of international visitors, accounting for 25 per cent of all overnight stays. Domestic tourists are more attracted to the recreational activities on the island, while foreign visitors find the viewing of wildlife and scenery, and the experience of staying in a rural area of Australia, more appealing.

Organization

There are a number of agencies involved in managing tourism on Kangaroo Island:

- At local level:
  - the two District Councils on Kangaroo Island
  - Tourism Kangaroo Island
  - the KI Economic Development Board.
- At state level:
  - South Australia Tourism Commission
  - Department of Environment and Natural Resources.

It is the nature of Kangaroo Island as a significant natural resource (30 per cent of the area is protected, with national or conservation park status), and also as a thriving rural community, that has given rise to the debate over the island's future, particularly in terms of tourism. In response a range of planning and management initiatives have been implemented:

- As tourism expanded, a tourism policy for the island was implemented in 1991 dividing Kangaroo Island into 11 tourism zones, identifying the resources in each of the zones and the potential for future development.

- The tourism policy stimulated considerable debate and community consultation that eventually culminated in a Sustainable Development Strategy for the island in 1995. The mission statement of this strategy was:
  - ○ 'Kangaroo Island will be one of the world's pre-eminent nature-based tourist destinations with a strong rural industry selling its products to tourist, mainland and overseas markets, a high quality of life for residents and well managed natural resources.'
  - ○ In order to achieve this strategy an innovative approach to monitoring the island's tourism was developed, known as the tourism optimization model (TOMM). This involves extensive consultation as to the future of the island; identification of key indicators and benchmarks to monitor progress towards future conditions; and a system of monitoring to ensure the island is on track to achieve these conditions. TOMM has become internationally recognized as an effective approach to planning and managing sustainable tourism.
- In 2002 the South Australian Tourism Commission and Planning South Australia launched a consultation document on environmentally sustainable tourism development.

Kangaroo Island is therefore an excellent example of a disciplined and professional community-based approach to the management of tourism in a sensitive area.

Reflections on the case

Kangaroo Island is an important wildlife site, tourist destination and home to a thriving rural community and, as such, it has become a classic case study in the debate about the future development of tourism. The island has solved the problem by adopting an innovative planning and monitoring regime, which adjusts to changing circumstances, and places development decisions firmly in local control. This approach could act as a model for other destinations facing similar development issues.

Discussion points/assignments

1 **Explain the appeal of Kangaroo Island as a destination to a range of international and domestic tourism markets. To what extent is the island a 'microcosm' of Australia as a whole?**

2 **Carry out an investigation of the various constraints on tourism development on Kangaroo Island, such as bush fires, water supplies, infrastructure and the availability of labour.**

3 Explain what is meant by an Environmental Impact Statement (EIS) in the context of planning a tourism project. How effective is an EIS in protecting local ecosystems and ensuring sustainable development?

4 Hold a debate on the pros and cons of developing a 'holiday village' accommodating 300 guests on Kangaroo Island. Role players might include representatives from conservation groups, local farmers, the island's airline, and South Australia's business community.

Key sources

Hall, C. M. (1997) *Introduction to Tourism in Australia*. Longman, Harlow.

Manuel, M., McElroy, B. and Smith, R. (1996) *Tourism*. Cambridge University Press, Cambridge.

Mandis Roberts Consultants (1996) *Developing a Tourism Optimization Model (TOMM). A Model to Monitor and Manage Tourism on Kangaroo Island South Australia*. Mandis Roberts, Surry Hills, NSW.

South Australia Tourism Commission (2003) *Kangaroo Island Tourism Profile*. SAC, Adelaide.

Thomson, F. L. and Thomson, N. J. (1994) Tourism, tax receipts and local government: the case of Kangaroo Island. *Journal of Tourism Studies*, 5 (1), 57–66.

Websites

www.kangaroo-island-au.com/
www.tourism.sa.gov.au/
www.southaustralia.com/
www.tourkangarooisland.com.au/

Case 31

The re-visioning of tired destinations: Australia's Gold Coast

Introduction

Across the world, destinations that were created for mass tourism after the Second World War are beginning to feel their age. In many destinations, both the infrastructure and the physical fabric are beginning to reach the end of their useful life and markets are declining. This has prompted a response to rejuvenate and reposition destinations by reformulating the product and diversifying markets. In this case study, the Gold Coast in Queensland, Australia, has undergone a significant and innovative 'visioning' exercise to determine its future direction. On completion of this case you will:

1 Recognize the issues related to 'stagnating' destinations.
2 Understand the reasons why 'stagnating' destinations engage in 'visioning' and strategic planning.
3 Recognize the particular characteristics of the Gold Coast as a destination.
4 Be familiar with the innovative approach used to 'vision' the future of the Gold Coast.
5 Understand the outcomes of the Gold Coast visioning process.

Key issues

There are five key issues in this case:

1 The Gold Coast has become a low yield, high volume tourism destination dependent upon mass-market tourism and, as a result, has decided to reposition itself.

2 The Gold Coast is one of a number of 'stagnating' destinations worldwide that has decided to 'vision' its future as a destination by an extensive planning and consultation exercise.
3 The 'visioning' exercise involved an innovative 'whole of destination' approach, including consultation with the increasing number of residents moving into the area.
4 The visioning exercise is firmly rooted in a sustainable tourism approach.
5 The visioning exercise has had significant outcomes in terms of the organization and perception of tourism in the destination.

The Gold Coast

In Australia, Queensland's Gold Coast is a long strip of coastline stretching from Southport in the north to Coolangata on the New South Wales border, backed by stunning mountain and rainforest scenery, much of which has national park status. The coastline is heavily developed, particularly around the core of the destination at Surfer's Paradise – where significant high-rise developments continue to be constructed. The Gold Coast is recognized as Australia's major tourist area, with the largest concentration of bedspaces in the country. Not only is it a significant domestic destination, but it also attracts substantial numbers of international visitors, particularly from Asia. Of course this means that the Gold Coast is vulnerable to fluctuations in the Asian outbound market, initially caused by the currency crisis in 1997–98, but more recently by incidents such as the SARS outbreak in 2003 and the continuing recession in the Japanese economy.

As a destination, the Gold Coast is dependent upon an attractive mix of both natural and man-made attractions. The natural attractions include the area's subtropical climate, the long clean beaches, the Pacific surf and the hinterland of national parks, rainforest and mountains. The man-made attractions include three of Australia's largest theme parks – Seaworld, Movieworld and Dreamworld – as well as a major water park. Along the coast itself there are many smaller attractions and innovative products such as the 'Aquaduck' tours that utilize amphibious craft for a combination of land and water tours; mini-golf, surf schools and nature-based hinterland trips.

Visioning strategies for stagnating destinations

The visioning of the Gold Coast is recognition of the need for strategic planning at the destination level. In a turbulent environment for tourism, particularly post-9/11, it is important for destinations to take control of their own future by embarking on such planning exercises. For 'tired' destinations this is particularly important, as the next stage of their evolution is 'decline'. The best framework to consider for this approach is the Tourist Area Life Cycle (TALC) (Figure 31.1). Many destinations

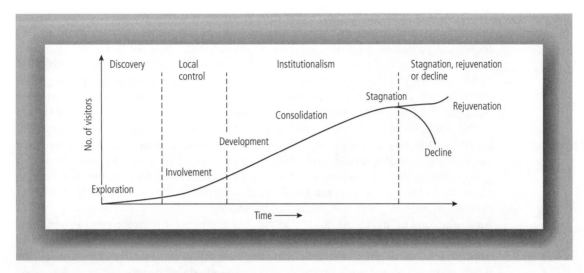

Figure 31.1 The tourist area life cycle
Source: Butler, 1980

have reached the stagnation stage of the cycle and it is these destinations that are exemplified by the Gold Coast. Indeed, across the world destinations such as Waikiki (Hawaii), Pataya Beach (Thailand), Acapulco (Mexico) and many cold water resorts in Europe and on the eastern seaboard of the USA have embarked upon such exercises. Perhaps the first to do so was Atlantic City in the USA.

For the Gold Coast, and other destinations, the real dangers of the stagnation phase are:

- The dominance of increasingly low-yield, mass-market, short-stay tourists who choose the destination on the basis of price. This leads to a low-yield, high-volume destination (sometimes termed 'profitless volume destinations').
- The danger of tourism exceeding carrying capacity limits in terms of both the tolerance of the local community and the quality of the environment of the destination.
- The fact that the destination becomes a low-yield destination means that reinvestment and refurbishment are difficult and the 'quality' of the destination declines – including the public sector infrastructure as well as private sector facilities.
- The products on offer become increasingly out of step with the demands of the market.
- Market share is eroded by newer destinations that can compete for tourists more effectively as they are more fashionable.

These threats mean there are significant benefits to a strategic planning exercise. In any tourist destination there are bound to be conflicting interests, stakeholders, 'destination creators' and groups that can be brought together by a strategic planning exercise. These varied interests can be harnessed to work together for the collective good of the destination. In the strategy planning literature this is known as developing a 'strategic conversation'. Not only do these many stakeholders (such as residents, business, government and charities) begin to work together and collaborate, but they also work out their own roles in the exercise, and often key performance indicators (KPIs) are decided upon. These might include a KPI to increase a particular market spend by a certain percentage; or to reduce the environmental impact of tourism in a particular way – such as reducing litter. An obvious benefit of the strategic approach is the long-term perspective of development that it brings. Effectively day-to-day actions and decisions (the notorious short-term perspective of tourism) can be placed within the context of a longer-term vision.

The strength of such an approach is that it demands a 'whole of destination' outlook. This means that every element of the destination – including the host community – is considered, and in so doing it can act as a 'circuit breaker' to jolt groups into action. It also ensures that the important linkages between the various elements in the destination are considered, and particular sectors (such as accommodation) are not given special treatment and do not develop out of step with visitor attractions or transportation. Visioning is the newest development of strategic planning and adopts a more flexible approach than previous strategic planning approaches, but at the same time it crafts and promotes a clarity of vision for the destination which is then communicated across all stakeholders.

The Gold Coast visioning process (GCV)

The Gold Coast visioning exercise (GCV) was essentially concerned to map out the future for the Gold Coast as a tourism destination, but also took into account the growing residential population of the area. The Gold Coast/Brisbane corridor is the fastest growing part of Australia in terms of population, partly as a result of the phenomenon known as 'sea change' where retiring 'baby boomers' (the generation born in the years immediately following the Second World War) move to coastal areas with high amenity values.

The objectives of the GCV were:

- to provide a systematic and comprehensive overview of the current status of Gold Coast tourism
- to develop scenarios for future global, national and local trends and assess their impact upon the Gold Coast
- to combine these scenarios with sustainable tourism principles to deliver a shared vision for the future of the Gold Coast
- to utilize this shared vision to generate a set of core values for the Gold Coast that could be used to assess future developments
- to arrive at a consensus on preferred tourism development options consistent with the vision.

Effectively this represents a shift from a 'destination marketing' to a 'destination management' approach, bringing together all the elements involved in tourism.

The approach of the GCV is shown in Figure 31.2. The elements of the approach were:

- 'scoping studies' to discern the key issues, including impacts, sustainability, and the attitudes of residents

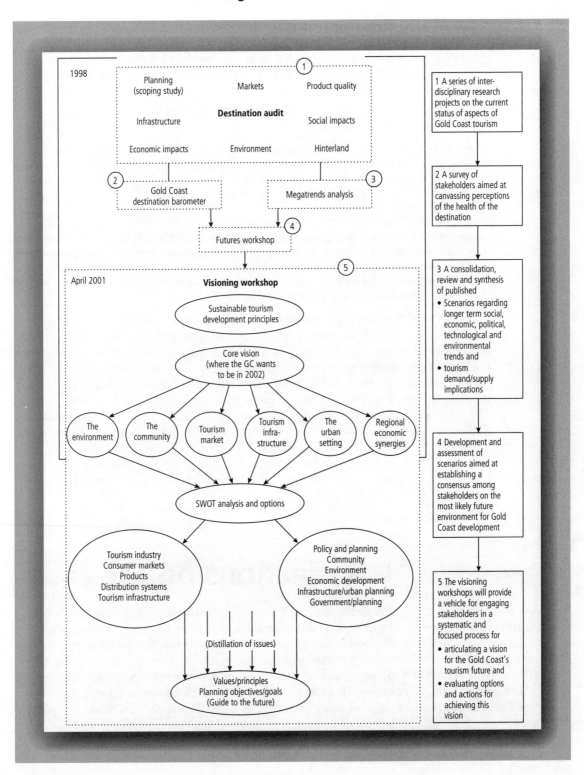

Figure 31.2 The Gold Coast visioning process
Source: Faulkner, 2003

- an audit to elicit the characteristics of tourism on the Gold Coast.
- a survey of tourism industry stakeholders on the status of Gold Coast tourism
- futures and visioning workshops held on the Gold Coast to synthesize the findings of the surveys, work out their implications, and reach a consensus.

To summarize the outcomes of the approach, the Gold Coast has published its preferred future (Faulkner, 2002: iii):

> The Gold Coast will become one of the great leisure and lifestyle destinations of the world. The region will be renowned for sustainable management of its natural and built environment, its sense of self-confidence, the vibrancy and depth of its service economy, the continuing well being of its community, and the unique sense of place of a thriving and dynamic resort.
>
> The destination will be safe, clean, well serviced and uniquely Gold Coast in style. The region will have leading-edge organizational, management and marketing structures that will be underpinned by new partnerships between business, community and government. It will have developed a brand and market awareness which positions the Gold Coast as a market leader in targeted domestic and international markets. The Gold Coast will set the pace as the lifestyle and leisure capital of the 'Pacific Rim'.

The GCV has delivered its promise. The Gold Coast has been prompted into thinking about its future direction as a destination and is acutely aware of the dangers of drifting into decline. The GCV has articulated a set of core tourism values and principles that now underpin the preferred future for the destination in the medium to long term. It has jolted the Gold Coast out of an *ad hoc* and uncoordinated approach to tourism into a more professional and systematic approach. The GCV has also prompted a rethink of the administration of tourism on the Gold Coast, with a new tourism unit set up within the Gold Coast City Council and a change in leadership of the Gold Coast Tourism Bureau. Whilst the GCV may not be entirely responsible for these changes, the destination is now in a position to utilise tourism research and strategy more effectively and has a shared vision for its future.

Reflections on the case

There is no doubt that a number of destinations across the globe are suffering from the same syndrome as the Gold Coast. Yet destinations at the stagnation stage of the life cycle are not a fashionable part of tourism; industry leaders tend to focus on growth and expansion, brushing more problematic issues under the carpet. Yet for destinations reaching the latter stages of the life cycle, there are recognized solutions to preventing decline – solutions that are a combination of business strategy, public sector leadership, marketing and planning. In the case of the Gold Coast, a highly innovative visioning process has prompted a rethink of tourism in Australia's premier resort area.

Discussion points/assignments

1 Compare Queensland's Gold Coast with a Mediterranean mass-market destination which is also in the stagnation stage of the life cycle, and discuss how a visioning exercise could reverse the drift into decline.

2 Compare the Gold Coast with Florida in terms of climate, natural and man-made attractions, tourism markets and infrastructure.

3 The stagnation stage of the life cycle of a resort is often characterized by the increasing cost of public services and the lowering of the 'quality of life' for many residents. Describe this situation from the viewpoint of (i) older residents living in the community, many of whom are 'incomers' from industrial cities in other parts of the country and (ii) a well-educated middle class couple with young children, who are staying in the resort for their main holiday.

4 Select key performance indicators in order of priority, as part of a strategy for improving a resort on the brink of decline. Give reasons for your choice of indicators.

Acknowledgements

This case is based upon the work of the late Professor Bill Faulkner who championed the Gold Coast visioning process. Figure 31.1 is reproduced from Butler (1980) Figure 31.2 is reproduced from Faulkner (2003) by permission of Channelview Publications.

Key sources

Butler, R. W. (1980) The concept of a tourist area cycle of evolution. *Canadian Geographer*, 24 (1).

Faulkner, W. (2002) *Our Gold Coast: The Preferred Tourism Future.* CRCST, Gold Coast.

Faulkner, W. (2003) Rejuvenating a maturing tourist destination: the case of the Gold Coast, in E. Fredline, C. Jago and C. P. Cooper (eds), *Progressing Tourism Research.* Channel View, Clevedon, pp. 34–86.

Heath, E. and Wall, G. (1992) *Marketing Tourism Destinations.* Wiley, New York.

Ritchie, J. R. B. (1999) Crafting a value-driven vision for a national tourism treasure. *Tourism Management*, 20 (3), 273–282.

3.4
The Americas

Case 32

Tourism in New York City

Introduction

New York is one of the world's great tourist cities, although the attacks of 9/11 have diminished the numbers of visitors. This case examines the functioning of tourism in New York. On completion of this case you will:

1 Recognize the scale of the impact of 9/11 on New York's tourism.
2 Understand the economic contribution of tourism to the city.
3 Be aware of New York's advantageous location.
4 Appreciate the range of premier attractions in the city.
5 Recognize the range of tourist facilities and the scale of organization of tourism in New York.

Key issues

There are three key issues in this case:

1 New York is one of the world's top tourist cities. The true scale and economic contribution of tourism to New York was only fully realized when the attacks of 9/11 significantly reduced the volume and value of tourism to the city.
2 New York has a large range of premier attractions located in a relatively small area, making it the ideal tourist city.
3 The support facilities, particularly transportation and accommodation, and the organization of tourism in New York are impressive and testify to the importance of tourism in the city.

New York

The terrorist attacks of 9/11 have highlighted the importance of New York City (NYC) as one of the world's top ten tourist destinations. Tourism is of major significance to the city's economy, generating almost 25 billion dollars and supporting 282 000 jobs. Although it is not the national capital – or even the capital of the state of New York (which is Albany) – New York is the country's primary city in many other respects. It is, for example, the USA's leading financial centre and conference venue, and it is also a major centre for fashion and the arts. Until the 1960s it was the unchallenged 'gateway to America', and the Statue of Liberty in New York Harbor was for most immigrants and visitors their first sight of the New World. Nowadays few visitors arrive by sea, but New York remains the leading point of entry for tourists from Europe. New York plays an international role as the seat of the United Nations Assembly, while events in Wall Street have an even greater impact on the world economy.

New York stands on one of the world's finest harbours, created by the confluence of the Hudson and East Rivers, which also divide the city into a number of peninsulas and islands, linked by bridges, tunnels and ferries (see Figure 32.1). New York City, as distinct from the rest of the metropolitan area in New Jersey and New York State, has an area of almost 800 square kilometres and a population of 8 million. It consists of five boroughs, namely:

- Manhattan, which is one of the most densely populated and ethnically mixed areas in the world. High land costs have resulted in the distinctive landscape of skyscrapers, particularly in the 'midtown' commercial area south of Central Park. Although Manhattan accounts for only 7 per cent of New York's land area, it is the main focus of tourist activity.
- Brooklyn and Queens contain some well-defined ethnic neighbourhoods.
- The Bronx is mainly known for urban decay, but also contains Yankee Stadium – 'the home of baseball' – and the New York Botanical Gardens.
- Staten Island is a relatively quiet residential area.

New York's appeal is its cultural diversity and dynamism as 'the city that never sleeps'. The downside is the excessive crowding and hustle in a city that has fewer green open spaces than London or Paris. Summers are notoriously hot and humid, with episodes of high air pollution, while winters are cold and Central Park is often blanketed in snow. More than most cities, New York has suffered from a negative image of urban decay, sleaze and violent crime. In fact it is by no means the most dangerous city in the USA, and a policy of zero tolerance by the civic authorities has greatly reduced the incidence of crime on the subway and in the streets, making most of New York safe for tourists.

Attractions

The fact that New York has so many attractions within a tightly packed area means that there are 'multipass' admission offers – such as the Culture Pass and the City

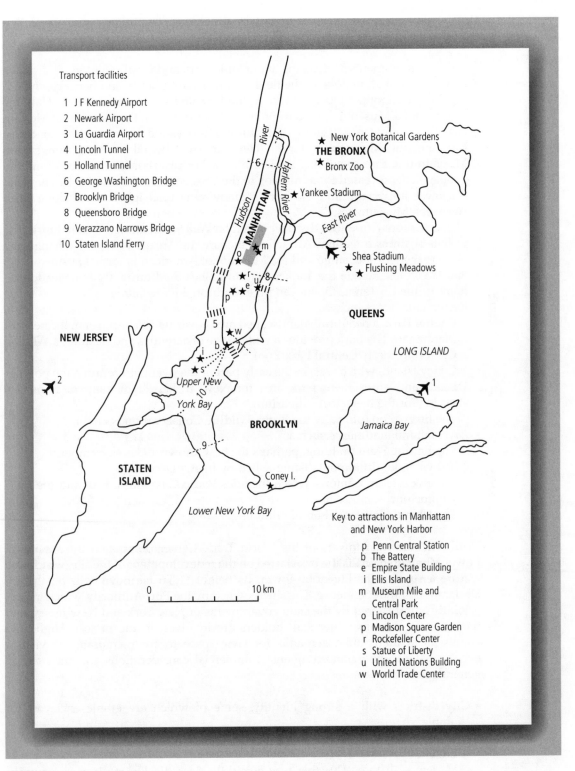

Transport facilities

1 J F Kennedy Airport
2 Newark Airport
3 La Guardia Airport
4 Lincoln Tunnel
5 Holland Tunnel
6 George Washington Bridge
7 Brooklyn Bridge
8 Queensboro Bridge
9 Verazzano Narrows Bridge
10 Staten Island Ferry

★ New York Botanical Gardens
THE BRONX
★ Bronx Zoo
★ Yankee Stadium

Hudson River
Harlem River
East River

MANHATTAN

★ Shea Stadium
★ Flushing Meadows

QUEENS

NEW JERSEY

LONG ISLAND

Upper New York Bay

BROOKLYN

Jamaica Bay

STATEN ISLAND

★ Coney I.

Lower New York Bay

0 ——————— 10 km

Key to attractions in Manhattan and New York Harbor

p Penn Central Station
b The Battery
e Empire State Building
i Ellis Island
m Museum Mile and Central Park
o Lincoln Center
p Madison Square Garden
r Rockefeller Center
s Statue of Liberty
u United Nations Building
w World Trade Center

Figure 32.1 New York City

Pass – allowing multiple visits to certain attractions. The following is a selection from the variety New York can offer the tourist:

- Historic monuments such as the Statue of Liberty and Castle Clinton.
- Major cultural attractions in the fields of music, art, science and heritage, including the Metropolitan Opera House in the Lincoln Center and Carnegie Hall, the Guggenheim Museum, the Metropolitan Museum of Art, the Museum of Modern Art, the American Museum of Natural History, the Intrepid Sea–Air–Space Museum, the Museum of Jewish Heritage and the Ellis Island Immigration Museum (the former holding station in New York Harbor where over 12 million people were processed for admission to the USA between 1890 and 1954). Some of the most important of New York's many museums are located along Fifth Avenue's 'Museum Mile'.
- The 'downtown' financial district centred on Wall Street attracts leisure tourists as well as business travellers. Attractions include the American Stock Exchange, the New York Stock Exchange and the Museum of American Financial History.
- Sports venues include the Yankee Stadium, Shea Stadium, Flushing Meadows – home of the US Tennis Open – and the Madison Square Garden.
- Recreational areas include:
  ○ Central Park, a beautifully landscaped area covering 340 hectares in the heart of Manhattan. The park provides a wide range of activities and includes a Wildlife Center (formerly Central Park Zoo).
  ○ Coney Island, which was, in the early part of the twentieth century, the popular beach and amusement park area for New Yorkers. Nowadays it is mainly visited for the New York Aquarium.
  ○ The Bronx Zoo (officially the Bronx Wildlife Conservation Society).
- Architectural landmarks such as:
  ○ The Empire State Building, perhaps the best-known 1930s skyscraper.
  ○ The Chrysler Building – distinguished by its Art Deco spire.
  ○ The Rockefeller Center – which includes Radio City Music Hall and the NBC Studio Tour.
  ○ The United Nations Assembly Building.

Until 9/11 the twin towers of the World Trade Center dominated the skyline of Lower Manhattan. In 2004 work started on the redevelopment of the site, which will feature a spectacular Freedom Tower, its height (1776 feet) symbolizing the US Declaration of Independence. The site is owned by the Port Authority, which in turn is jointly administered by the state governments of New York and New Jersey, and the interests of many other stakeholders are involved in the project. High land values mean that public demands for civic space to commemorate the victims of 9/11 have to be balanced against commercial considerations and the need to generate tax revenues.

- City districts with a strong identity, some of which are ethnic enclaves, for example:
  ○ Chinatown
  ○ Little Italy
  ○ Harlem – in the 1920s this was a middle class Black American community, famous for its contribution to the development of jazz; after a long period of decline it is now undergoing regeneration

- Spanish Harlem – the *barrio* occupied by Puerto Ricans and other Spanish-speaking immigrants
- Greenwich Village and Soho, which are historic neighbourhoods, defined by their associations with artists, writers and craft industries
- the theatre district, located around Times Square, between 42nd and 50th Streets and the midtown section of Broadway, and which boasted no less than 38 theatres in 2001
- South Street Seaport – a section of New York's waterfront that has undergone extensive restoration, featuring historic ships, a maritime museum, shops and restaurants.

- Shopping attractions: shopping weekends to New York's Fifth Avenue stores such as Macy's, Bloomingdales, Saks Fifth Avenue and Tiffany's, are becoming popular with the European market, encouraged by competitive air fares.
- Dining – with around 18 000 restaurants, New York offers cuisine from all over the world, and there are also a large number of themed restaurants.
- A range of event attractions, the best known being the St Patrick's Day parades.

Transport

The main international air gateways to New York are:

- La Guardia (LGA) 13 kilometres to the east of midtown Manhattan, used mainly for domestic flights but with some services to Canada and Mexico.
- John F Kennedy (JFK) 20 kilometres south-east of midtown Manhattan.
- Newark International (EWR) 26 kilometres to the south-west in New Jersey.

Domestic and charter carriers also use:

- MacArthur Airport
- Stewart International Airport (only international for livestock!)
- Teterboro Airport
- Westchester County Airport.

The Metropolitan Transportation Authority (MTA) oversees the extensive transport network within the city. Bus companies such as Gray Line and New York Apple Tours provide 'hop-on, hop-off' sightseeing circuits, and companies such as Circle Line or New York Waterway offer sightseeing river cruises. Public transport includes rapid transit overland services as well as the underground railway system – the famous subway. The Staten Island Ferry is a favourite with visitors, with its views of the Statue of Liberty and the Manhattan skyline. The city has a number of major transport terminals such as Penn Central Station and the Port Authority bus station. Visitors can purchase passes that allow multiple rides on the public transport systems, although many opt to use the yellow taxi cabs. New York has a number of companies offering tailor-made walking tours and personal greeters can be organized to show visitors around the city.

Accommodation

In 2001, New York City had a hotel capacity of some 66 500 rooms, mainly concentrated in Manhattan. Hotels range from budget to luxury in price, from boutique (small upmarket hotels of character) to themed hotels (on a particular period, for example), and from suites to self-catering apartments. Accommodation is at a premium, particularly in Manhattan, where occupancy rates generally exceed 80 per cent and hotel tariffs are higher than average for the USA. However, the terrorist attacks of 9/11 impacted upon the accommodation sector in the last quarter of 2001 and occupancy rates fell to around 70 per cent.

Organization

The main tourist organization for New York City is NYC & Company (formed in 1999 and formerly the New York Convention and Visitors Bureau). This is the city's official marketing agency and has been in existence since 1935 in various forms. It is a private, non-profit-making organization with a large membership of 1400 tourism businesses. It sees the business and convention market as vital to the city's economy. The New York State government has also played an important role, with its 'I love New York' campaign of the 1980s. This was remarkably successful in turning around NYC's negative image and generating a greater volume of visitors. The City has also been a pioneer in facilitating the use of locations for film and TV productions, guaranteeing worldwide recognition.

Demand

The events of 9/11 only momentarily decreased the numbers of visitors to New York. Out of the estimated 36.2 million visitors in 2000, almost 20 per cent were international and over half were day visitors. New York is the number one destination for foreign visitors to the USA, ahead of Los Angeles, Miami and Orlando. In fact New York City receives over 20 per cent of the USA's international visitors. In terms of staying tourists, the UK is the main contributor (over 15 per cent), followed by Canada (13 per cent), Germany, Japan, France and Italy. Of course much of this is VFR travel, given the very diverse ethnic mix of New York.

Reflections on the case

New York is one of the world's top tourist cities and this is reflected in the scope of this case. Simply scanning the attractions, the accommodation, transport links and scale of demand to New York demonstrates this. However, it also demonstrates how vulnerable tourism destinations are to terrorist attacks, as witnessed by 9/11, and the need for destinations to have in place crisis and risk management plans to cope with future events.

Discussion points/assignments

1 Debate the proposals for the redevelopment of the World Trade Center site and assign key roles representing the various stakeholders to members of the class.
2 Explain the growth in popularity of New York as a short-break destination for tourists from Britain and other European countries since the 1980s.
3 You have been asked by the editor of your college magazine to write a report on two of New York's visitor attractions. Your report should include information on access, the nature of the product, the target market, product interpretation and visitor management, on-site catering and merchandising (the sale of materials to promote the attraction).
4 Evaluate the strengths and weaknesses of New York as a venue for a major international sporting event such as the 2012 Olympic Games.
5 Discuss the influence of two of the following – films, TV, theatrical productions, popular literature and music – in raising awareness of New York as a destination, using specific city locations as examples.

Website
www.nycvisit.com

Case 33

Nunavut: the involvement of indigenous communities in tourism in the Canadian Arctic

Introduction

This case examines the issues surrounding the involvement of indigenous communities in the Canadian Arctic. On completion of the case you will:

1 Be aware of the geographical and cultural features of Nunavut.
2 Recognize that technology has made Nunavut more accessible for tourism than in the past.
3 Understand how the Inuit communities can benefit from tourism.
4 Recognize the tourism resource base of Nunavut and the constraints that this places upon development.
5 Understand how tourism can act as a medium for the Inuit to engage with the wider world.

Key issues

There are five key issues in this case:

1 Nunavut is a newly designated Canadian territory in the Arctic. Its role in the history of exploration, and the heritage and culture of the Inuit make it attractive to visitors.
2 Nunavut has benefited from improvements in transport technology and cold weather clothing and equipment, enabling the opening up of vast territories to visitors in a way that was not possible in the 1950s.
3 Tourism brings with it a range of economic and social benefits for the Inuit people, providing access to the wider world and yet sustaining their culture.
4 Tourism development can utilise Nunavut's natural and cultural resource base but the inhospitable climate and the remoteness of most of the territory also place constraints on the level and type of tourist development.
5 There are a variety of initiatives in Nunavut that have allowed the Inuit communities to engage in tourism.

Nunavut

In 1999 the Canadian government created a new territory – Nunavut – out of the Northwest Territories and settled land claims to some 350 000 square kilometres with the indigenous population. These are the Inuit – 'the people', but better known to the outside world as Eskimos (the name given to them centuries ago by the Cree Indians, meaning 'eaters of raw meat').

Nunavut, which means 'our land' in the Inuktitut language, is a vast and challenging wilderness that includes most of Canada's Arctic archipelago, and the tundra region known as the 'Barren Lands' lying between Hudson Bay and the Arctic Ocean. It covers an area of 1.9 million square kilometres – as large as Alaska and California combined – and yet contains only 26 000 inhabitants, widely dispersed in 28 isolated communities (see Figure 33.1). The Inuit make up 85 per cent of the population, the rest being mainly incomers, such as professional and technical workers, from southern Canada. As the majority, the Inuit will gain political control of the territory and its potential wealth in mineral resources. Tourism also offers prospects for development, and is a sector in which Inuit guides and *outfitters*, with their unrivalled knowledge of the country and skills in improvisation, are already playing an important role. Inuit communities are involved in the management of the national parks that have been designated for the territory.

As we saw in the cases of Lapland and Svalbard, the Arctic regions are nowadays perceived as unspoiled wilderness areas, and visits there are part of the growing ecotourism movement. This contrasts with the earlier view of the Arctic as a 'white hel', a grim test of endurance for expeditions seeking the North West Passage to Asia or a route to the North Pole. Explorers such as Peary and Amundsen, who were prepared to learn survival skills from the Inuit and adapt to the environment, were invariably more successful than those who carried their cultural baggage around with them, like the ill-fated Franklin expedition. Tourists can now retrace these

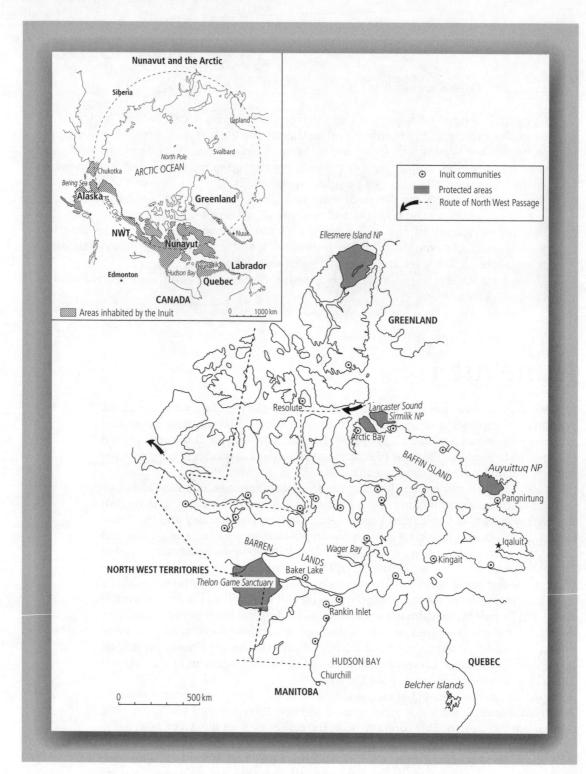

Figure 33.1 Nunavut

journeys in comfort and in a matter of a few days rather than the months or years it took the explorers, thanks to:

- the accessibility brought about by aviation, especially Twin Otter charter aircraft that are capable of landing on either ice or gravel airstrips
- advances in cold weather technology applied to clothing, equipment and shelter
- the ending of the Cold War, which has opened up areas of the Arctic formerly closed by Russia or the Western powers for strategic reasons – for example, it is now possible for tourists to cruise through the North West Passage from the Atlantic as far as Provediniya on the Russian side of the Bering Strait in a single summer season.

Tourism should also help to revive the culture of the Inuit as well as their economic well-being. In the 1950s their age-old way of life was still based on the hunting of caribou and sea mammals for subsistence, although they traded Arctic fox furs with the Hudson Bay Company in exchange for guns, tobacco and tea. Changes in fashion and the subsequent collapse in fur prices resulted in the Inuit becoming much more dependent on the social welfare programmes introduced by the Canadian government. Permanent settlements of identikit wooden buildings replaced the skin tents used in summer and the winter igloos. Dog teams have been largely replaced by skidoos (snowmobiles) that in the words of one young *Inuk* are 'fast, don't eat meat, and don't stink' (quoted by Davis, 1998). Nevertheless, the traditional image persists in the outside world.

While the material improvements have made life less hazardous for the Inuit, they have suffered from a high degree of social dislocation due to the rapidity of change from a nomadic Stone Age culture with a communal ethos, to one dominated by Western technology and value systems. The resulting social problems include a great deal of alcohol and drug abuse, and a suicide rate six times the Canadian average. A low level of educational attainment leaves Inuit communities vulnerable to manipulation by outside commercial interests. The birth rate is much higher than in southern Canada, posing a demographic 'time bomb' as more young people come on to the labour market with unrealistic expectations of what the new territory can provide. All this has implications for Nunavut's economic development, including its fledgling tourism industry.

Tourism development

Nunavut's rigorous climate, vast distances and forbidding terrain discourage independent travel. With seas, lakes and rivers frozen for eight months or more, and with no roads outside the main settlements, most tourist transport is by air. Tourism development faces the following problems:

- **High development costs** Building hotels on permafrost is expensive, as special provision has to be made for utilities and waste disposal. Businesses are also 60 per cent more expensive to operate than in southern Canada, due primarily to high transport costs. Since Nunavut has no agriculture or manufacturing industry, almost everything has to be brought in by supply ship during the brief Arctic summer, or airlifted at even greater expense.

- **Limited accommodation** In 2001 there were only about 1400 bed spaces in the entire territory, mainly in lodge-style accommodation. Even the capital, Iqaluit had insufficient hotel capacity to house guests at the inauguration ceremonies for the new territory.
- **Limited air transport** Although several regional airlines operate scheduled services between the main communities in Nunavut and cities in southern Canada, interconnections between communities often involve a flight back to Iqaluit. This makes travel time-consuming and expensive. Airport delays are also frequent due to unpredictable weather throughout the year.
- **Seasonality** Despite attempts to promote snow-based activities such as sledging, snowmobiling and cross-country skiing during the late winter and early spring, most tourism takes place during the very short summer season.
- **Cultural differences** The environmental sensibilities of Western tourists, particularly animal lovers, are at odds with the attitudes of Inuit communities with their hunting traditions. In a society where nothing is wasted, what appear to be unsightly piles of garbage contain butchered carcasses and machine parts. The Inuit see hunting as an escape route from welfare dependency and a renewal of their close relationship with the land. This is generally accepted by the Canadian government, which has allocated hunting quotas to Inuit communities. What is more controversial is the fact that polar bear hunting tags are then sold to wealthy American tourists seeking trophies.

We can summarize Nunavut's resource base for tourism as:

- A vast wilderness of tundra and glacial mountains, threaded by pristine lakes, rivers and fjords.
- The wildlife of the tundra and the marine life – whales, narwal and walrus – of the Arctic seas.
- The traditional culture of the Inuit, perfectly adapted to one of the world's harshest environments.
- The heritage of polar exploration, particularly the quest for the North West Passage and the race for the North Pole.

Baffin Island

Baffin Island offers the largest share of Nunavut's attractions and amenities, including the territory's capital – Iqaluit. The town is set to grow as a regional hub for air services, with connecting flights to Nuuk and Kangerlussuaq (Sondre Stromfjord) in Greenland. Specialist *outfitters* based in Iqaluit and other communities, such as Pangnirtung and Arctic Bay, provide transport and equipment to access the following tourism resources:

- The spectacular scenery of the eastern part of Baffin Island, with its serrated mountains, extensive glaciers, and a rugged coastline deeply indented by fjords. This culminates in the Auyuittuq National Park, which attracts growing numbers of adventure-seeking tourists.
- Other opportunities for adventure tourism include fishing for Arctic char in the island's lakes and rivers, and sea kayaking (the kayak was an Inuit invention).

Wildlife tours focus on the coastal waters of Lancaster Sound, the summer habitat of vast numbers of migratory birds and whales.

- Inuit communities, notably Kingait (Cape Dorset) and Pangnirtung, are centres for handicrafts such as soapstone carving and print-making using local materials and traditional skills. These are marketed throughout Canada by a native-run cooperative, thus benefiting the local economy. The designs are popular with tourists, because they are inspired by Arctic wildlife and Inuit nostalgia for the past.

The Barren Lands

The Barren Lands, accessed from communities such as Rankin Inlet and Baker Lake, offer a different type of tourism experience. Here the scenery is low key compared to eastern Baffin Island, but the effects of past glaciation are evident in a tundra landscape seamed with gravel-strewn eskers and pitted with countless lakes. Although the autumn migration of vast caribou herds is rarely seen nowadays, wildlife resources are abundant in the Thelon Game Sanctuary and around Wager Bay, where the Sila Lodge provides facilities for ecotourism. The many rivers attract canoeists, but with a season restricted to a few weeks of unpredictable weather, the risks are higher than in southern Canada.

The Ellesmere Island National Park

The Ellesmere Island National Park, situated in the northernmost part of Canada, only 800 kilometres from the North Pole, represents the extremely cold and dry climate conditions and glacial terrain characteristic of the High Arctic. Here tourists number less than a hundred annually, compared to the thousands visiting Svalbard. This is mainly because access is limited to expensive charter flights from the airbase at Resolute, the most northerly community on the scheduled air network, which lies 1000 kilometres to the south. Even a limited number of visitors may make a severe impact on the fragile plant cover, which is extremely slow to regenerate, and on the animal life – including musk oxen and Arctic hare – that show little fear of humans in this remote location.

Nunavut and the wider world

Nunavut is forging links through sport and cultural events with the peoples of other Arctic lands, such as the Sami of Lapland. One notable example is Inuit participation in the Riddu-Riddu summer music festival, held at Mandalen in northern Norway. Nunavut is now more closely associated with other Inuit communities living in the Northwest Territories, Nunavik (northern Quebec) and Labrador, and outside Canada – in Greenland, Alaska and Chukotka in north-eastern Siberia.

The Inuit language and traditions are declining in some areas, and all these communities face similar problems, namely:

- a high birth rate
- economic dependence on a few primary products
- the effect of global warming in reducing the ice cover of the Arctic Ocean and consequently the habitat for the polar bear and Arctic sea mammals
- the impact of pollutants, carried by winds and ocean currents from industrialized regions to the south, on Arctic ecosystems; this has grave consequences for the traditional food supplies and health of the Inuit people.

Nunavut is opposed to the ban on commercial seal hunting, imposed by the Canadian government in 1989, seeing a market for sealskin products in the Far East. Its leaders are nevertheless showing the way forward in environmental campaigns to persuade the Canadian government to implement the Stockholm Convention on the control of industrial chemicals and pesticides, and the Kyoto Protocol on the control of greenhouse gases.

Reflections on the case

Although previously difficult to access, and despite the hostile Arctic environment, the newly created Canadian territory of Nunavut is developing a fledgling tourism industry. The industry is benefiting Inuit communities in the territory, not only in terms of their economy and culture, but also as a medium of wider engagement with the world. Nunavut is a good example of community involvement in tourism.

Discussion points/assignments

1 Describe particular initiatives that have encouraged Inuit involvement with the tourism sector.
2 Explain why Westerners have for long been fascinated by the Inuit way of life. Suggest a code of conduct for present day tourists visiting Inuit communities.
3 Discuss the future prospects for tourism in Nunavut stemming from developments in transport, communications (including information technology), building technology, and education.
4 Put together a tour itinerary for a group of wealthy Americans who propose to retrace the route taken by Sir John Franklin and other explorers in search of the North West Passage.
5 Design a 'mini-guide' giving advice and information for a group of college students planning an expedition using canoes or kayaks on the lakes and rivers of the Barren Lands.

Key sources

Anderson, M. J. (1991) Problems with tourism development in Canada's Eastern Arctic. *Tourism Management*, 12 (3), 209–220.

Butler, R. and Hinch, T. (1996) *Tourism and Indigenous Peoples*. International Thomson Business Press, London.

Davis, W. (1998) The Arctic. *Condé Nast Traveler*, January, 110–121, 197–200.

Hall, C. M. and Johnston, M. (1995) *Polar Tourism*. Wiley, Chichester.

Mason, P. (1994) A visitor code for the Arctic. *Tourism Management*, 15 (2), 93–97.

Mason, P. (1997) Tourism codes of conduct in the Arctic and sub-Arctic region. *Journal of Sustainable Tourism*, 5 (2), 151–165.

Mason, P., Johnston, M. and Twynam, D. (2000) The World Wide Fund for Nature Arctic Tourism Project. *Journal of Sustainable Tourism*, 8 (4), 305–323.

Notzke, C. (1999) Indigenous tourism development in the Arctic. *Annals of Tourism Research*, 26 (1), 55–76.

Selwood, J. and Heidenreich, S. (2000) Tourism in Nunavut: problems and potential, in M. Robinson *et al.* (eds), *Reflections on International Tourism Management, Marketing and the Political Economy of Travel and Tourism*. Sheffield Hallam University, pp. 415–426.

Twynam, G. D. and Johnston, M. E. (2002) The use of sustainable tourism practices. *Annals of Tourism Research*, 29 (4), 1165–1168.

Wight, P. A. and McVetty, D. (2000) Tourism planning in the Arctic: Banks Island. *Tourism Recreation Research*, 25 (2), 15–26.

Website

www.nunanet.com/nunatour

Case 34
Tourism in Hawaii

Introduction

Hawaii is one of the iconic tourism destinations in the world with an image based on Hollywood films and TV programmes. This case examines tourism in Hawaii and the consequent impacts. On completion of this case you will:

1 Appreciate that Hawaii is a chain of volcanic islands in the Pacific Ocean.
2 Be aware of the historical development of tourism on Hawaii.
3 Recognize the scale of Hawaii's attractions and support facilities for tourism.
4 Understand the key dimensions of the market for tourism in Hawaii.
5 Be aware of some of the impacts of tourism on the islands.

Key issues

There are five issues in this case:

1 Hawaii is widely recognized as an iconic tourism destination with an image based upon Hollywood portrayals of idyllic Pacific islanders, whereas in fact the islands are highly developed for tourism and large-scale commercial agriculture.
2 Hawaii has a long history of tourism development and in the twenty-first century the environmental and cultural impacts of tourism are being questioned and this is influencing future developments.
3 Hawaii's market is complex and made up of both domestic and international visitors.
4 Hawaii's tourist attractions are based upon its natural and cultural resources.
5 Tourism in Hawaii has a number of negative impacts that are the subject of planning and management.

Hawaii

Many millions of people the world over, who have never visited the islands, have a clear perception of Hawaii. The image of a 'tropical South Pacific paradise', exotic but safe, was largely created by the American media – particularly the Hollywood film industry in the 1930s. This image has spawned a multi-billion dollar industry and attracted over 6 million visitors a year to the islands at the beginning of the twenty-first century. Hawaii's location in the mid-Pacific sets it apart as a destination from the rest of the United States, but its popularity is mainly due to the American connection.

Hawaii consists of a chain of volcanic islands that originated as a geological *hot spot* in the ocean floor of the North Pacific – in fact the state takes its name from the largest of these islands. Hawaii is geographically isolated – 4000 kilometres from the North American mainland but an even greater distance from Asia and the rest of Polynesia. The islands were first settled by Polynesians from Tahiti and the Marquesas Islands between 500 and 800 AD. However, it was not until 1795, shortly after Captain Cook's arrival, that the various tribes were united by Kamehameha the Great, founder of the Hawaiian monarchy. In the course of the nineteenth century, Hawaii came increasingly under American influence through the activities of whalers, missionaries and traders, some of whom became plantation owners after acquiring tribal lands. Labour was imported from China, Japan and other countries to work the plantations, eventually resulting in the multi-racial society that now characterizes the islands. These developments had a number of environmental and social impacts:

- Most of the native plants and animals, which had previously been protected by isolation, were displaced by introduced species, and are now found only in remote mountain areas.
- The native Hawaiians became a marginalized minority in their own country, with their traditional culture in danger of disappearing.

Tourism development

Although the first tourist facility on the islands opened as early as 1872, this catered mainly for business travel. Leisure tourism did not really develop until after Hawaii became a territory of the United States in 1898. In 1901 the Moana Hotel opened, the first of many resort hotels along Waikiki Beach, but catering strictly for a monied clientele. In 1903 the Hawaiian Promotion Committee was formed, but in the early part of the twentieth century the islands were expensive to reach, involving a voyage lasting from four to six days, by luxury liner out of San Francisco or Long Beach. It was not until the 1950s that a rapid expansion of tourism took place as a result of:

- Economic prosperity on the US mainland following the Second World War, during which large numbers of American servicemen had been stationed on the islands.

- The introduction of cheaper and more frequent air services, using jet aircraft, which ended the comparative isolation of the islands.
- The use of Hawaii as a location for film and TV productions.
- The achievement of statehood in 1959, which integrated Hawaii more fully into the mainstream of American life.

Tourism stemmed out-migration from the islands and provided an alternative source of employment to a declining agricultural sector based on sugar and pineapple production. By the 1970s, inclusive air tours had brought Hawaii within reach of Americans on modest incomes and the age of mass tourism had arrived. Between 1950 and 1980 the number of visitors grew from 46 000 to 4 million, a rate of increase almost without parallel in any other destination. After reaching a peak in 1990 with almost 7 million arrivals, tourism stagnated during the next decade, largely as a result of the first Gulf War and the Asian currency crisis. Since then the major resorts have repositioned themselves to meet changing demands, and in 2002 arrivals stood at 6.3 million.

Most tourism development has been concentrated on Oahu, the third largest of the islands in area, but the most important in other respects, as it contains 75 per cent of the population, the bulk of the tourist accommodation, and the capital Honolulu. Although the majority of tourists staying in Oahu visit one or more of the 'neighbor islands', such visits tend to be brief. There is little doubt that mass tourism has had an undesirable impact on Oahu, particularly at Waikiki where development has been largely unplanned. The state government has therefore encouraged projects on the other islands, and these are generally of a higher standard. On Maui, for example, most of the development consists of condominiums, with some apartments owned on a time-share basis, catering mainly for wealthy Americans. However, these projects have been criticized for contributing even less to the community than the large high-rise hotels that characterize Waikiki. The Japanese have invested heavily in Hawaii, not just in hotel developments, but in golf courses, travel agencies and real estate.

Although Hawaii is not lacking in cultural and other attractions, the bulk of the demand is for beach tourism, and is generated from the following countries:

- **The United States and Canada**   The United States mainland accounts for two-thirds of all visitors to Hawaii. Thanks to cheap domestic air fares and competitive tour pricing, visitors from cities in the Middle Atlantic and Mid-Western states can reach the islands almost as easily as those from California.
- **Japan**   The Japanese tend to spend much more per capita than the Americans; however, this market has declined since the late 1990s. Young Japanese are particularly attracted to the islands as a honeymoon destination. Honolulu is a major hub on the network of trans-Pacific air services, bringing Tokyo as close to Hawaii as many cities in the USA.
- **Australia and New Zealand**   These are important markets, due to increased accessibility.
- **Western Europe**   The region generates less demand due to the greater distance and higher cost of air travel, with relatively few tourists visiting islands other than Oahu. All travel between the islands and to the mainland is by air, except for cruises based on Honolulu, and there is virtually no public transport on the islands.

Tourism resources

Hawaii's appeal as a tourist destination is due to a combination of factors – a favourable climate, beautiful coastal and mountain scenery, the opportunities for surfing and a wide range of outdoor activities – and not least the Polynesian culture. We will now look at some of these resources in more detail.

Climate

The Hawaiian islands lie in the path of the prevailing north-east trade winds, which strongly influence the climate, moderating the heat and humidity of these tropical latitudes. However, from time to time, the trades are interrupted by *kona* winds blowing from the south or south-west that bring spells of more humid weather and have an important effect on surf levels off the beaches. As the islands are mountainous, there are also striking differences in climate and vegetation between the leeward and windward slopes. Most of the resort developments are on the more sheltered south and west coasts of the islands that enjoy a dry climate with abundant sunshine.

Surfing beaches

Hawaii can claim to be the home of surfing, and offers some of the most powerful waves in the world. These often originate as a result of winter storms in the Aleutian Islands, 4000 kilometres to the north. There is no intervening landmass to diffuse the ocean swells, and no continental shelf to reduce their impact before they reach the beaches. The northern coast of Maui and the better known North Shore of Oahu are the favoured locations for experienced surfers seeking the big waves in the winter months. At Pipeline surfers *ride the tube*, challenging waves shaped into hollow cylinders by a combination of a powerful swell and a shallow reef. Summer is the best time for surfing at Waikiki, where white American settlers adopted the sport from the native Hawaiians and introduced it to California and Australia in the 1920s. Since the Second World War, light fibreglass boards, undergoing constant improvements in design, have replaced the heavy long-boards made from native hardwoods, while the film, music and clothing industries and a professional competition circuit have spawned an international surf culture. A recent development is *power surfing*, using jet skis as tow-in craft to tackle the really big waves – needless to say this is decried by purists.

Hawaiian culture

Islanders of part-native Hawaiian descent form the largest ethnic group on Hawaii, accounting for 40 per cent of the population. There is some resentment of the *haole* (white American) domination of the economy, but race relations have generally been better than in the mainland United States. Islanders from all ethnic groups now take pride in the native Hawaiian heritage, but this has changed considerably since Captain Cook's time. The question of authenticity is a matter for discussion, given the way cultural traditions are presented as part of the tourist image. These include:

- the *lei* or garland of welcome presented to visitors at the airport on arrival, symbolizing *Aloha*, the islanders' tradition of hospitality
- the *luau* or banquet staged in the hotels, featuring a pig baked in an earth oven, recalling the harvest festivals
- Hawaiian music and dance, of which the *hula* is the best known; this originally served a religious purpose, recounting the history and legends of the people through facial expressions, hip movements and hand gestures; however, Hawaiian music has adopted elements from other cultures, such as the ukulele (introduced by Portuguese immigrants), and was largely re-invented by the American entertainment industry in the 1930s.

The marine environment

The seas around the Hawaiian Islands provide opportunities for a range of activities including:

- diving, based on the coral reefs along the leeward coasts of the islands; since the 1980s it has also become possible to explore the underwater world in safety and comfort using submersible craft
- yachting and windsurfing, particularly off Maui
- whale watching, especially off Maui where it is a major business; however, this very popularity may threaten the survival of the humpback whale as a species.

The natural heritage

The US National Park Service protects outstanding examples of the natural heritage of the islands, the best known being the Volcanoes National Park on the 'Big Island' of Hawaii. Hiking tours and ecotourism are developing in the interior of the islands, providing an alternative to the high-consumption tourist lifestyle, based on the beach and the shopping mall, that is typical of the resorts. Although certain features are common to all the islands, such as surfing beaches, waterfalls and volcanic scenery, each of the major islands has a distinct character:

- **Oahu** Aptly known as the 'Gathering Place', Oahu is the most visited of the islands. The features that make Honolulu different from other large American cities are:
  - the world-famous beach at Waikiki, with the landmark of volcanic origin known as Diamond Head
  - the Bishop Museum – one of the world's finest collection of Pacific arts and crafts
  - the Iolani Palace, with its reminders of the Hawaiian monarchy.
  The naval base at Pearl Harbor, of Second World War fame, is situated near Honolulu. Another major attraction is the Polynesian Cultural Centre at Lae, which combines education with entertainment as a living showcase for the folklore of the seven Polynesian nations of the Pacific.

- **Maui** The green 'Valley Isle' contains a number of exclusive resorts such as Kapalua and Kaunapaali – which is now integrated with the former whaling port of Lahaina. Major attractions include the Haleakala Crater, one of the world's largest, and the Seven Pools of Hana.
- **Kauai** The 'Garden Isle' is particularly renowned for its lush scenery, exemplified by:
  - the Fern Grotto at Wailua
  - the Waimea Canyon
  - the beaches of Hanalei – world famous as the location for 'Bali Hai' in the film *South Pacific*.

  Much of the island is only accessible by helicopter, boat or hiking trail. Kauai was badly affected by the *Iniki* hurricane disaster of 1992, which caused the island authorities to revise their tourism policy to favour small locally owned enterprises and native Hawaiian communities.
- **Hawaii** The 'Big Island' offers the greatest contrasts in climate, due to the high volcanic peaks of Mauna Loa and Mauna Kea. Kilauea is one of the world's most active volcanoes, and its frequent eruptions have created a lunar landscape of firepits, craters and lava caves in the south-eastern part of the island, and the characteristic beaches of black and green sand. Elsewhere cattle ranches, coffee plantations and rainforests add variety to the landscape.
- **Molokai, Lanai** and **Niihau** The other inhabited islands have as yet been little influenced by tourism. The main attraction of Molokai – 'the Friendly Isle' – is the rugged coastal scenery of the Kaleapapa National Park, site of a former leper colony. Lanai until recently depended on its pineapple plantations but has now diversified into upmarket tourism, while sparsely populated Niihau has rejected tourism altogether.

The impacts of tourism

Tourism has provided economic benefits to Hawaii, but at a cost to the environment and the island lifestyle. The dominance of the tourism sector is particularly opposed by native Hawaiian activists, who see it as threatening their agricultural lands, sacred sites, water supplies and fishing grounds, as well as trivializing their cultural traditions. Golf courses not only make enormous demands on water resources but are also a major source of pollution, due to the constant applications of fertilizer and weed killer that are needed. The owners of large hotels have been accused of denying locals access to public beaches. Tourism has also been blamed for a rising crime rate, family breakdown and rising land prices that deny local people access to the housing market. Nevertheless, since the 1980s, efforts have been made to introduce conservation measures and curb inappropriate tourism developments. At the same time the larger resorts such as Waikiki have begun to reposition themselves away from high volume, low yield mass tourism, with environmental improvements and investment in the accommodation stock. The biggest long-term threat may not be from the growth of tourism as such, but from population growth, caused by immigration from the mainland of the United States.

Reflections on the case

Despite its image as an idyllic Pacific paradise, Hawaii is the major tourism destination in the Pacific with a large and professional tourism sector. Tourism development has a long history in Hawaii and in the twenty-first century the islands are paying heed to the impacts of tourism and developing sustainable tourism products and repositioning some of the older resorts.

Discussion points/assignments

1 Most people have stereotyped images of foreign countries, peoples and faraway places which are referred to in the tourism industry as 'icons', and these are often portrayed in travel brochures and posters. Identify those features of the culture and landscapes of Hawaii that might qualify as icons. To what extent do these images give a misleading impression to potential visitors and differ from the reality of life for Hawaiians?

2 You have been asked to give a presentation on surfing in Hawaii to your class, taking into account the *demand* for surfing worldwide as well as the *supply* of resources and facilities for the sport.

3 Investigate the part played by feature films, television and popular literature in publicizing Hawaii as a holiday destination, using some of the locations portrayed as examples.

4 Native Hawaiians claim that their traditions have been debased for tourist consumption, while some tourists are disappointed by what they see as commercialization and 'staged authenticity' in the presentation of Hawaiian culture. Discuss whether these views are justified by the evidence.

5 Despite their geographical location in the middle of the world's largest ocean, the Hawaiian Islands are well served by a number of airlines. With reference to the ABC World Airways Guide, compare the frequency of flights from London, Sydney, New York and Tokyo to Honolulu with those to another Pacific island destination such as Tahiti.

Key sources

Bowen, R. L., Cox, L. J. and Fox, M. (1991) The interface between tourism and agriculture. *Journal of Tourism Studies*, 2 (2), 43–54.

Cockerell, N. (1993) Hawaii. *International Tourism Reports*, 4, 50–70.

Farrell, B. H. (1982) *Hawaii: The Legend that Sells*. University of Hawaii Press, Honolulu.

Fujii, E., Im, E. and Mak, J. (1992) Airport expansion, direct flights and consumer choice of travel destinations: the case of Hawaii's Neighbour Islands. *Journal of Travel Research*, 30 (3), 38–43.

Gee, C. Y. and Patoskie, J. D. (1993) Maui and Lanai: a study of luxury resort development. *World Travel and Tourism Review*, 3, 270–275.

Lynch, R. (1997) Tourism in independent Hawaii. *Contours*, 7 (11/12), 24–26.

Mak, J. and Moncur, J. E. T. (1995) Sustainable tourism development: managing Hawaii's 'unique' tourist resource: Hanauma Bay. *Journal of Travel Research*, 33 (4), 51–57.

Sheldon, P. J. and Abenoja, T. (2001) Resident attitudes in a mature destination: the case of Waikiki. *Tourism Management*, 22 (5), 435–443.

Tamirisa, N. T., Loke, M. K., Leung, P. and Tucker, K. A. (1997) Energy and tourism in Hawaii. *Annals of Tourism Research*, 24 (2), 390–401.

Tarlow, P. E. (2000) Creating safe and secure communities in economically challenging times. *Tourism Economics*, 6 (2), 139–149.

Wyllie, R. W. (1998) Not in our backyard: opposition to tourism development in a Hawaiian community. *Tourism Recreation Research*, 23 (1), 55–64.

Wyllie, R. W. (1998) Hama revisited: development and controversy in a Hawaiian tourism community. *Tourism Management*, 19 (2), 171–178.

Websites

http://www.gohawaii.com/

http://www.state.hi.us/dbedt/tourism.html

Case 35

The regeneration of Rio de Janeiro

Introduction

Rio de Janeiro (or Rio as it is popularly known) is one of many world-class resorts that are looking to re-vision themselves for the twenty-first century. This case examines tourism in Rio and the re-visioning process. On completion of the case you will:

1 Understand the reasons for Rio's reputation as one of the world's great tourist cities.
2 Be aware of Rio's trajectory on the destination area life cycle.
3 Recognize the range of attractions and facilities for tourism in Rio.
4 Understand the social and environmental problems that have emerged for this destination in the past twenty-five years.
5 Be aware of Rio's process of re-visioning and the steps taken to reposition the city in the international tourism market.

Key issues

There are four key issues in this case:

1 Rio is one of the world's great tourist cities and has completed virtually all of the stages of the destination area life cycle.
2 Rio's development as the leading resort in Brazil over many years has brought with it a range of social and environmental problems that have threatened the sustainability of the city's growth and its markets for the future.
3 Like many other resorts in the world, Rio has embarked upon an ambitious revisioning plan to reposition itself for the visitors of the twenty-first century.
4 Rio's re-visioning integrates tourism with other economic and social sectors of the city, and to date has been a success.

Rio

Rio de Janeiro is one of the world's great tourist cities for the following reasons:

- It provides the best-known images of Brazil, a country that is widely regarded as exotic, with a 'liberated' lifestyle, and an economy full of promise for the future.
- The spectacular beauty of its setting, between one of the world's finest harbours – Guanabara Bay – and a number of granite peaks, including Sugar Loaf and Corcovado, which is crowned by the famous statue of Christ the Redeemer.
- Some 80 kilometres of fine sandy beaches, the most celebrated being Copacabana and the more fashionable Ipanema. These are ideal for people-watching (but not for bathing due to the heavy Atlantic surf). The beach is a fashion parade, and although beachwear is minimal, 'topless' sunbathing by female visitors is regarded with disapproval. The need for 'Cariocas' to look good is all-important, so not surprisingly cosmetic surgery is a lucrative industry. Some beaches are used by certain social groups, or for a particular activity, such as Copacabana for football and volleyball, Arpoador for surfing.
- The uninhibited dance rhythms and extravagant costume parades of *Carnaval*, one of the greatest shows on Earth, which serves to break down social barriers between rich and poor in a country where millions do not even earn the $80 a month minimum wage.

To complement these resources the city has a good transport infrastructure, including two major airports, and world-class hotels that are concentrated in the Copacabana area.

Yet, despite these resources, in the last quarter of the twentieth century Rio reached the later stages of the tourism area life cycle and began to suffer from a number of problems. These are related to the fall in tourist demand for Rio, the changing nature of that demand and competition from other, newer destinations. In addition, many of the city's problems stem from the fact that not only was Rio replaced by Brasilia as the national capital, and the loss of political influence this entails, but also São Paulo has overtaken Rio as a commercial centre. At the same time the city still acts as a magnet for a massive influx of poor rural immigrants, while the rugged topography makes it difficult to carry out physical planning for growth. Aside from the *favelas* (shanty towns on the hillsides), Rio is divided by the Serra da Carioca mountain range into a northern zone (*zona norte*) and a southern zone (*zona sul*), where most of the tourist attractions are situated.

In response to these problems, Rio embarked upon a major regeneration initiative. This fits in well with the Brazilian government's aims of:

- creating a modern and efficient state
- reducing social and regional inequalities
- modernizing the economy
- enhancing Brazil's competitiveness in world markets.

The development of tourism in Rio

In the nineteenth century Rio not only attracted the Brazilian elite, but also wealthy visitors from Europe and the USA, but it was not until the late 1950s that tourists arrived in large numbers, attracted by the beaches and the climate.

- **Growth of tourism: 1960s and 1970s** Growth in both tourist numbers and facilities was rapid between 1960 and 1975, with international visitors complementing the domestic market. In the early 1970s the Galeão International Airport opened, providing the impetus to attract the major hotel chains.
- **The emergence of problems: 1980s and early 1990s** By the 1980s problems were emerging, based on the city's lack of planning and uncoordinated approach to tourism. Between 1985 and 1993 international arrivals declined substantially from 621 000 to 378 000, and average hotel occupancies fell to 50 per cent. Visitors were increasingly concerned about security and not getting value for money. By this stage of Rio's tourism development the specific problems included:
  ○ lack of integration between the public and private sectors
  ○ lack of professionalism in the tourism industry
  ○ lack of tourist information at key attractions
  ○ a scarcity of employees speaking English or a language other than Portuguese
  ○ minimal diversification of the product away from beach tourism
  ○ an expanding population competing with tourists for services and infrastructure
  ○ beach pollution
  ○ price inflation due to the unstable Brazilian currency
  ○ crime against tourists.
- **The regeneration strategy: 1990s** It was at this time that the authorities decided that a concerted regeneration strategy was needed, both for the city itself and also for tourism.

The regeneration of Rio

In 1993 the Mayor of Rio, with the support of the private sector, drew up the city's first strategic plan. This was followed in 1997 by a strategic plan specifically for tourism in cooperation with Embratur, the national tourism organization. The plan is designed to run until 2006 with rolling reviews of the plan's five major programmes. The main objectives of the plan are to:

- increase receipts from tourism
- maintain Rio's leading competitive position in domestic tourism
- make Rio competitive in the international market
- reposition the image of Rio.

We can summarize the five programmes and their key objectives as follows:

- **Programme 1   New product development to attract new and existing markets**
  - Diversification of entertainment facilities:
  - Development of new products, such as ecotourism. Here Rio is fortunate in having the Tijuca National Park – a surviving example of coastal rainforest within the city limits.
  - Development of products relating to the city's culture and history. Rio is well known for its samba schools and contribution to world music, but it also boasts a rich artistic heritage, dating back to the long colonial period and the reign of Dom Pedro II, who brought stability to Brazil in the nineteenth century.
  - Development of sport tourism. Rio boasts the Maracaná Stadium, one of the world's largest, and Brazil is internationally celebrated for its achievements in football and motor racing.
- **Programme 2   Upgrading of current tourism products to both enhance quality and reposition the resort:**
  - Conservation of existing features such as the famous Sugar Loaf.
  - Improvement of access and signposting to the city's attractions.
  - Conservation of streetscapes and other features to enhance the quality of the visitor experience.
  - Encouragement of private sector involvement in upgrading tourism products.
- **Programme 3   Development of a database for tourism and the enhancement of tourist information in the city:**
  - Development of a statistical database for tourism.
  - Development of tourist information centres.
- **Programme 4   Implementation of a disciplined marketing approach for Rio:**
  - Creation of a new image of a culturally vibrant city – 'Incomparable Rio'– and the promotion of this new image to the travel trade, the media and the public.
  - Development of a public relations campaign targeted at the local population and the media.
- **Programme 5   Development of a skilled and professional workforce for the tourism sector:**
  - Development of a tourism education system in Rio.
  - Establishment of a quality management system for tourism in Rio.

Discussion

The regeneration strategy for Rio is a good example of a disciplined response to a problem in a tourist destination. The strategy has had a range of positive outcomes. For example:

- The city is now in a better position to bid for the 2012 Olympic Games.
- International visitors have reached over 2 million, whilst domestic visitors are estimated at 5 million arrivals a year.
- The various stakeholders at the destination are working together with a more unified purpose. Rio's coordinating agencies – the Rio Convention Bureau and the city's tourism agency, Riotur – have taken a leading role in the regeneration process.

On the other hand, in 2003 the city authorities rejected a proposal to build a Guggenheim Museum in the port area, despite the proven success of a similar project in Bilbao.

Although much has been done to improve security for tourists (by the creation of a special police force, for example) and to improve the image of the city overall, tourism has so far done little to benefit the more than one million people who live in the 500 or so *favelas*. These shanty towns are only a short distance from the affluent areas they overlook, but lack basic infrastructure and any privacy for their inhabitants, and are places where gang rule generally prevails over the rule of law. Rocinha, the largest of these slums, has been the scene of a private initiative to train local guides who can show visitors the 'hidden side of Rio'. An award-winning film based on another *favela*, called *Cidade de Deus* (City of God), had greater impact, persuading the Brazilian government in 2003 to allocate much needed funding to these deprived areas.

Reflections on the case

Rio is one of the world's great cities, but in the past 25 years has reached the stagnation stage of the destination area life cycle. In order to maintain its position as a leading international resort, Rio has embarked upon an ambitious programme of re-visioning and regeneration which integrates tourism with the city's other economic and social sectors. This is having a number of positive outcomes, although so far tourism has had little effect in narrowing the gulf between rich and poor.

Discussion points/assignments

1 Evaluate the importance of Rio de Janeiro as a venue for sport tourism, bearing in mind the city's bid for the 2012 Olympics.
2 Debate the pros and cons of *favela* tours, from the viewpoint of the tour organizers, local people representing the visited communities, the city authorities, and the tourists themselves. Assign roles to members of the class.
3 Describe the social and environmental problems that threaten Rio's prospects as a sustainable tourist destination. What is being done to address these problems?
4 Investigate the features that make Rio's Carnival one of the world's great event attractions, and assess its economic and social impact on local communities.

Acknowledgement

This study is mainly adapted from Railson Costa de Souza (1998) The Evolution of Rio de Janeiro as a Destination and Its Regeneration Process. Unpublished MSc dissertation, Bournemouth University.

Key source

Santana, G. (2001) *Tourism in South America*. Haworth, New York.

Websites
http://www.embratur.gov.br/
http://www.rioconventionbureau.com.br
http://www.rio.rj.gov.br

Case 36

Ecotourism in the Ecuadorian Amazon

Introduction

The fate of the world's largest rainforest and its native inhabitants is a matter of global concern. This case study focuses on ecotourism in Ecuador's share of the Amazon Basin, as an alternative to less sustainable forms of development. On completion of this case you will:

1 Appreciate the biodiversity of Ecuador's rainforests and their potential for ecotourism.
2 Understand the challenges facing Indian communities in the Amazon and the role of community-based ecotourism as an economic alternative to the petroleum and logging industries.
3 Recognize that community-based tourism accounts for only a small share of Ecuador's tourism market.
4 Be aware of the range of ecotourism projects in the Ecuadorian Amazon and the types of accommodation and transport used by ecotourists.

Key issues

There are five key issues in this case:

1 The need for ecotourists and non-governmental organizations to work together to convince governments of the need to conserve the rainforest resource.
2 The dilemma facing a developing country like Ecuador, which finds it difficult to promote sustainable development in the face of pressing economic problems.
3 The fact that well-managed ecotourism can deliver economic and social benefits to indigenous communities.
4 The many challenges facing indigenous communities in developing self-sufficiency and self-reliance through ecotourism.
5 The need for responsible behaviour on the part of tourists and tour operators visiting such communities.

The scope of ecotourism

Ecotourism is the sector of the international tourism industry that has shown the fastest growth since the mid-1990s. The value of this sector to the economy of a developing country like Ecuador is significant, but difficult to measure with any precision. According to the Travel Industry Association of America, 83 per cent of US tourists are prepared to spend more with environmentally responsible companies (Szuchman, 2001). Tour operators in South America are only too ready to add the eco-label to their products to attract tourists concerned about environmental issues, but in practice few hotels meet recognized eco-certification standards. There is no generally accepted definition of ecotourism, but it is more than just nature-based travel, and most destinations are far from being uninhabited wilderness. Wherever there are local communities, the indigenous people should gain long-term economic benefits from such tourism rather than being excluded, as has too often been the case in the national parks and game reserves of Africa, for example. Ecotourism should accept the resource as it is, with the understanding that this may limit the number of visits over a given period, and promote ethical responsibilities and behaviour in the actions of all those involved.

If we apply ecotourism to Leiper´s model of a tourism system, the tourist-generating area – for example, the UK – has a deficit of wildlife resources and accounts for much of the demand, whereas Ecuador has an abundant supply, including many unique species of plants and animals. In the generating area the ecotourist will be motivated by attitudes of 'responsible consumption' towards nature-based products and will be educated to an above-average level. Many individual tourists will be far from wealthy (although they may be perceived as such by the host community), and for them it is likely to be the 'holiday of a lifetime', involving months of preparation – the *anticipation phase* of the trip – as well as *recollection* of the experience to other potential tourists long after their return to their country of origin. In the destination area, nature will be the main attraction, while the ancillary services (accommodation, catering and guiding) should be well managed and 'environmentally friendly'. Participation in a learning experience is the primary objective of the trip, while shopping, night-time entertainment and recreation facilities are of less concern than is the case for other types of tourism. In the *transit zone*, where the tourists' journeys take place, the ecotourist would ideally seek locally owned transport operators and non-polluting modes of transport. This might be an option for internal travel, from, say, the tourist's base on arrival in the destination country to the national park or other protected areas that are to be visited. However, ecotourism destinations like the Ecuadorian Amazon are almost by definition remote places, and reaching them from generating areas such as Britain requires a journey halfway across the world by air. Since aircraft emissions are a prime source of pollution and possibly contribute to 'global warming', this is the weakest link in the argument that ecotourism is the 'greenest' form of tourism.

Ecotourism in Ecuador

Some 17 per cent of Ecuador is officially protected with national park or nature reserve status. Although it is one of the smallest countries of South America,

Ecuador boasts a great variety of life zones and scenic attractions in its section of the Andes, including the volcanic peaks of Cotopaxi, Chimborazo and Sangay, all within a short distance of the capital, Quito. The Pacific coastline now features on the international surfing circuit, but has been largely undeveloped for beach tourism. Cultural tourism, based on the Indian and Spanish colonial heritage of the Sierra, Ecuador's Andean region, has been overshadowed by better-known attractions in neighbouring Peru. The fall in oil prices in the mid-1990s and a huge foreign debt contributed to the near-collapse of the economy and the adoption of the US dollar as the nation's currency in place of the *sucre*. This has helped to raise the profile of tourism, and it is now second only to exports of petroleum and bananas as an earner of foreign exchange. Ecotourism, followed by adventure tourism in the form of river running, trekking and horse riding, are the major growth sectors.

Nevertheless, Ecuador lacks an effective programme of tourism promotion involving both the private and public sectors. Although there is a Ministry of Tourism and a national tourist organization (CETUR), government support for the industry has been inconsistent. CETUR is funded by taxation and tourism businesses, but many of these are not officially registered as they form part of the country's large informal economy. The transport infrastructure is inadequate, and moreover the money raised from airport departure taxes is diverted to other projects rather than funding much-needed improvements to terminal facilities at Quito and Guayaquil.

Ecotourists are attracted primarily to the Galapagos Islands, the subject of a previous case study, rather than the mainland of Ecuador. Other significant resources include the mangrove swamps of the Pacific coast (now much diminished due to the growth of the lucrative shrimp-farming industry), the *paramos* (moorlands) and cloud forests of the High Andes, and the rainforests in the north-west and east of the country. In north-west Ecuador the Cotocachi–Cayapas Reserve, lying between the Andes and the Pacific coastal lowlands, has been the focus of an international project for a 'rainforest corridor' extending to the Choco region in western Colombia.

A much more extensive area of primary forest lies to the east of the Andes in the region known to Ecuadorians as El Oriente, which forms part of the vast Amazon Basin. Although Ecuador's share of Amazonia is small compared to that of Brazil, it is richer in biodiversity than any other part of the world, including Costa Rica, which is much better known as a ecotourism destination. The forests, rivers and freshwater lagoons of the region provide a variety of habitats for wildlife. In primary rainforest the larger trees form a dense leaf canopy at a height of 30–45 metres, preventing sunlight from reaching the forest floor, which is relatively free of undergrowth. In between there is an understorey of smaller trees and a layer of shrubs, festooned with lianas and epiphytes (air plants such as orchids). In the Cuyabeno Reserve there are over 400 species of birds, dolphins (at a distance of 4000 kilometres from the Atlantic Ocean!), not to mention the abundance of fish species. However, this biodiversity is not only a tourism resource; there is also the trade in animals and birds destined largely for private collections, and the issue of 'bio-piracy', where American companies have sought to secure patents on medicinal plants as yet unknown to science. Since the late 1960s the rainforest of the Oriente has diminished considerably in extent, for the following reasons:

- The discovery of oil and the associated development, which has caused widespread disturbance to wildlife and the contamination of water resources. Even the

Yasuni National Park, which is designated by UNESCO as a World Biosphere Reserve, is under threat from the international oil companies.

- The commercial logging of tropical hardwoods, much of it illegal. Since these trees rarely occur in pure stands and are widely scattered throughout the forest, indiscriminate felling is almost inevitable.
- The influx of large numbers of settlers from the Sierra and the Pacific coastal lowlands who have cleared land for agriculture.

Even so the six provinces that comprise the Oriente only account for 6 per cent of the population of Ecuador, and this region has a frontier character. Although the oil industry has provided a transport infrastructure in the northern Oriente that can be used by tourism, most localities can only be accessed by motor-canoe along navigable rivers such as the Napo, or by light aircraft.

The rise of community-based ecotourism

The rainforest of the Oriente is home to nine indigenous groups who are facing severe pressures. Most of these groups now number less than a thousand individuals. Their age-old way of life was based on hunting, fishing and gathering, with some subsistence agriculture on small clearings in the forest. In the course of the twentieth century some elements of the traditional culture were discarded, largely as the result of missionary influence. The most warlike of these Indians – the Huaorani (formerly known as Aucas) – were responsible for the killing of American missionaries in 1956, while artefacts of the Shuar (Jivaros), such as blowguns and *tsantsas* (the shrunken heads of defeated enemies), are found in many museum collections. The lowland Quechua, who speak the same language as the Indians of the Sierra, are by far the largest group and have been in the forefront of community-based ecotourism projects. From the late 1960s the indigenous people increasingly faced the loss of their hunting grounds through the encroachment of the oil and logging industries, and the movement of settlers into the region. The growth of ecotourism persuaded the government to set aside areas as national parks or nature reserves, but this was done without consulting local communities. Moreover some Quito-based tour operators presented the native people as a curiosity or exploited them as cheap labour.

As a consequence, the indigenous peoples of the Oriente are increasingly turning to community-based ecotourism (CBE) as one of a number of strategies towards self-reliance. Political organization plays an important role in this process. Considering their small numbers relative to the Indian population of the Sierra, groups from the Oriente have been active in the *Pachacutik* movement which seeks greater representation in the National Congress in Quito, and the recognition in the Ecuadorian Constitution of the special rights of indigenous communities to retain their languages and traditions. With the help of NGOs (non-governmental organizations), they have fought to legalize the communal ownership of their ancestral lands. Finally, indigenous organizations have emphasized their conservation role as 'guardians of the forest', as INEFAN (the government agency responsible for nature reserves) is under-resourced.

Community-based enterprises in their purest form are owned and managed by the community, with its members employed on a rotation basis so that income from tourism is spread evenly. There are problems with this approach; if the building of an airstrip or tourist accommodation does not produce income or jobs in the short term the community may lose interest in the project. A more flexible form of CBE involves particular families taking on responsibility for management, yet providing work for others according to the pattern of tourism demand. A third type involves joint ventures between an indigenous group and an outside partner, usually a tour operator based in Quito. The tour operator provides the tourists, transportation and a bilingual guide, and offers training and marketing expertise, while the community takes care of the day to day arrangements for its guests. In the case of the Kapawi Eco-Lodge, which is situated in a reserve near the Peruvian border, the tour operator obtained a long-term lease for the development on land belonging to the Achuar tribe. It is intended that they will take over full responsibility for managing the project in 2011.

The majority of ecotourists to the Ecuadorian Amazon stay in hotels of varying standard in the gateway towns of Puyo, Tena and Misahualli and use these as bases for their tours, which may involve a lengthy trip by river transport. Others stay in lodges close to the reserves, which are usually in more remote locations and managed by large national or international tour companies. One of the perceived advantages of CBE is that the host community has made a conscious choice in favour of tourism, so that the visitor feels like a welcome guest rather than an intruder. The indigenous guide not only has an unrivalled knowledge of the forest and its wildlife, but due to differences in temperament shows little of the *machismo* that characterizes Latin American male attitudes. To keep negative social impacts to a minimum, no more than 12 visitors are allowed on any one tour, while visits may be limited to one group per month. The tourist accommodation is likewise sited some distance from the village, and is built in the traditional style using local materials, usually as open-sided *cabañas* with a thatched roof, elevated on stilts to take advantages of any breezes. Tour programmes are flexible and unhurried, giving visitors the opportunity to interact with village life and for cultural exchange between hosts and guests. In some areas the forest trails have been improved for hiking tours, with boardwalks, rope bridges and even observation towers, while river journeys are undertaken in dugout canoes.

The disadvantage of most CBE enterprises for conventional tourism is their lack of sophistication, as it has been a steep learning curve for indigenous people to adjust to the requirements and expectations of Western tourists. Some of these are unrealistic; tourists looking for 'authenticity' will be disappointed by the fact that their hosts aspire to live in modern houses with tin roofs and wear Western-style clothing, while others may disapprove of the continuing importance of hunting. As yet there are few English-speaking guides, so tourists need to be adequately prepared for their visit. Lodging and catering facilities are fairly basic, except in a few joint enterprises such as the Kapawi Eco-Lodge. Although some food is produced locally, most supplies have to be brought in from the nearest town, which may involve a lengthy journey by motor-canoe. Access to an assured tourist market is a major problem, as most communities lack modern means of communication. Here visitors can play an important role by 'spreading the word' to potential tourists on returning to their country of origin.

Community-based ecotourism has brought benefits to indigenous groups, allowing them to retain aspects of their traditional lifestyle and embrace change on their own terms. A limited amount of employment has been provided in the community for guides, canoeists and cooks, while other households gain income from the sale of handicrafts such as basketwork, hammocks (an Amerindian invention), pottery and woodcarvings, and these also help to revive traditional skills. Involvement in CBE encourages protection of the forest and its resources, and generates pride in the native culture. At the same time it improves communication with the wider world. Some money is now available for access to modern health care in Quito, but more exposure to the market economy results in greater dependence on imported consumer goods. Taking a short-term view, there is an 'opportunity cost' for those involved in CBT, since by doing so they forego more stable and better paid jobs with the oil companies. Logging and oil can provide more immediate income than tour groups, and community leaders find it difficult to resist the blandishments of the oil companies. Community enterprises also face competition from cut-price tour operators, who are less concerned about ethics and environmental issues. In a wider sense the development versus conservation dilemma is faced by the whole of Ecuador with its faltering economy.

Reflections on the case

The ultimate aim of ecotourism is to help indigenous peoples retain their traditional lifestyle, since they know best how to achieve sustainable management of the rainforest. In community-based ecotourism as practised in the Ecuadorian Amazon, the forest Indians have assumed control over the numbers and activities of tourists in their territories. Ecotourism not only generates income for communities living in remote areas with few other resources, but also encourages them to value their culture. However, there is constant pressure from the oil industry and other drivers of change, and these communities need outside help from NGOs and supportive tour operators to improve their product and maintain their way of life.

Discussion points/assignments

1 As indigenous communities cannot rely solely on ecotourism for a livelihood, suggest a number of activities related to an ecotourism programme that could generate additional income.
2 Discuss the opinion that the reality of ecotourism in the Ecuadorian Amazon falls some way short of the ideal.
3 Draw up a code of conduct for tourists visiting an Indian community in the Amazon.
4 Like other forms of tourism, ecotourism responds to changes in fashion, and indigenous communities have to compete with established tour operators for a share of the market. Suggest ways in which indigenous communities can stay ahead of the competition by specializing in a niche market.

5 A retired school teacher living in Manchester is planning 'the trip of a lifetime' to the Ecuadorian Amazon. Put together all the components of the tourism experience, including:
 • the 'anticipation phase', including advice on preparing for the trip
 • the journey to the destination, including all stopovers and transfers
 • a detailed itinerary for the visit, which involves staying in Indian communities
 • advice on networking, so that our client can effectively spread the word about CBE.

Key sources

Braman, S. and Fundación Acción Amazonia (2001) Practical strategies for pro-poor tourism: Tropic Ecological Adventures – Ecuador. *PPT Working Paper 6.*

Colvin, J. (1994) Capirona: a model of indigenous tourism. *Journal of Sustainable Tourism,* 2 (3), 174–177.

Jeffreys, A. (1998) Tourism in northwest Ecuador. *Geography Review,* January, 26–29.

Leiper, N. (1990) *Tourism Systems: An Interdisciplinary Perpsective.* Massey University, Auckland.

Mann, M. (ed.) (2002) *The Good Alternative Travel Guide.* Earthscan/Tourism Concern.

Szuchman, P. (2001) Eco-credibility. *Condé Nast Traveler,* August, 46.

Wesche, R. and Drumm, A. (1998) *Defending our Rainforest: A Guide to Community-based Ecotourism in the Ecuadorian Amazon.* Acción Amazonia, Quito.

Woodfield, J. (ed.) (1994) *Ecosystems and Human Activity.* Collins Educational, London.

Websites

www.gn.apc.org/tourismconcern
www.planeta.com

Part 4
Useful Sources

4.1

Sources to support work on the case studies

This section of the book is designed to support your work on the case studies. Whilst we have provided a set of relevant sources at the end of each case study, there is also a range of other material that you will find useful when tackling the cases. These include abstracting services, handbooks and dictionaries of tourism and the academic tourism journals. We have not provided a listing of trade publications (such as *Travel Trade Gazette*) for two reasons; first, there will be different trade journals and newspapers available to you depending upon which part of the world you live in, and secondly, in our view, the material tends to date rapidly.

The World Wide Web is now a major source of information about tourism and destinations. Of course, the Web is disorganized and lacks any form of information quality control, but the official tourism sites in particular provide instant access to countries, cities and resorts. Other sites are now available that provide destination accounts, photographs and statistics. Because we feel that this is such a valuable source for everyone working on the cases in this book, we have provided a list of the website addresses of national tourist organizations of the major tourism countries in the world. In addition, the companion website to the book provides a comprehensive listing of travel and tourism websites, including search engines. However, we would not recommend that you use only Internet sources in your approach to these cases, but use the Web to supplement print sources.

This list of sources is organized to cover the following types of reference material:

- general texts on tourism and the geography of travel and tourism
- reports, dictionaries, yearbooks and encyclopaedias
- abstracting services
- statistical sources
- tourism journals
- website addresses of national tourism organizations.

General texts on tourism and the geography of travel and tourism

Ashworth, G. (1984) *Recreation and Tourism*. Bell & Hyman.

Bierman, D. (2003) *Restoring Destinations in Crisis*. Allen and Unwin.

Boniface, B. and Cooper, C. (2005) *Worldwide Destinations: The Geography of Travel and Tourism*, 4th edn. Elsevier Butterworth-Heinemann.

Bull, A. (1998) *The Economics of Travel and Tourism*. Longman.

Burkhart, A. J. and Medlik, S. (1991) *Tourism, Past, Present and Future*. Heinemann.

Burns, P. M. and Holden, A. (1995) *Tourism: A New Perspective*. Prentice Hall.

Burton, R. (1995) *Travel Geography*. Addison Wesley Longman.

Butler, R. W. and Pearce, D. G. (1993) *Tourism Research*. Routledge.

Callaghan, P. (1989) *Travel and Tourism*. Business Educational.

Coltman, M. (1989) *Introduction to Travel and Tourism*. Van Nostrand Reinhold.

Conlin, M. V. and Baum, T. (1995) *Island Tourism*. Wiley.

Cooper, C. P., Fletcher, J., Gilbert, D. and Wanhill, S. (1998) *Tourism Principles and Practice*. Addison Wesley Longman.

Crotts, J. C. and Van Raaij, W. F. (1993) *Economic Psychology of Travel and Tourism*. Haworth Press.

De Kadt, E. (1979) *Tourism: Passport to Development*. Oxford University Press.

Drakakis-Smith, G. and Lockhart, D. (1997) *Island Tourism: Trends and Prospects*. Pinter.

Dumazedier, J. (1967) *Towards a Society of Leisure*. Free Press.

Fennell, D. A. (2003) *Ecotourism*. Routledge.

Frechtling, D. (2001) *Forecasting Tourism Demand*. Elsevier Butterworth-Heinemann.

Gee, C. Y., Choy, D. J. L. and Makens, J. C. (1997) *The Travel Industry*. Van Nostrand Reinhold.

Glyptis, S. (1993) *Leisure and the Environment*. Wiley.

Goeldner, C. R. and Ritchie, J. R. B. (2004) *Tourism: Principles, Practices, Philosophies*. Wiley.

Gunn, C. A. (1997) *Vacationscape: Designing Tourist Regions*. Van Nostrand Reinhold.

Gunn, C. and Var, T. (2002) *Tourism Planning*. Routledge.

Hall, C. M. (1994) *Tourism and Politics*. Wiley.

Hall, C. M. and Jenkins, J. M. (1994) *Tourism and Public Policy*. Routledge.

Hall, C. M. and Page, S. (2002) *The Geography of Tourism and Recreation*. Routledge.

Harrison, D. (1994) *Tourism and the Less Developed Countries*. Wiley.

Holloway, J. C. (2001) *The Business of Tourism Sixth edition*. Addison Wesley Longman.

Harrison, D. (2002) *Tourism in the Less Developed World*. CABI.

Horner, S. and Swarbrooke, J. (2003) *International Cases in Tourism Management*. Elsevier Butterworth-Heinemann.

Howell, D. W. (1993) *Passport: An Introduction to the Travel and Tourism Industry*. South Western.

Hudman, L. E. (1980) *Tourism: A Shrinking World*. Wiley.

Hudman, L. E. and Jackson, R. H. (1999) *The Geography of Travel and Tourism*. Delmar.

Ioannides, D. and Debbage, K. G. (1998) *The Economic Geography of the Tourist Industry*. Routledge.

Inskeep, E. (1991) *Tourism Planning: An Integrated Planning and Development Approach*. Van Nostrand Reinhold.

Jeffries, D. (2001) *Governments and Tourism*, Elsevier Butterworth-Heinemann.

Jennings, G. (2001) *Tourism Research*. Wiley.

Kelly, J. R. (1990) *Leisure*. Prentice Hall.

Lennon, J. J. (2003) *Tourism Statistics*. Allen and Unwin.

Leiper, N. (1990) *The Tourism System*. Massey University Press.

Likorish, L. and Jenkins, C. L. (1997) *An Introduction to Tourism*. Butterworth-Heinemann.

Lundberg, D. E. (1975) *The Tourist Business*. Van Nostrand Reinhold.

Lundberg, D. E., Stavenga, M. H. and Krishanmoorthy, M. (1995) *Tourism Economics*. Wiley.

Medlik, S. (1995) *Managing Tourism*. Butterworth-Heinemann.

Mercer, D. (1980) *In Pursuit of Leisure*. Sorret.

Middleton, V. T. C. and Hawkins, R. (1998) *Sustainable Tourism: A Marketing Perspective*. Elsevier Butterworth-Heinemann.

Mill, R. C. (1990) *Tourism: The International Business*. Prentice Hall.

Mill, R. C. and Morrison, A. (1992) *The Tourism System: An Introductory Text*. Prentice Hall.

Mowforth, M. and Munt, I. (1998) *Tourism and Sustainability*. Routledge.

Murphy, P. E. (1991) *Tourism: A Community Approach*. Methuen.

Newsome, D., Moore, S. and Dowling, R. (2001) *Natural Area Tourism*. Channel View.

Page, S. (2003) *Tourism Management: Managing for Change*. Elsevier Butterworth-Heinemann.

Page, S., Brunt, P., Busby, G. and Connell, J. (2001) *Tourism. A Modern Synthesis*. Thomson Learning.

Pearce, D. (1989) *Tourist Development*. Longman.

Pearce, D. (1992) *Tourist Organizations*. Longman.

Pearce, D. (1995) *Tourism Today: A Geographical Analysis*. Longman.

Pearce, D. and Butler, R. (1993) *Tourism Research: Critiques and Challenges*. Routledge.

Pearce, D. and Butler, R. (1995) *Change in Tourism: People, Places, Processes*. Routledge.

Pearce, D. G. and Butler, R. W. (2001) *Contemporary Issues in Tourism Development*. Routledge.

Poon, A. (1993) *Tourism, Technology and Competitive Strategies*. CAB.

Ritchie, J. R. B. and Goeldner, C. R. (1994) *Travel, Tourism and Hospitality Research: A Handbook for Managers and Researchers*. Wiley.

Ritchie, J. R. B. and Crouch, G. I. (2003) *The Competitive Destination*. CABI.

Robinson, H. (1976) *A Geography of Tourism*. Macdonald & Evans.

Ross, G. F. (1996) *The Psychology of Tourism*. Hospitality Press.

Ryan, C. (2002) *The Tourist Experience*. Continuum.

Ryan, C. (2003) *Recreational Tourism*. Channel View.

Sharpley, R. (1994) *Tourism, Tourists and Society*. Elm.

Sharpley, R. and Telfer, D. (2002) *Tourism and Development*. Channel View.

Shaw, G. and Williams, A. (1994) *Critical Issues in Tourism*. Blackwell.

Sinclair, T. and Stabler, M. (1991) *The Tourism Industry: An International Analysis*. CAB.

Sinclair, T. and Stabler, M. (1997) *The Economics of Tourism*. Routledge.

Smith, S. L. J. (1983) *Recreation Geography*. Longman.

Smith, S. L. J. (1996) *Tourism Analysis: A Handbook*. Addison Wesley Longman.

Smith, V. L. (1989) *Hosts and Guests*. University of Pennsylvania Press.

Smith, V. and Brent, M. (2003) *Hosts and Guests Revisited*. Cognizant.

Smith, V. L. and Eadington, W. R. (1995) *Tourism Alternatives: Potential Problems in the Development of Tourism*. University of Pennsylvania Press.

Swarbrooke, J. (2001) *The Development and Management of Visitor Attractions*. Elsevier Butterworth-Heinemann.

Theobald, W. F. (1994) *Global Tourism: The Next Decade*. Butterworth-Heinemann.

Towner, J. (1994) *An Historical Geography of Recreation and Tourism*. Belhaven.

Tribe, J. (1995) *The Economics of Leisure and Tourism: Environments, Markets and Impacts*. Butterworth-Heinemann.

Turner, L. and Ash, J. (1975) *The Golden Hordes: International Tourism and the Pleasure Periphery*. Constable.

Vellas, F. and Becherel, L. (1995) *International Tourism*. Macmillan.

Wahab, S. (1993) *Tourism Management*. Tourism International Press.

Weaver, D. (2001) *The Encyclopaedia of Ecotourism*. CABI.

Weaver, D. and Lawton, L. (2002) *Tourism Management*. Wiley.

Weaver, D. (2002) *Ecotourism*. Wiley.

Williams, S. (1998) *Tourism Geography*. Routledge.

Williams, S. (2004) *Tourism, Critical Concepts in the Social Sciences*. Routledge.

Witt, S., Brooke, M. Z. and Buckley, P. J. (1995) *The Management of International Tourism*. Unwin Hyman.

Reports, dictionaries, yearbooks and encyclopaedias

In addition to books, journals and trade press coverage of tourism destinations and cases, there are a number of useful sources to be found in consultant's reports (including those on-line such as www.euromonitor.com), tourism dictionaries, yearbooks and encyclopaedias. Some of the key sources include:

Cooper, C. and Lockwood, A. (1989) *Progress in Tourism, Recreation and Hospitality Management*. Vols 1–6. Belhaven and Wiley.

Economic Intelligence Unit publications.

Euromonitor publications.

Europa Publications (annual) *The Europa World Yearbook*. Europa Publications.

INSIGHTS, English Tourist Board.

Jafari, J. (2000) *The Encyclopedia of Tourism*. Routledge.

Khan, M., Olsen, M. and Var, T. (1993) *Encyclopedia of Hospitality and Tourism*. Van Nostrand Reinhold.

Medlik, S. (2002) *Dictionary of Transport, Travel and Hospitality*. Butterworth-Heinemann.

Paxton, J. (annual) *The Statesman's Yearbook*. Macmillan.

Ritchie, J. R. B. and Hawkins, D. (1991–1993) *World Travel and Tourism Review*. Vols 1–3. CAB.

Seaton, A., Wood, R., Dieke, P. and Jenkins, C. (eds) (1994) *Tourism: The State of the Art: The Strathclyde Symposium*. Wiley.

Witt, S. F. and Mountinho, L. (1995) *Tourism Marketing and Management Handbook.* Student edition. Prentice Hall.

Abstracting services

Using electronic searching and abstracting services is a very effective way of searching the available literature and a great way to begin a case. The key services include:

Articles in Tourism (monthly) Universities of Bournemouth, Oxford Brookes and Surrey.
International Tourism and Hospitality Data Base CD-ROM. The Guide to Industry and Academic Resources. Wiley.
Leisure, Recreation and Tourism Abstracts (quarterly) CAB.
The Travel and Tourism Index. Brigham Young University Hawaii Campus.
Tour CD – Leisure Recreation and Tourism on CD-ROM.

Statistical sources

There is still a limited range of sources that draw together tourism statistics and trends. None the less, the WTO's increasingly user-friendly reports are well worth consulting for both global and regional trends – but beware the distinctions between travellers, tourists and day visitors in the tables. The key sources are:

Organization for Economic Co-operation and Development (annual) *Tourism Policy and International Tourism in OECD Member Countries.* OECD.
Pacific Asia Travel Association (PATA) (annual) *Annual Statistical Report.* PATA.
World Tourism Organization (annual) *Compendium of Tourism Statistics.* WTO.
World Tourism Organization (annual) *Tourism Highlights.* WTO.
World Tourism Organization (annual) *Yearbook of Tourism Statistics.* WTO.
World Tourism Organization (monthly) *World Tourism Barometer.* WTO.
World Tourism Organization (1994) *Recommendations on Tourism Statistics.* WTO.
World Tourism Organization (1999) *Tourism Market Trends,* 6 vols. WTO.
World Tourism Organization (2001) *Tourism 2020 Vision – Global Forecast and Profiles of Market Segments.* WTO.
World Tourism Organization (2001) *Tourism Forecasts,* 6 vols. WTO.

Journals

The growth in tourism journals has brought with it a rich source of case study and statistical material. In addition, the geographical and leisure journals are increasingly publishing tourism-related papers. Journals with content relevant to the geography of travel and tourism include:

Annals of Leisure Research
Annals of Tourism Research

ASEAN Journal of Hospitality and Tourism
Asia Pacific Journal of Tourism Research
Australian Journal of Hospitality Management
Current Issues in Tourism
e-Review of Tourism Research (http://ertr.tamu.edu)
Event Management
Festival Management and Event Tourism
Geographical Geography Review
Hospitality and Tourism Educator
International Journal of Contemporary Hospitality Management
International Journal of Hospitality and Tourism Administration
International Journal of Hospitality Management
International Journal of Service Industry Management
International Journal of Tourism Research
Journal of Air Transport Geography
Journal of Air Transport Management
Journal of Convention and Exhibition Management
Journal of Ecotourism
Journal of Hospitality and Leisure Marketing
Journal of Hospitality and Tourism Research
Journal of Hospitality, Leisure, Sport and Tourism
Journal of Leisure Research
Journal of Sport Tourism
Journal of Sustainable Tourism
Journal of Teaching in Travel and Tourism
Journal of Tourism and Cultural Change
Journal of Tourism Studies
Journal of Travel and Tourism Marketing
Journal of Travel Research
Journal of Travel and Tourism Research
Journal of Vacation Marketing
Leisure Futures, Henley Centre for Forecasting
Leisure Management
Leisure Sciences
Leisure Studies
Managing Leisure
Pacific Tourism Review
Progress in Tourism and Hospitality Research
Scandinavian Journal of Hospitality and Tourism
Service Industries Journal
The Tourist Review
Tourism Analysis
Tourism and Hospitality Research
Tourism Culture and Communication
Tourism Economics
Tourism Geographies
Tourism in Focus
Tourism Management
Tourism Recreation Research

Tourist Studies
Travel and Tourism Analyst
World Leisure and Recreation Association Journal

Website addresses of national tourism organizations

The World Wide Web is now a rich source of material for anyone researching tourism cases. Destinations, organizations, companies and individuals provide millions of web pages containing material and information that was previously only available by contacting the organization concerned. Of course this source of information needs to be used with care, as there is no quality control of much of the material that is available on the Web. The companion website for this book provides an annotated list of useful travel and tourism websites. It is the aim of this section of the compendium to provide the reader with a list of the official tourism sites of governments and tourist boards for each country in the world. This is a good source of initial information about a country, and, as well as providing excellent destination information, many sites have web pages for professionals and students, providing statistics and useful material about planning, marketing and policy for tourism in the country concerned. Nonetheless, even within regions, the quality of the websites is variable – the official site for Hungary, for example, is excellent, providing comprehensive tourism information for the professional as well as the traveller, whilst the site for Poland, in our view, is completely inadequate.

At the time of writing (mid-2004) these addresses were correct, but you must remember that they may change and you will need to use a search engine to find the new address. The companion website to this book provides hints about searching the World Wide Web.

Country	Website
Algeria	http://www.mta.gov.dz/
Andorra	http://www.turisme.ad
Angola	http://www.angola.org/
Anguilla	http://net.ai/
Antigua and Barbuda	http://www.interknowledge.com/antigua-barbuda/
Argentina	http://www.sectur.gov.ar/
Aruba	http://www.interknowledge.com/aruba
Australia	http://www.australia.com
Austria	http://www.austria-tourism.at/
Bahamas	http://www.interknowledge.com/bahamas/
Bangladesh	http://www.bangladesh.com
Barbados	http://barbados.org/
Belgium	http://www.visitbelgium.com/
Belize	http://www.travelbelize.org/
Bermuda	http://www.bermudatourism.com
Bhutan	http://www.tourisminbhutan.com
Bolivia	http://www.bolivia.com/noticias/tourismo.asp
Bonaire	http://www.interknowledge.com/bonaire/index.html
Brazil	http://www.embratur.gov.br/

Bulgaria	http://mi.government.bg/eng/tur/pol/orgs.html
Cambodia	http://www.tourismcambodia.com
Cameroon	http://www.compufix.demon.co.uk/camweb/
Canada	http://www.visitcanada.com
Cayman Islands	http://www.caymanislands.ky
Chile	http://www.turismochile.cl
China	http://www.chinatour.com
Colombia	http://www.presidencia.gov.co/
Costa Rica	http://www.tourism-costarica.com
Croatia	http://www.vlada.hr/
Cuba	http://www.cubaweb.cu/
Curaçao	http://www.interknowledge.com/curacao/
Cyprus	http://www.cyprustourism.org/
Czech Republic	http://czechtourism.com
Denmark	http://www.visitdenmark.com
Ecuador	http://www.ecuador.us
Egypt	http://www.egypttourism.org/
Estonia	http://www.tourism.ee/
Ethiopia	http://www.ethiopia.ottawa.on.ca/tourism.htm
Falkland Islands	http://www.tourism.org.fk/
Federated States of Micronesia	http://fsmgov.org/
Fiji	http://www.BulaFiji.com
Finland	http://www.finland-tourism.com
France	http://www.maison-de-la-france.fr
French Guiana	http://www.guyanetourisme.com/
Gabon	http://www.tourisme-gabon.com
Gambia	http://www.gambiatourism.info
Georgia	http://www.parliament.ge/TOURISM
Germany	http://www.germany-tourism.de/
Gibraltar	http://www.gibraltar.gi/tourism/
Greece	http://www.greektourism.gr
Greenland	http://www.greenland-guide.dk
Grenada	http://www.interknowledge.com/grenada/
Guadeloupe	http://www.antilles-info-tourisme.com/guadeloupe/
Guam	http://www.visitguam.org/
Guatemala	http://www.visitguatemala.com
Guyana	http://www.turq.com/guyana.html
Hawaii	http://www.hawaii.gov/tourism/
Honduras	http://www.turq.com/honduras.html
Hong Kong	http://www.hkta.org
Hungary	http://www.hungarytourism.hu/
Iceland	http://www.icetourist.is/
India	http://www.tourindia.com/
Indonesia	http://tourismindonesia.com
Iran	http://www.itto.org/
Ireland	http://www.ireland.travel.ie
Isle of Man	http://www.isle-of-man.com/

Israel	http://www.infotour.co.il
Italy	http://www.enit.it/
Jamaica	http://www.visitjamaica.com/
Japan	http://www.jnto.go.jp/
Jersey	http://www.jtourism.com
Jordan	http://www.jordanembassyus.org
Kenya	http://www.bwanazulia.com/kenya/
Korea (South)/(Republic of Korea)	http://www.knto.or.kr
Laos	http://www.mekongcenter.com
Lebanon	http://www.Lebanon-tourism.gov.lb
Liechtenstein	http://www.news.li/touri/index.htm
Luxembourg	http://www.etat.lu/tourism
Macau	http://www.macautourism.gov.mo/ login.html
Macedonia	http://www.tarm.org.mk
Malaysia	http://tourism.gov.my/
Maldives	http://www.visitmaldives.com/intro.html
Malta	http://www.tourism.org.mt/
Martinique	http://www.martinique.org/
Mauritius	http: www.mauritius.net/
Mexico	http://www.mexico-travel.com/
Micronesia	http://www.visit-fsm.org/
Monaco	http://www.monaco.mc/monaco/ guide_en.html
Mongolia	http://www.mongoliatourism.gov.mn/
Morocco	http://www.tourisme-marocain.com
Myanmar	http://www.myanmartourism.com
Namibia	http://www.namibiatourism.co.uk
Nepal	http://www.visitnepal.com
Netherlands	http://www.visitholland.com/
New Zealand	http://www.purenz.com
Nicaragua	http://www.intur.gob.ni/
Nigeria	http://www.nigeria-tourism.net
Northern Ireland	http://www.nitb.com
Norway	http://www.tourist.no
Palau	http://www.visit-palau.com/
Palestine	http://www.pna.org
Panama	http://www.panamainfo.com/
Papua New Guinea	http://www.pngtourism.org.pg
Peru	http://www.peruonline.net
Philippines	http://www.tourism.gov.ph/
Poland	http://www.polandtour.org
Portugal	http://www.portugal.org
Puerto Rico	http://www.gotopuertorico.com
Romania	http://www.turism.ro/
Russian Federation	http://www.interknowledge.com/russia/ index.html
Saba	http://www.turq.com/saba/
Saint-Pierre and Miquelon	http://www.saint-pierre-et-miquelon.com
Scotland	http://www.travelscotland.co.uk

Senegal	http://www.earth2000.com
Serbia	http://www.serbia.sr.gov.yu
Seychelles	http://www.seychelles.com/
Singapore	http://www.visitsingapore.com
Slovakia	http://www.scar.sk
Slovenia	http://www.slovenia-tourism.si
South Africa	http://www.environment.gov.za/
Spain	http://www.tourspain.es
Sri Lanka	http://www.lanka.net/ctb/
St Barthelemy	http://www.st-barths.com/
St Eustatius (Netherlands Antilles)	http://www.turq.com/statia/
St Kitts & Nevis	http://www.interknowledge.com/ stkitts-nevis/
St Lucia	http://www.st-lucia.com/
St Maarten	http://www.st-maarten.com/
St Martin	http://www.interknowledge.com/st-martin
St Vincent & The Grenadines	http://www.turq.com/stvincent
Sudan	http://www.sudan.net/
Sweden	http://www.visit-sweden.com
Switzerland	http://www.switzerlandtourism.ch/
Syria	http://www.syriatourism.org
Taiwan	http://www.tbroc.gov.tw/
Tanzania	http://www.tanzania-web.com
Thailand	http://www.tourismthailand.org
Tibet	http://www.tibet-tour.com/
Trinidad and Tobago	http://www.visittnt.com/
Tunisia	http://www.tourismtunisia.com/
Turkey	http://www.turkey.org/
Turks & Caicos	http://www.interknowledge.com/ turks-caicos
Uganda	http://www.uganda.co.ug/tour.htm
United Kingdom	http://www.visitbritain.com/
USA	http://www.tinet.ita.doc.gov/
Uruguay	http://www.turismo.gub.uy
US Virgin Islands	http://www.usvi.net/
Vanuatu	http://www.vanuatu.net.vu/
Venezuela	http://www.venezlon.demon.co.uk
Vietnam	http://www.vn-tourism.com/index.htm
Wales	http://www.visitwales.com
Western Samoa	http://www.visitsamoa.com
Yemen	http://www.yementourism.com
Zambia	http://www.africa-insites.com/zambia/
Zanzibar	http://www.zanzibar.net/zautalii/ index.html
Zimbabwe	http://www.zimbabwetourism.co.zw/ defaulta.htm

Index